The Anti-New York Times

Rebuttals to the Lies, Omissions, Half-Truths & Globalist Bias of "the Paper of Record"

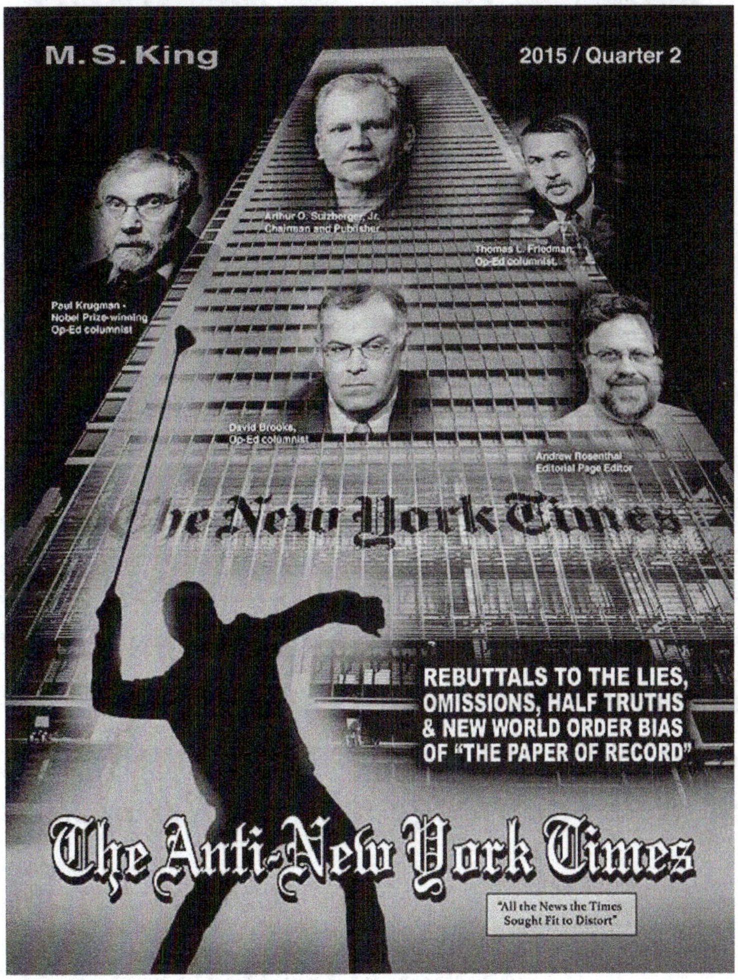

QUARTER 2, 2015

APR – MAY - JUN

By M. S. KING

"Nothing can now be believed which is seen in a newspaper. Truth itself becomes suspicious by being put into that polluted vehicle. The real extent of this state of misinformation is known only to those who are in situations to confront facts within their knowledge with the lies of the day."

- ***Thomas Jefferson (1743-1826)***

Author of the Declaration of Independence
3rd President of the United States

From: Letter to John Norvell, 1807

About the author

M. S. King is a private investigative journalist and researcher based in the New York City area. A 1987 graduate of Rutgers University, King's subsequent 30 year career in Marketing & Advertising has equipped him with a unique perspective when it comes to understanding how "public opinion" is indeed scientifically manufactured.

Madison Ave marketing acumen combines with 'City Boy' instincts to make M.S. King one of the most tenacious detectors of "things that don't add up" in the world today. Says King of his admitted quirks, irreverent disdain for "conventional wisdom", and uncanny ability to ferret out and weave together important data points that others miss: *"Had Sherlock Holmes been an actual historical personage, I would have been his reincarnation."*

King is the webmaster of **TomatoBubble.com** – which also features **The Anti-New York Times** for select readers. He is also the author of:

- *The Bad War: The REAL Story of World War II*
- *Planet Rothschild: The Forbidden History of the New World Order*
- *The War Against Putin: What the Government-Media Complex Isn't Telling You About Russia.*
- *The Real Roosevelts: An Omitted History*
- *God vs Darwin: The Logical Supremacy of Intelligent Design over Evolution*

King's other interests include: the animal kingdom, philosophy, chess, cooking, literature and history *(with emphasis on events of the late 19th through the 20th centuries).*

CONTENTS

INTRODUCTION

Since its founding in 1851 by Republican Henry Jarvis Raymond, ***The NY Times*** has been a big player in shaping public opinion. But it was not until 1896 that the *Times* took a turn to the internationalist Left when it was purchased by a German-Jew named Adolph Ochs. In 1897, Ochs himself would coin the paper's now famous self-serving slogan, printed on its masthead every day ever since: ***"All the News That's Fit to Print".***

Adolph Ochs

Ochs' daughter married Arthur Hays Sulzberger, who became publisher when Adolph died. Ochs' great grandson Arthur Ochs Sulzberger, Jr. is the publisher of the NY Times today. So, for 1.2 centuries, America's most influential propaganda sheet has been in the hands of the same Zionist-Marxist family. Count on *The Times* to promote big government, Globalism, phony environmentalism, Israel, the Fed, and endless wars.

Just how powerful is what your fighting author likes to refer to "Sulzberger's Slimes"? The erudite writer Gore Vidal may have been a morally degenerate sodomite who was wrong about many things, but his reference to the Slimes as *"the Typhoid Mary of American journalism"* was as spot-on as it was witty. One need only glance at the morning headlines of "the paper of record", and then take note of how the superficial infomercials known as "the Nightly News" will so often pick up on whatever front page fairy-tale that the Manhattan Mendacity Machine spun that very same morning.

Like some journalistic plague; the virus of lies, half-truths and cherry-picked data then infects the unguarded minds of the whole country, and indeed, the world. Such is the indisputable power and undeserved "prestige" of this dreadful "Orwellian" institution.

The Anti-New York Times was originally established as, and still is, a pay-to-view daily sub-page of **TomatoBubble.com.** Beginning in 2015, the collected rebuttals to the Slimes' Spin were published in Quarterly book format – which you now hold in your hands. To best understand the bare-knuckled and often humorous rebuttals, it is recommended that readers also purchase and study, ***Planet Rothschild: The Forbidden History of the New World Order.*** That will give you a firm grounding in REAL history while **The Anti-New York Times** informs you of the contemporary world which had grown out of that tragic history.

When gathered in one place, the rebuttals expose The Slimes as a deceitful naked Emperor. If the Slimes is the disease of deception, let **The Anti-New York Times** be your antidote of truth.

The New York Times

REBUTTED BY

The Anti-New York Times

APRIL, 2015

NY Times: Russian History Receives a Makeover That Starts With Ivan the Terrible

By NEIL MacFARQUHAR and SOPHIA KISHKOVSKY

The 16th-century czar's reputation was scrubbed in one of several exhibitions that have presented a generous view of the country's history.

REBUTTAL BY

The Anti-New York Times

New York Marxists just love making fun of a nation's heroes. To the Globalist, the idea of patriotism and honoring one's heritage is all so quaint; unless of course you are glorifying Old Testament psychos, Marxist scum, or the founders of Israel. It's 'OK' to be proud of that!

So it comes as no surprise that a patriotic-themed Moscow museum exhibition is being slimed by the snobby scribblers of Sulzberger's Slimes. Here is a typical wise-crack:

"Ivan the Terrible, the Russian czar, should really be considered Ivan the Not So Bad, according to a wildly popular historical exhibition held recently near the Kremlin."

Will the real Ivan please stand up?
Could it be that Ivan the Terrible was given a "bum-rap" because the Jews hated him?

From the Jewish Encyclopedia: In his time (1500's) the prejudice against the Jews in the Muscovite dominions was very pronounced. They were feared as magicians and proselytizers.

Translation: The Jews were making mischief, as always.

The undertone of the Slimes' piece is that the Russian art and academic world is bending to the will of the big bad Putin; a charge which the museum's directors strongly deny. As if Russians need to be told to respect their heritage! The story quotes a "Russian" accuser with a clearly Jewish-sounding surname:

"History is being used as an ideological tool," said Nikita P. Sokolov, a historian and editor. The message of some of the biggest shows, he said, was that "Russia is a besieged fortress that needs a strong commander, and anyone trying to democratize Russia and shake the power of the commander is trying to undermine this country."

The Slimes then quotes a museum historian who denies the allegation:

"Not once has any government representative told me how history should be written," said Yuri A. Nikiforov, a World War II historian. "It's just not true that Russian historians dance to the president's tune."

Fair and balanced reporting, right? Both sides are presented, right? **But therein lies the art of journalistic hokus-pokus.** You see, once a baseless accusation is thrown at the intended target, the damage is already done, regardless of whether or not the target gets a chance to respond. The reader has been programmed to believe, or at least suspect, that the big bad Putin is pressuring Russian museums to alter history. Even though an opposing voice of denial is briefly presented, the stink of the smear doesn't come off. The Slimes understands this marketing tactic, which is why we call it, The Slimes.

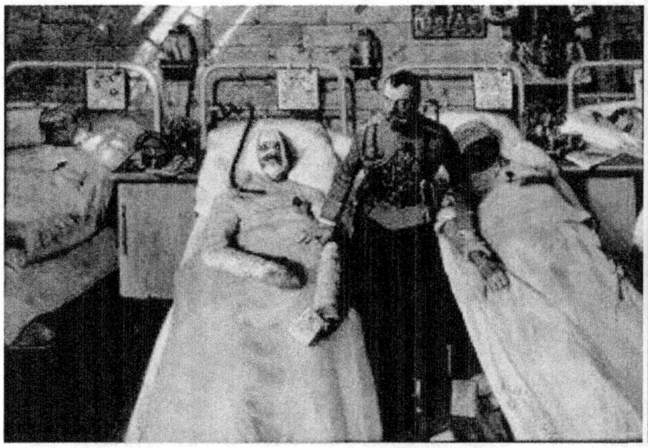

1- Czar Nicholas II is shown in a painting with wounded soldiers.
2- Painting of a modern unit of the Russian military, part of the exhibit covering the history of the country's armed forces.

APRIL, 2015

NY Times: In Nigeria's Election, Muhammadu Buhari Defeats Goodluck Jonathan

By ADAM NOSSITER

Mr. Buhari, a former military strongman, defeated Mr. Jonathan, whose government has been criticized for its handling of an Islamist insurgency and sinking economy.

REBUTTAL BY

The Anti-New York Times

The 'Boku Haram' terrorist scam worked! Having been blamed for failing to adequately protect his people from the CIA-Mossad front group, incumbent President Goodluck Jonathan was defeated by the Globalist candidate-of-choice, Muhammadu Buhari. The Slimes explains why Jonathan's 'goodluck' had run out:

"On Mr. Jonathan's watch, Nigeria has been pummeled by Boko Haram, its economic fortunes have plunged with falling oil prices."

.

Boku Haram - rigged by the United States! Falling oil prices - rigged by U.S. ally Saudi Arabia! Get the picture?

#BringBack
Our Girls

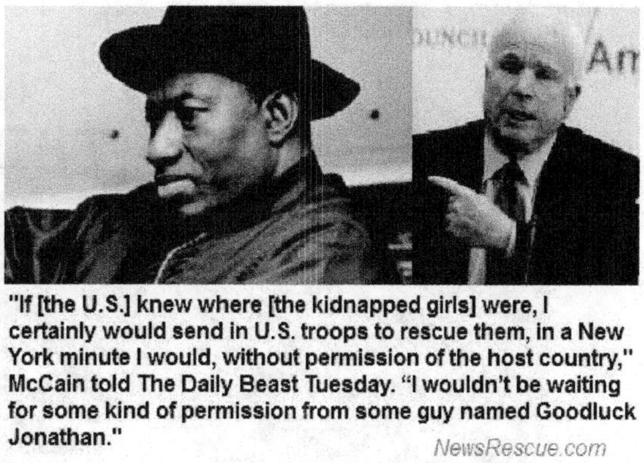
"If [the U.S.] knew where [the kidnapped girls] were, I certainly would send in U.S. troops to rescue them, in a New York minute I would, without permission of the host country," McCain told The Daily Beast Tuesday. "I wouldn't be waiting for some kind of permission from some guy named Goodluck Jonathan."
NewsRescue.com

The First Tranny's 'Bring Back Our Girls' stunt paid off.

"If they knew where they were, I certainly would send in US troops to rescue them, in a New York minute I would, without permission of the host country, I wouldn't be waiting for some kind of permission from some guy named Goodluck Jonathan," (Nigeria's president)

- John McCain (A Soros Stooge)

An article appearing in the 'Nigerian Voice' entitled ***(Is George Soros Eyeing Nigeria's Presidential Election?)*** accuses the notorious Globalist billionaire of targeting Nigeria for subversion. Olagoke Abayomi writes:

"Soros has set his eyes on Nigeria's presidential election, slated for March 28. The billionaire has substantial economic interests in Africa's largest country, directed through the Helios Investment Partners hedge fund. In recent years, the fund has invested billions in all sectors of Nigeria's economy, ranging from shopping malls to pension funds, oil and gas joint ventures and mobile phone infrastructure."

"Let's not forget that Buhari, a former military ruler who rose to and was deposed from power in a coup d'état in the 1980s, has mounted an aggressive media campaign that sought to whitewash the multiple abuses perpetuated by his oppressive regime. To this end, he received the backing of multiple international experts from Soros' clique, including the International Crisis Group and the OSI who considerably swayed the Western media coverage of the March elections."

TNV THE NIGERIAN VOICE

Soros
I can make him sing, talk, or even destroy entire economies without moving my lips.

The 'Nigerian Voice' sees the hidden hand of the evil George Soros at work in Nigeria.

Buhari's Party is known as the **'All Progressive Congress'** (APC). In 2014, the APC was admitted as a consultative member into the **Socialist International**. It doesn't get any more 'One World' than that. The extent to which Buhari will sell out Nigeria to the West remains to be seen. Surely he understands that the N.W.O. gang put him in power and, through Boku Haram, has the ability to take him down just as quickly.

With both the United States and China deploying troops into Africa *(The U.S. for conquest; China to protect its nationals from Boku Haram);* events in oil-rich Nigeria are worth monitoring.

China does a lot of business with Nigeria, which is why the U.S. proxy Boku Haram had kidnapped Chinese workers.

APRIL, 2015

NY Times: Norway Reverts to Cold War Mode as Russian Air Patrols Spike

By ANDREW HIGGINS

The Russian moves have set off debate over military spending and highlighted how quickly President Vladimir V. Putin has shredded the certainties of the post-Cold War era.

REBUTTAL BY

The Anti-New York Times

Sulzberger's war prep Yellow Press propaganda continues with this latest Russo-phobic bit of tommy-rot from Bodo, Norway. Yes, even the gentle Norwegians are potential targets of the big bad Putin. From the article:

"From his command post burrowed deep into a mountain of quartz and slate north of the Arctic Circle, the 54-year-old commander of the Norwegian military's operations headquarters watches time flowing backward, pushed into reverse by surging Russian military activity redolent of East-West sparring during the Cold War."

One day, it's Ukraine's turn to publicly wring its hands over the threat of the Russian Bear; the next, Lithuania; the next, Latvia; the next, Estonia; the next, Finland; the next, Sweden, and now Norway. With every new whine comes a a front page poop-pie served up by one of Sulzberger's slanderous scribblers. These numerous countries can't possibly *all* be wrong about Russia, can they? Allegations which come from *multiple* sources serve as corroborating evidence, do they not? Or so the uninformed mind might reason. And therein lies the scam of "consensus". You see, there is no "all". There are no "multiple sources". **There is only one entity** and that's the NATO / European Union beast; itself a sub entity of the U.S.-led New World Order.

As it was during World War II, so it is today. Then, as now, the governments of smaller countries such as Norway, Denmark, Belgium, Holland, Luxembourg etc all came under the domination of the same "Western" entity *(US, UK, France)*. In essence, Hitler did not actually invade multiple countries because Germany's enemy was only one, with lots of junior subsidiaries pretending to be "neutral".

1- The entrance tunnel to a bunker in Bodo, built during the Cold War and modeled after American installations, that now houses the Norwegian military command.
2- Many sub-leaders ('capi' or 'capos') - same Mafia

There is, however, a positive note in regard to Norwegian public opinion. It appears as though, unlike the foolish Poles and Ukrainians, Norwegians aren't buying this crap. An unidentified squadron commander is referenced as follows:

"But he (squadron commander) questioned whether public opinion had caught up with the fact that a predictable post-Cold War era of East-West comity was now over. 'The problem in Norway is that we are so rich, fat and happy that we are not worried enough.' he said."

Like most degenerate zombies of the decadent West, the average Norwegian may indeed be fat, materially satisfied and contented to watch sports and idiotic TV shows as civilization burns down around him. But evidently, there is a remnant of intelligence left; which is more than we can say for many of the paranoid warmongering Slavs of Eastern Europe.

April 1940: The Germans occupied Norway in order to prevent the then Lord of the Admiralty, Winston Churchill, from establishing bases there.

APRIL, 2015

NY Times: Somali Militants Kill 147 at Kenyan University

By JEFFREY GETTLEMAN, ISMA'IL KUSHKUSH and RUKMINI CALLIMACHI

Shabab militants claimed responsibility for an attack in which gunmen forced their way into dormitories, leaving 147 people dead.

REBUTTAL BY

The Anti-New York Times

A new CIA super-villain is on the loose, this time in the African nation of Kenya. Move over ISIS, move over Boku Haram, it's time for 'Shabab' to have its 15 minutes of fame. Actually, the group has been around since 2012, but this latest anti-Christian attack *(or make-believe attack?)* marks its boldest act yet. It's bad news for Kenya. The Slimes reveals:

"Kenya's tourist industry, one of the pillars of its economy, has been badly damaged by the terrorist attacks, and the bloodshed on Thursday is sure to make things worse. There are also fears that the Shabab's relentless emphasis on singling out Christians could inflame religious strife in a country already wrestling with tensions between a Muslim minority, which has complained about government persecution, and a Christian majority that increasingly feels under attack."

Sandy Hook style photo-op fakery in Kenya? That 's the same girl being carried by two different men! Same face, same shirt, same under-shirt, same pants, same dirt-stain pattern on left thigh, same shoes. The only change is the bloodless bandage added in the 2nd image.

What could Kenya have possibly done to bring the wrath and subversion of the West's clandestine forces upon itself? Why is Obongo going to Kenya in July? It is said that a picture is worth 1,000 words. So, here are "2,000 words" to consider:

China and Kenya are very close business partners.

The Globalists want Africa to stay backwards and dependent upon them. China's mutually beneficial economic activities on the continent do not fit in with that agenda. That is why Qaddafi of Libya was murdered; that is why Boku Haram is destabilizing Nigeria; that is why the Ebola virus was planted and built into a "crisis"; and that is why Shabab is attacking *(or pretending to attack?)* Kenya. These false-flag terror attacks are designed to achieve a Trifecta of objectives for the Globo-Zionists:

1- Drive China out of Africa   2- Intimidate Christians   3- Slander Muslims

There has been no shortage of past stories linking the money and influence of the **demonic** George Soros to the deadly subversion of Kenya. t is all so gosh-damn sickening! Soros, the NGO's and the CIA target innocent Christians while Islam takes the blame – and Africa descends into chaos.

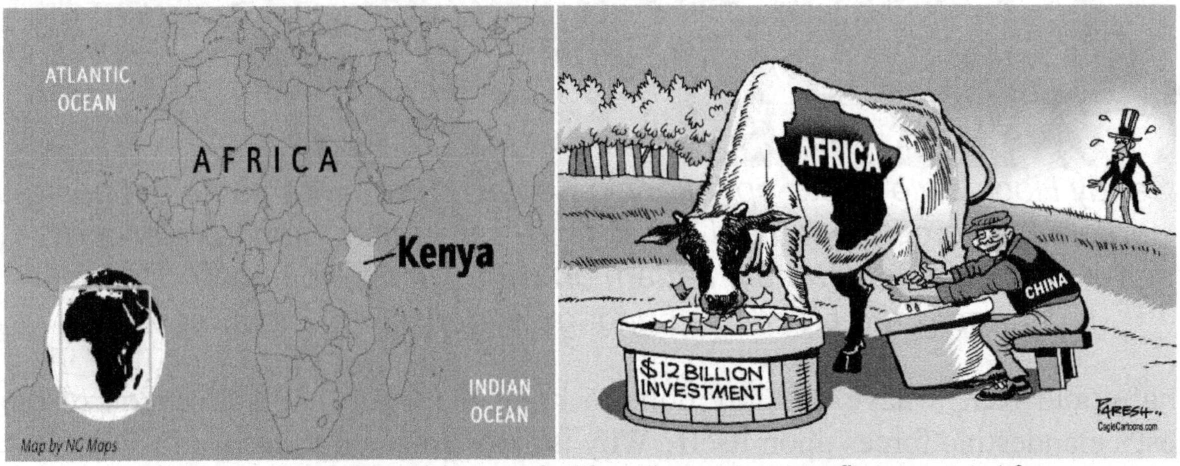

Western cartoons often mock China's positive influence in Africa.

APRIL, 2015

NY Times: G.O.P.'s Israel Support Deepens as Political Contributions Shift

By ERIC LIPTON

Republicans are more fervently pro-Israel than ever, partly a result of ideology, but also a product of a surge in campaign spending on their behalf by a small group of wealthy donors.

REBUTTAL BY

The Anti-New York Times

Safe and secure in the knowledge that they can say and do whatever the hell they bloody want, the Zionists at the Jew York Slimes have come right out and essentially stated, *on the front page*, that Zionist billionaires now own the Republican Party. There are no code-words here, no euphemisms, no 'beatin' round the bush'. It's just a straight up admission that "wealthy donors" are now dictating the pro-Israel foreign policy of GOP. Even the Sheldon Adelson connection is openly publicized:

"Over all, the most significant contributor by far to Republican supporters of Israel has been Sheldon Adelson, the casino magnate, who with his wife has invested at least $100 million in conservative causes over the last four years."

This explains why the Republi**cant's**, who can never seem to muster the courage to fight Homo-Obongo on any matter of domestic substance, suddenly turn into hungry tigers when it pertains to all matters Israeli. Obongo can have his Global Warming regs, his socialized medicine, his voter fraud etc, but the moment he softened up on Iran, the Republi**can'ts** suddenly found some "courage" and attacked. Only when they have the support of some big money Jews behind them do these gutless whores, including Rancid Paul, start acting all tough.

Senator Tom Cotton of Arkansas, left, a leading critic of negotiations with Iran, has drawn support from pro-Israel donors.

America Jewry is divided on going to war with Iran. On the one hand, the Likudnik 'Neo-Cons' have been itching to bomb Iran for years. On the other, the "moderate" Zionists fear what Iran can deliver back to Israel in retaliation. There is also a concern over what impact the Palestinian situation and the possibility of a Middle East War might have on the Globo-Jews drive for a New World Order.

But what neither Jewish faction seems to fear anymore is public exposure and American public opinion. In the past, journalists or politicians who dared to state in soft terms what this article states rather boldly would have been crucified. That was then. Today, no one even cares. Big Jewry has the population on mental lock-down. There is no need for them to even hide their control anymore.

Rival gangsters -- Billionaire Jews Adelson & Soros disagree on Iran and wage war against each other via proxies. But apart from the Israel issue, both are on the same page when it comes to the subversion of America.

APRIL, 2015

NY Times: Waving Cash, Putin Sows E.U. Divisions in an Effort to Break Sanctions

By ANDREW HIGGINS

The Russian president has mended issues with Cyprus and has courted Greece as Moscow seeks to assert influence in some of Europe's most troubled corners.

REBUTTAL BY

The Anti-New York Times

In a devilish display of typical psychopathic "projection", Sulzberger's Slimes accuses Russia of doing exactly what the U.S. has been doing for decades, namely, buying up the loyalty of foreign governments. Here a small whiff of today's front page excrement:

"The shift from fury to declarations of eternal friendship displayed Mr. Putin's well-known flair for tactical back flips. But it also showed his unbending determination to break out of sanctions imposed on Russia by the United States and the European Union for ***Moscow's annexation of Crimea*** *and support for armed rebels in eastern Ukraine."*

McCain's incitement of a violent Kiev rent-a-mob is ALWAYS conveniently ignored, as is Victoria Nuland (Nudelman's) hand-picking of the new puppet leaders of Ukraine.

"Moscow's annexation of Crimea ", eh? The violent CIA-NGO coup that overthrew an elected government, *prior* to the "annexation", is not mentioned; nor is the fact that the Crimean people voted by a margin of 97% - 3% to return to their original Russian sovereignty; nor is the fact that the eastern rebels are resisting a tyrannical regime in Kiev which was installed by outside forces; nor is the fact that the U.S. State Department, by its own admission, poured 20 million dollars into "pro-democracy" organizations in Ukraine *(subversive propaganda aimed at whipping up rent-a-mobs).* It's amazing what a false image one can paint simply by omitting certain inconvenient details.

The fact that tiny Cyprus and now, Greece, are moving closer to Russia has less to do with "Putin's cash" and his "sowing of divisions", than it does with the growing realization that the European Union was a really bad deal for them. If a control-freak degenerate were to cheat and beat his girlfriend until she finally leaves him; do we blame the break-up on the nice new boyfriend that she starts dating?

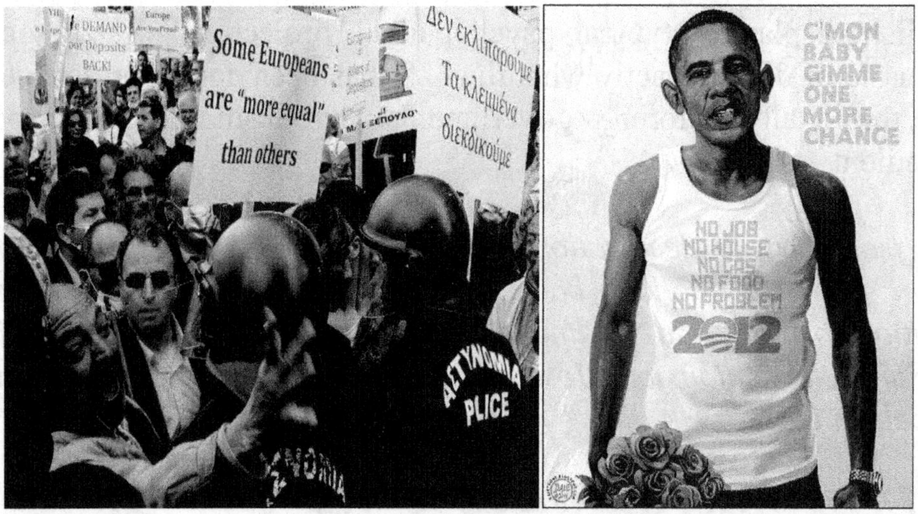

Depositors in the now-defunct Laiki Bank, which closed during Cyprus's 2013 financial crisis, protested when their bank accounts were subjected to an EU-mandated "haircut". Many Cypriots and Greeks now want to dump the US-EU Axis of Evil

APRIL, 2015

NY Times: South Carolina Officer Is Charged With Murder in Black Man's Death

By MICHAEL S. SCHMIDT and MATT APUZZO

The North Charleston officer had said that the man took his stun gun, but a video shows the officer firing eight times as the man, who was apparently unarmed, fled.

REBUTTAL BY

The Anti-New York Times

Assuming, for the sake of argument, that this stunning video from South Carolina is not part of a staged "crisis actor" stunt; it is clear that Sulzberger's Slimes, with this massive front page / full page coverage, is trying to fan the flames of anti-White hatred. Not since the 9/11 false-flag has "the paper of record" carried such a massive front page barrage of emotion-based images. We now learn that the video was *originally* sent to The Slimes, making the whole affair even more suspicious.

#NEWS
MOMENT OF FATAL SOUTH CAROLINA POLICE SHOOTING

People are being killed like flies all across America, and many of these cases are being caught on hidden camera. **But it's only when a White kills a Black that Sulzberger sounds the Pavlovian alarm bells, triggering the inevitable and inane "national conversation" about "racism" and "police brutality".** And yet for some odd reason, the brutality of law enforcement officers on the Federal level is never exposed, even when it is White on Black.

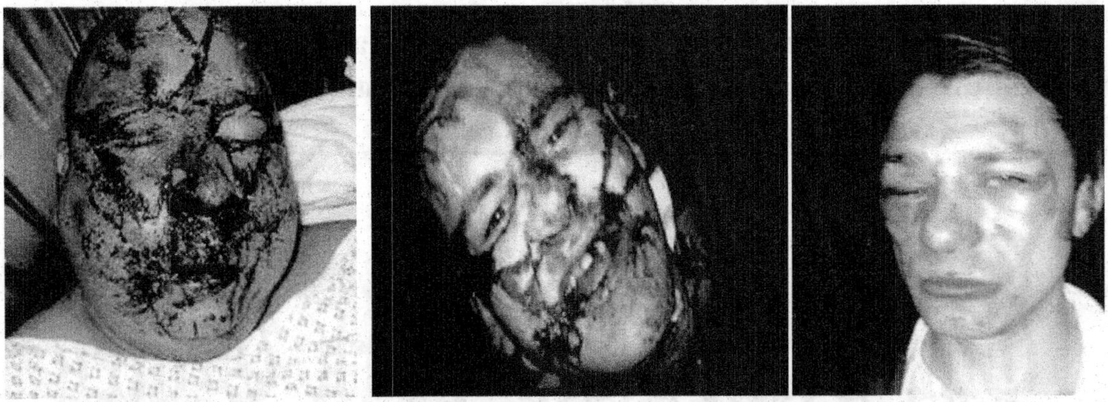

*When are the **hundreds** of White victims of the brutal "knockout game' going to get some front page love from the Slimes?*

Many of the attacks have been caught on video. Some cases have even resulted in death. Why no front page frame-by-frame coverage?

Case in point: In October of 2013, Miriam Carey, an unarmed **34 year old Black woman,** was killed after a car chase from the White House to Capitol Hill. Carey, a dental hygienist, was driving with her 1 year old daughter. Carey was shot dead by **White Federal agents** after her car had already stopped. Details of this strange case in which Carey drove away in fear after hitting a Fed cop car remain murky. But the fact remains, the Feds shot at her 7 times ***after her car had already broken down.***

Though the Black family of the victim expressed their justifiable sorrow and outrage, Obongo was silent. Jesse JackAss was silent. Al Charlatan was silent. The Black Panthers, NAACP, and the Congressional Black Caucus were all silent. You see, when you become a Fed cop, you become untouchable. If you think you have problems with localized police now, just wait and see what happens when have a ***Federalized*** police force, brought about due to Sulzberger's hyping of incidents like the one that just *allegedly* happened in South Carolina.

If real, this is a horrible killing that just happened in South Carolina. But we must 'keep our eye on the ball' here and not lose our minds. For Jewish-Marxist supremacists like Sulzberger care not a rat's arse about "police brutality" nor about "racism". The two-fold agenda behind this disproportionate hype is about:

a) inciting Blacks against Whites, and

b) placing local police under the authority of the Department of Homeland Security.

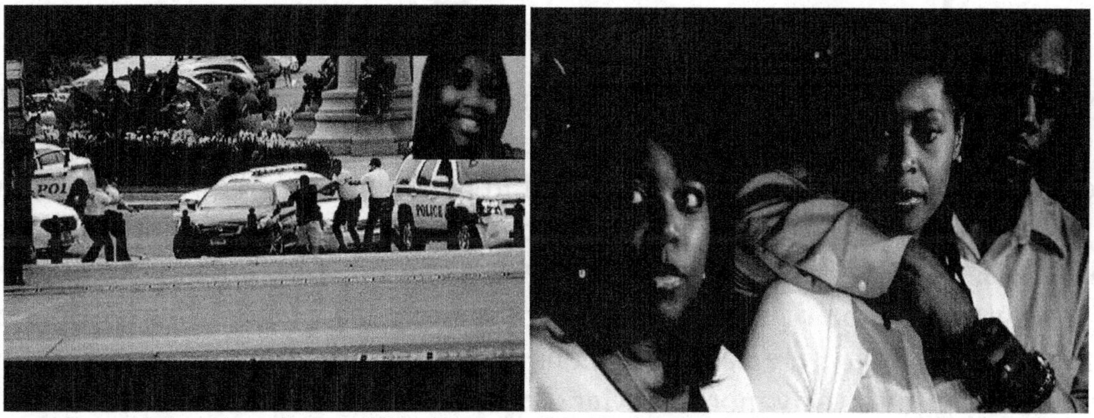

An odd double-standard. The thugs St. Trayvon Martin of Sanford, FL and St. Michael Brown of Ferguson, MI were lionized, but the family of the truly executed Miriam Carey got no sympathy from Sulzberger.

APRIL, 2015

NY Times: Malaysia Resurrects Detention Without Trial, Alarming Government Critics

By THOMAS FULLER

Three years after abolishing detention without trial, the Malaysian government revived the practice on Tuesday with the passage into law of a highly contentious antiterrorism bill that opposition leaders fear could be used against government critics.

REBUTTAL BY

The Anti-New York Times

Why does Sulzberger's Slimes even pay salaries to its foreign affairs reporters? All that these commie clowns do is use the same template every day when attacking a target nation. One need only fill in the blank with the "bad guy" country of the day. One day it's Russia; the next, China; the next, Myanmar; the next, Syria; the next, Malaysia, and on and on the same old song goes. The only other variance would be the offense-in-question. One day it's "human rights violations"; the next, "corruption"; the next, "weapons of mass destruction" and on and on the same old song goes. Any moronic Marxist with a mouse can 'cut & paste' for the Slimes!

As usual, the article fails to provide the proper context for Malaysia's latest crackdown on terrorism and subversion; an initiative dubbed 'the Sedition Act." The Slimes' open-mouthed retard readership is expected to gobble down the misleading slop that Malaysia is restricting "free speech". But things aren't that simple. You see, when a nation is being targeted by the CIA-NGO-Soros-Mossad Axis of subversion, measures must be taken to stop the cancer from spreading. Legitimate internal criticism of government policy is a healthy thing; but the incitement by puppet-traitors in service to outside paymasters is quite another.

In regard to the currency crisis of 1997, former Malaysian Prime Minister Mahathir Mohamad accused George Soros of ruining Malaysia's economy with "massive currency speculation". Mohamad also stated: "The Jews rule the world by proxy."

As always, The Slimes uses the old "critics say" trick to mask what is actually its own attack. Here:

"Critics say the law is a further slide toward authoritarianism in Malaysia and a definitive reversal of personal freedoms that Prime Minister Najib Razak vowed to introduce soon after assuming power in 2009....'Now free speech is being exterminated', Michelle Yesudas, a Malaysian lawyer, said in a Twitter post. She circulated a modified picture on social media of the board game Monopoly in which nearly every square said, 'Go to jail'...

Malaysia has already survived an attempted 'Color Revolution' (2011-12) and endured not one, but *two* very mysterious airplane disappearances of Malaysia Airlines passenger jets (2014). Rather than destabilizing Malaysia, it appears that these pathetic attempts at subversion have backfired. The article reveals that about 20 high-profile subversives, including journalists, "opposition" politicians and a university professor, have been charged with sedition over the past year.

The rent-a-mobs of Malaysia have been neutered.

Good for you Malaysia! Lock your traitor libtards up and throw away the key. Better yet, shoot them. Let's hope Mr. Putin and friends will soon do likewise to "western integrationists" who are still embedded within certain Russian institutions.

In addition to Malaysia being a long-time target of the Soros Globalists, Bibi Satanyahu's Likudniks have long had the knives out for the predominately Muslim southeast Asian country as well. In December of 2013, a Malaysian Tribunal actually declared Israel guilty of war crimes in association with Operation Cast Lead (2010). Again, we say: good for you, Malaysia!

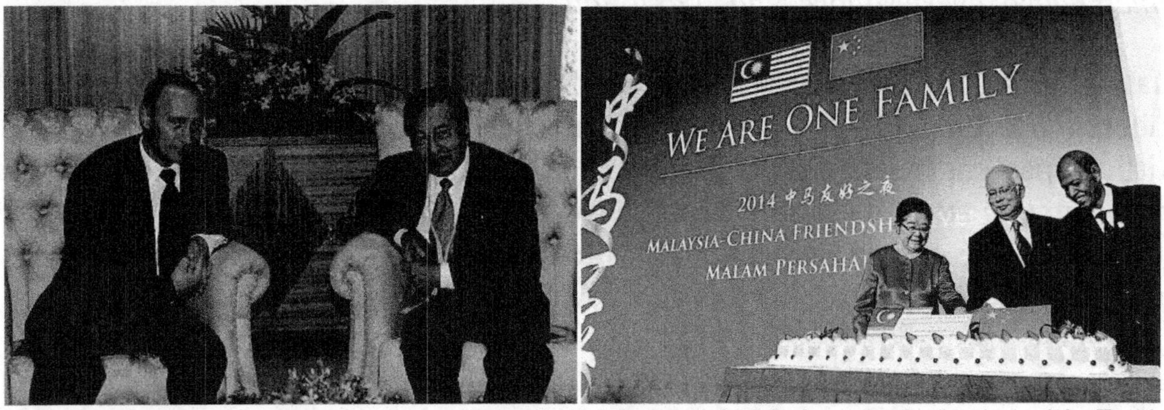

The "anti-Semitic conspiracy theorist" Mahathir Mohamad chats with Putin in 2003 / Malaysia getting chummy with the big bad China.

APRIL, 2015

NY Times: Leader of Iran Challenges U.S. on Pact Details - Doubt on Nuclear Deal

By THOMAS ERDBRINK and DAVID E. SANGER

Iran's supreme leader, Ayatollah Ali Khamenei, declared on Thursday that all sanctions would have to be lifted on the day any deal is signed and that military sites would be strictly off limits to foreign inspectors.

REBUTTAL BY

The Anti-New York Times

Today's "liberal" Slimes along with the "neo-con" Wall Street Urinal and the Internet-based Sludge Report are all dumping front-page cold water on the much talked-about "Iranian Nuclear Deal" **TM.** It appears that the big bad Ayatollah of Iran has had the unmitigated audacity, the temerity, the gall, the chutzpah to say that sanctions against Iran should be lifted on the same day that the accord is signed. Imagine that. How dare he?!

IRAN

Four Good Reasons Why Iran Doesn't Trust America

A brief survey of justifiable Iranian resentment

We must always be careful in accepting, at face value, what could be out-of-context or mistranslated quotes from the mendacious manipulators of the Marxist mainstream media. But even accounting for any possible exaggeration or embellishment, it is clear that the Ayatollah is concerned about possible dirty tricks being played 'down the road' on Iran. Who can blame him? The U.S. is notorious for its backstabbing.

Let's have a look at Uncle Sam's illustrious resume:

- Late 1890's-1900's: The U.S. promises Philippine rebels that they will have independence after the Spanish are defeated in the Spanish-American war. After the war, mostly during the Presidency of the deranged Teddy Roosevelt, the U.S. wages a 5 year war on the Philippines. In addition to 5,000 dead Americans, an estimated 20,000 Filipinos are killed in the fight, with 80,000 more dead of disease and other indirect causes.
- 1918: The U.S. promises the Germans that they will be treated fairly and as an equal if they lay down their weapons and sign an Armistice. Germany was then raped by the Treaty of Versailles.
- 1940's: The U.S. incites Chinese leader Chiang Kai Shek to ignore Japanese peace proposals and continue fighting. After Japan is defeated, Chiang is betrayed as the U.S. State Department throws its weight behind the Communist Mao Tse Tung.

1- Philippine independence fighters; dumped in a ditch after believing America's promises.
2- The 'Big 4', led by Wilson, destroy a deceived and unarmed Germany after World War I.
3- Chiang helped FDR and Churchill to defeat Japan. Behind Chiang's back, a 'Big 3' deal at Yalta handed Japanese Manchuria over to Joe Stalin, who then passed it along to the Chinese Communist Rebels of Mao Tse Tung. In 1949, Chiang and his followers were forced to flee for their very lives to the island of Taiwan.

- 1980's: The U.S. supports Saddam Hussein in Iraq's war against Iran. After the war, the U.S. / Israel Axis sets its sights on destroying Iraq, which it has.
- 1990's: After the collapse of the Soviet Union, Russian leader Mikhail Gorbachev is reassured that NATO will never expand eastward. Since that time, the U.S. controlled war machine has gobbled up Poland, Hungary, Romania, Bulgaria, the former Yugoslavia, the former Czechoslovakia, Latvia, Lithuania, Estonia; with Georgia and Ukraine in the pipeline.
- 2000's: The U.S. offers normalized relations to Libya's Muammar Qaddafi if he agrees to give up his "weapons of mass destruction" *(chemical, biological).* After de-fanging and de-clawing his armed forces, Qaddafi was rewarded with a bayonet jammed up his rectum.

So you see, my dear Ayatollah. You are worried about nothing. Relax man. The Zio-Globalist U.S. would never break a promise!

1- Gorbachev was played for a fool. Today, the might NATO sits right on Russia's borders.
2- Saddam was used to weaken Iran. He was then discarded like a used-up lemon and eventually hanged.
3- Upon learning of Qaddafi's murder, Hillary cackles: "We came. We saw. He died."

APRIL, 2015

NY Times: Scientists Question Environmental Impact of China's Winter Olympics Bid

By IAN JOHNSON

According to Beijing's bid, the impact from the Games would be "eco-friendly." But conservationists say that holding the Games in a water-stressed environment would be devastating.

REBUTTAL BY

The Anti-New York Times

The envious losers of America's PRC *(Predatory Ruling Class)* cannot stand to witness the grand spectacles of culture and entertainment that China and Russia are known to put on for events such as the Olympics. They whined in dismay as Beijing dazzled the world in 2008, and Sochi in 2014: *"They spent too much money!"*, the suddenly budget-conscious Slimes did allege.

Beijing 2008 / Sochi 2014

So it is to be expected that Sulzberger's Slimes would again attempt to throw cold water on China's bid to host the 2022 Winter Olympics. The International Olympic Committee inspected the region's facilities last week, and it is expected to make a final decision in July. If Beijing wins, it will be the first city to host the Winter and the Summer Games, which it held in 2008.

The phony pretext for The Slimes underhanded opposition to another Chinese Olympics is the shortage of water and natural snowfall in Beijing. How good of Sulzberger to be so concerned!

A ski resort near Zhangjiakou, China, that will be used as a venue for some events if China holds the 2022 Winter Olympics. "Artificial" snow makes up for a shortfall of the real thing.

The article quotes Zhang Junfeng, described as an "independent water expert":

"It just doesn't snow in Beijing. People get ideas by watching television and sports and think it's a great pastime, but it's not sustainable."

Another cherry-picked quote comes from Hu Kanping, a retired hydrologist:

"Of course they shouldn't have ski resorts."

Kanping writes reports for the Chinese NGO *(Nongovernmental Organization)* 'Friends of Nature'. As our regular readers should know by now, in most cases, NGO = CIA = NWO. Presumably, Professor Kanping would throw the people who work at such resorts out of their jobs!

自然之友
FRIENDS OF NATURE

"NGO warfare" - Never trust the claims of an NGO!

And finally, a French professor, Carmen de Jong, adds her two Euros in about China's plans to rely upon "artificial" snow:

"This kind of development is a Martian-like plan. It's completely artificial."

"Martians", eh? *(Face - Palm - Shaking head)* Ms. De Jong is an admitted Global Warmist. That alone should tell you who is buttering this egghead's French bread.

All this drama over "artificial snow" is based on junk science and Globalist politics. You see, "artificial snow" is produced by forcing water and pressurized air through a snow-gun or snow-cannon. Many resorts also add an agent to ensure that as much water as possible freezes and turns into snow. These products are non-toxic and biodegradable.

Water + cold air = "artificial snow". Oh horrors! Are these environmentalist goof-balls also opposed to the "artificial" ice used for indoor skating rinks? What about the "artificial" bodies of water used for indoor swimming?

There may be some legitimate local concerns regarding the diversion of water needed to make the snow. But of course, as usual, this matter has nothing to do with Sulzberger's concern for the environment of Beijing. It's all about the Globalist agenda; an agenda which includes bashing China and any other nation that refuses to submit to the New World Order.

"To the Olympics!"

APRIL, 2015

NY Times: Mighty Rio Grande Now a Trickle Under Siege

By MICHAEL WINES

A region confronts changing weather patterns that have shrunk snowpacks, spurred evaporation and reduced reservoirs to record lows.

REBUTTAL BY

The Anti-New York Times

The photo / article that dominates the front page immediately got your suspicious reporter here to guess that the story of the severe western draught would somehow contain the usual pseudo-scientific spin about "Global Warming" **TM**. Then the admonition of Sir Arthur Conan Doyle, speaking through his legendary character, Sherlock Holmes, came to mind: *"Never guess. It is a shocking habit,—destructive to the logical faculty."*

Indeed, the drought is becoming a big story on its own merit. Perhaps this one might actually be an informative and honest story after all, whispered Holmes. But just a few short paragraphs into the lengthy piece came the poison pill:

"Scientists say this is the harbinger of permanently drier and hotter West that global warming will deliver later this century. If so, the water-rationing order issued this month by Gov. Jerry Brown could be a sign of things to come."

Even Sherlock Holmes would be surprised at this level of treachery

But it gets even more stupid than that. The piece, citing a report from a Federal agency *(roll eyes)*, goes on:

"The 40-year increase (in Colorado & New Mexico temperatures), twice the global average, was beyond anything seen in the last 11,300 years."

What an astonishing bit of bull-shine! First of all, an area which accounts for about 1/4 of 1% of the earth's surface is not exactly what one would call a representative sample. If we are going to cherry-pick regions, let's talk about the three consecutive brutal winters that the northeastern United States has experienced; or the record level of Antarctic ice coverage; or the unusually high amount of ice chunks in the Great Lakes which only finished melting just a few weeks ago.

In regard to the past "11,300 years", we would like to ask: who was taking temperature readings in New Mexico 11,300 years ago; or for that matter, just 300 years ago? You see, Mr. Daniel Fahrenheit wasn't even born until 1686! His thermometer was introduced about 30 years later. *(Boy, those "barbaric" Germans sure are smart, aren't they?)*

Are we to believe that rock formations can somehow be used to magically divine the exact temperatures from 11,300 years ago, as well as every year ever since? Next thing you know, these clowns will be telling us that our great-great-great[x] grandmothers were single cells of algae-like organisms. Oh wait, they already told us that one.

It is truly amazing and indeed, *criminal*, what these crooked, grant-seeking "theoretical scientists" have been allowed to get away with; thanks to the unquestioning "theoretical journalists" at Sulzberger's Slimes.

Warmest weather of past 11,300 years? Mr. Fahrenheit calls Bull-Shine!

APRIL, 2015

NY Times: Atlanta School Workers Sentenced in Test Score Cheating Case

By RICHARD FAUSSET and ALAN BLINDER

The sentences imposed ranged from six months in jail to seven years in prison. The educators were convicted of falsifying test scores.

REBUTTAL BY

The Anti-New York Times

A story like this one illustrates the hypocrisy and tyranny of modern day America. Federal schemes such as Bush's "No Child Left Behind" and Homo-Obongo's "Common Core" place "testing" above real education and tie funding to "results". Of course, there are bad teachers out there, but the pressure on inner-city educators to miraculously turn dumb kids from dysfunctional broken homes into little Thomas Edisons is as immense as it is unrealistic. **If the "parents" are useless, it matters not how good the teacher is**. Add in a financial incentive to the mix and you have a recipe for government-induced fraud that a defense lawyer could plausibly condemn as a form of illegal entrapment.

$200 PER KID?
YEA, I'LL HAVE SOME MORE!
DIYLOL.COM

The fundamental problem behind failing inner city schools is that 75% of the kids are born to unmarried, uneducated, uninvolved and mostly teen-aged "baby mommas" on welfare. Test the young scholars all you want; but until the basic family structure and home discipline is restored, these kids will remain educationally disadvantaged.

This does not excuse the manipulation of test scores by educators and administrators; but to throw them in jail for as much as 7 years represents a far greater evil than the rigging of test-scores while under State pressure. The article explains:

"The racketeering charges carried a 20-year maximum sentence, and some defendants were also found guilty of lesser crimes. Prosecutors said the teachers had participated in a wide-ranging conspiracy to artificially inflate students' standardized test scores and give a false sense that struggling schools were improving, all within a system led by a superintendent, Beverly L. Hall, who demanded that administrators meet ambitious testing targets."

The Superintendent probably should do some jail time. As for the obedient underlings, it would have sufficed to have simply fired them and required a few hundred hours of community service. Apart from the injustice of the severe sentences for "crimes" induced by intense government pressure to "perform", the hypocrisy of the state is absolutely breathtaking. Not a day goes by when Federal or State agencies do not publicly falsify their own "test scores". The unemployment numbers are cooked; the inflation numbers are cooked, the GDP numbers are cooked, NASA temperature readings are cooked, foreign intelligence reports regarding "WMDs" and "Russians in Ukraine" are cooked; vote counts are cooked *(by both political parties),* the stock market, oil prices and gold prices are rigged, and the Federal Reserve engages in obscene levels of counterfeiting right in front of our collective noses. But that's "OK".

Whereas this test-score rigging, induced by government pressure, harms no one; the consequences of government data-rigging damage lives and kill innocent people. But no one is ever held accountable for those crimes. Instead, the "justice system" opts to throw some low level teachers and 'admins' in prison; while Sulzberger and friends show it off on the front page of America's "paper of record". Yeah, that ought to "send a message" to *Boobus Americanus* about the evils of rigging data.

It's "OK" when the Feds "cook the books".

APRIL, 2015

NY Times: Cuba to Be Removed From U.S. List of Nations That Sponsor Terrorism

By RANDAL C. ARCHIBOLD and JULIE HIRSCHFELD DAVIS

The White House announced on Tuesday that President Obama intends to remove Cuba from the American government's list of nations that sponsor terrorism, eliminating a major obstacle to the restoration of diplomatic relations after decades of hostilities.

REBUTTAL BY

The Anti-New York Times

Castro's Communist Cuba is not sponsoring terrorists, but it is still harboring fugitive terrorists wanted in the United States. First and foremost among them being **Joanne D. Chesimard**, who is on the F.B.I.'s list of most wanted terrorists for killing a New Jersey state trooper in 1973. She was granted asylum in Cuba after escaping from prison in 1979. Chesimard, who now goes by the name Assata Shakur, espouses revolution and terrorism against the United States. Oh how happy she must have been when Comrade Homo-Obongo was installed in 2008!

Though the article does briefly mention the Chesimard controversy, it does not mention the name of the deceased, Werner Foerster. Sulzberger's disrespectful scribblers refer to him only as, "a state trooper".

Trooper Foerster was shot and killed with his own weapon after backing up another trooper who had stopped a vehicle containing two men and a woman on the New Jersey Turnpike. The subjects started struggling with the troopers and disarmed Trooper Foerster *(a la St. Michael Brown)*. One of the men then opened fire, killing Foerster and wounding the other trooper.

Joanne Chesimard mugshot/1979, slain officer Werner Foerster

The young handsome man had a name, a face, a future and a wife and two children.

Werner Foerster wasn't the only law enforcement officer to be murdered by Black Panthers, Weathermen, or Black Liberation Army members during that turbulent period. The Communist terrorist scum that later spawned the demon seed Homo-Obongo also killed many others.

Related Line of Duty Deaths

Police Officer Donald W. Sager
Baltimore City Police Department, Maryland
End of Watch: Friday, April 24, 1970
Cause: Gunfire

Police Officer Harold Hamilton
San Francisco Police Department, California
End of Watch: Monday, October 19, 1970
Cause: Gunfire

Patrolman Joseph A. Piagentini
New York City Police Department, New York
End of Watch: Friday, May 21, 1971
Cause: Gunfire

Patrolman Waverly M. Jones
New York City Police Department, New York
End of Watch: Friday, May 21, 1971
Cause: Gunfire

Sergeant John Victor Young
San Francisco Police Department, California
End of Watch: Sunday, August 29, 1971
Cause: Gunfire

Officer James Richard Greene
Atlanta Police Department, Georgia
End of Watch: Wednesday, November 3, 1971
Cause: Gunfire

Police Officer Rocco W. Laurie
New York City Police Department, New York
End of Watch: Thursday, January 27, 1972
Cause: Gunfire

Police Officer Gregory P. Foster
New York City Police Department, New York
End of Watch: Thursday, January 27, 1972
Cause: Gunfire

Police Officer Sidney L. Thompson
New York City Transit Police Department, New York
End of Watch: Tuesday, June 5, 1973
Cause: Gunfire

Police Officer John G. Scarangella
New York City Police Department, New York
End of Watch: Friday, May 1, 1981
Cause: Gunfire

Sergeant Edward J. O'Grady, Jr.
Nyack Police Department, New York
End of Watch: Tuesday, October 20, 1981

Cause: Gunfire

Police Officer Waverly L. Brown
Nyack Police Department, New York
End of Watch: Tuesday, October 20, 1981
Cause: Gunfire

Though the sanctions against Cuba are outdated and useless, some of the American terrorists hiding there still need to be brought to justice. If we can demand the extradition and arrests of innocent 90-year old camp guards who served at the Auschwitz Soccer and Swimming Pool Clubs, then why is it so unreasonable to pressure Cuba into extraditing these *real* murderers back to the USA as a pre-condition for lifting sanctions? Can you just imagine if Chesimard had been a German SS guard hiding in Cuba? The lifting of sanctions would have been unthinkable. Heck, twenty different teams of Navy Seals would have been sent in to nab this bitch 30 years ago!

Does the life of one good man mean anything to anyone anymore? Does the concept of justice mean anything to anyone? Evidently not. All that Homo-Obongo and the Pinko Pope *(who pressed hard for the lifting of sanctions)* care about is self-aggrandizing photo ops and helping out a comrade.

Rest in peace, Trooper Foerster. Rest in peace.

It's just not right that this killer gets to retire to a tropical island.

The Pinko President & Pinko Pope threw the Castro brothers a no-strings-attached bone.

APRIL, 2015

NY Times: Preserving the Ghastly Inventory of Auschwitz

By RACHEL DONADIO

The aim of the foundation maintaining the site of the concentration camp is "to preserve authenticity." It is a moral stance with specific curatorial challenges.

REBUTTAL BY

The Anti-New York Times

To the simple-minded, this latest homage to Auschwitz is sure to be a tear-jerker. But to those who know better, it makes for a good reason to laugh, or vomit. Let's examine a few lines:

"After so many photographs and movies, books and personal testimonies, ***it is tempting to think of Auschwitz as a movie-set death camp****, the product of a gruesome cinematic imagination, and not the real thing.*

Alas, it is the real thing."

Unknowingly, in mentioning that Auschwitz struck her as *"a movie-set death camp"* , the subconscious mind of the naive writer - what some might call the "6th sense"- is actually sensing that something is fake about the whole thing. Sweetie, Auschwitz ***is*** a movie-set death camp. Alas, it ain't the real thing. Stick with your 'woman's intuition', honey. It's real and God-given.

"That is why, since its creation in 2009, the foundation that raises money to maintain the site of Auschwitz-Birkenau has had a guiding philosophy: 'To preserve authenticity.' The idea is to keep the place intact, exactly as it was when the Nazis retreated before the Soviet Army arrived in January 1945 to liberate the camp."

One would think; one would hope, that the dunderheads who kneel in Sulzberger's slop each day would pick up on this crucial detail that because it was the Soviets that liberated Auschwitz; we had to rely solely on the reports of the Joseph Stalin's monstrous henchmen which stated that it was an extermination camp. But Slimes readers aren't so discerning.

"It is a moral stance with specific curatorial challenges.....

Moral posturing always makes me puke.

"It means reinforcing ***the moss-covered pile of rubble that is the gas chamber*** *at Birkenau, the extermination camp a few miles away, a structure that the Nazis blew up in their retreat."*

This is an admission that the "gas chamber" shown to tourists is a reconstruction - a fake. What the writer leaves out, or probably does not even know, is that forensic tests conducted on the stone ruins of that "moss-covered pile of rubble" turned up negative when tested for poison gas residue....twice!

Images 1 & 2 are of the Soviet-era reconstruction of the "gas chambers". Image 3 depicts the ruins of the what is said to the original "gas chambers". The Polish curators and even the Jew York Slimes concede that what is shown to gullible tourists are NOT the actual "gas chambers".

The mushy propaganda continues:

"It means protecting that rubble from water seeping in from the adjacent ponds where the ashes of the dead were dumped."

Who said the ashes were dumped in those ponds? Stalin?

"And it means deploying conservators to preserve an inventory that includes more than a ton of human hair; 110,000 shoes; 3,800 suitcases; 470 prostheses and orthopedic braces; more than 88 pounds of eyeglasses; hundreds of empty canisters of Zyklon B poison pellets."

Zyklon B was an agent used to kill lice. This, plus the fact that "more than a ton of human hair" was cut off proves that the big-bad Germans were trying to *save* inmates from typhus outbreaks. We do know that the Germans would often shave the heads of inmates, but why would they save the hair? Why not dump it in the same pond where the ashes were supposedly dumped?

It is amazing what big liars and their controlled ignoramuses can get away with printing, simply due to the fact that people refuse to THINK.

The article mentions "children's shoes" (Oh horrors!), but not the Auschwitz Swimming Pool and Soccer Field.

APRIL, 2015

NY Times: A Police Shot to a Boy's Back in Queens, Echoing Since 1973

By JIM DWYER

No one could pull out a cellphone to make a video of Clifford Glover, a black 10-year-old who was fatally shot by a white officer while running away on a spring morning.

REBUTTAL BY

The Anti-New York Times

Assuming that the recent case in South Carolina was even real *(and the video seems very fake);* it has been a few weeks since a White cop shot an unarmed Black suspect. Because murder charges were immediately filed against the cop, Michael Thomas Slager, the anger associated with the aforementioned case has already subsided. So, what do the dirty Marxist agitators at Sulzberger's Slimes do to reheat the pot of racial tension? They dig up a case from ***1973*** and plaster it on the font page. Here is the inflammatory opening:

"It was 1973, long before anyone could imagine hashtag declarations of solidarity and protest, the kind of message to the world that today might read, #IamCliffordGloverInTheFourthGrade.

No one could pull out a phone to make a video of Clifford Glover, a 10-year-old running from a plainclothes police officer with a gun who had just jumped out of a white Buick Skylark in Jamaica, Queens, on a spring morning in 1973.

'I am sure a camera would have helped, but the ballistics were clear.' Albert Gaudelli, a former Queens prosecutor, said this week. 'The bullet entered his lower back and came out at the top of his chest. He was shot T-square in the back, with his body leaning forward. He was running away.'"

1- Clifford Glover
2- Officer Thomas J. Shea, center, celebrated his acquittal with his lawyers at a local restaurant.

The cop was responding to an armed robbery in which the child's step-dad may, *or may not*, have been involved in. The officer claimed that he thought he saw a gun and didn't realize the boy was 10. The prosecution claimed that the officer was reckless. It is pointless to even attempt to research and retry the case. All we can say is that it was not as 'Black & White' of a brutality case *(no pun intended)* as the Slimes would have us believe; and also ask, given that the event took place *42 years ago;* **why is it on the front page now?**

To paraphrase Saul Alinksy - the vile Chicago Communist who wrote 'Rules for Radicals' - the resurrection of this old story is intended to ***"rub raw the sores of social discontent"***. This is what Marxist Jews specialize in; firing up Black folks, inciting them to hatred of Whites, shaming weak-minded White libtards into pathetic self-hating guilt trips, and agitating for a Federal takeover of the nation's police departments. That is why this old story was resurrected.

1- Clifford's stepfather, mother, and baby sister, the day after Clifford was fatally shot in 1973. (She really doesn't seem to be that heartbroken). The article does reveal that Ms. Glover eventually left her husband; blaming him for her son's death and suspecting that he did indeed have a gun.

2- Killary Rotten Clinscum and Mr. & Mr. Obongo were all devotees of the Marxist race-baiting, rabble-rouser Saul Alinsky.

APRIL, 2015

NY Times: At Republican Gathering, All Talk Is of Hillary Clinton (None of It Is Good)

By PATRICK HEALY and JONATHAN MARTIN

During a gathering in New Hampshire, an energized, confident bench of 19 Republicans took turns taking apart Hillary Rodham Clinton or competing with her on policy ideas.

REBUTTAL BY

The Anti-New York Times

The Quadrennial Freak Show heats up as **Republican'ts** attack Killary Rotten Clinscum for committing the very same crimes and follies that the Bush / Cheney gang had committed. That is why we call it a Freak Show. The candidates are freaks; the breathless TV talking-heads who cover the "race" as if it were the Kentucky Derby are freaks; and the rank and file fools who get themselves all worked up over whether 'Tweedle-Dee' or 'Tweedle Dum' is the best man / woman/ queer for the job, are the biggest freaks of them all.

The opening paragraph of this article reveals just how stupid and hypocritical Republi**can't** candidates and activists truly are:

"They attacked her judgment on resetting American relations with Russia...."

Fools! First of all, Killary's "reset" was not an "appeasement" of Russia; it was a ploy. Killary is every bit as anti-Putin and pro-confrontation as any neo-con Republiscum warmonger. Secondly, Russia is not the cause of the chaos in Ukraine; the Globo-Zio U.S. is!

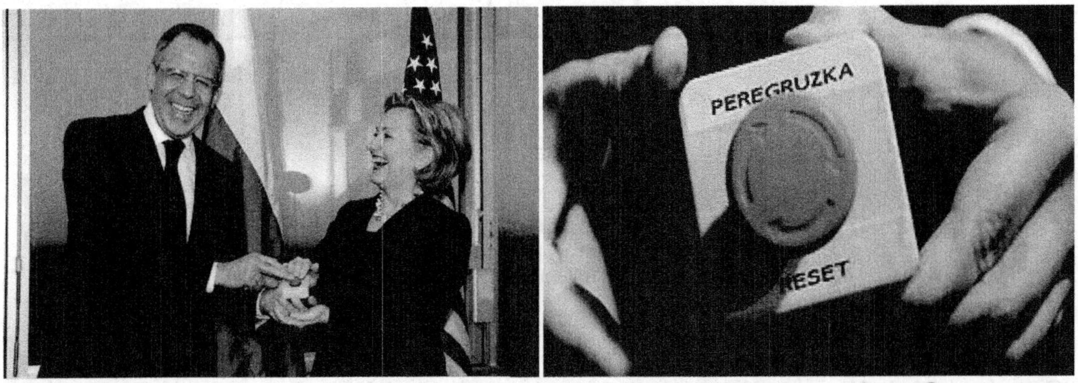

The cheap and erroneously translated "reset" button that Secretary Clinscum gave to the Russian Foreign Minister in 2009 was a ploy. Fear not Republi-dolts; the U.S., regardless of what Party controls the Presidency, has no intention of dealing honorably with Russia.

Continuing:

".....and protecting American diplomats in Libya."

The destabilization and destruction of Libya was a multi-year CIA project started under the Bush/Cheney gang. Qaddafi was a marked man long before Obongo took office and finished him off. Had we left Qaddafi alone, Libya would still be stable and that Ambassador would not have been killed at Benghazi.

"They slammed her as secretive for using a personal email account at the State Department and deleting messages in the face of scrutiny."

Ah yes. Killary was "secretive"; unlike the Bush/Cheney gang which was oh-so transparent in regard to the 9/11 attacks and the phony intelligence linking Iraq to 9/11 and "Weapons of Mass Destruction".

Evil, twisted, Satanic scum just kept on reading a children's book while thousands were burned to death, crushed to death, or forced to jump to their deaths during the false-flag attacks which he ***knew*** *were coming. The cold-hearted conspiratorial bastard then used grieving firefighters for a prop as he marched America off to fight Israel's war. And now, his brother Jeb wants the job. How could Killary do any worse?*

The piece continues:

"They mocked her recent campaign events in Iowa as inauthentic."

"Inauthentic", like Bush's "conversion" to Christianity? Or Romney's fake smile and patronizing "Who let the dogs out?" crack before a group of inner city kids? Or the really awful rug on Rancid Paul's head?

"and her unannounced lunch at Chipotle as antisocial."

Grow up Republitards, grow up.

"They even reached back to her husband's infidelity to disparage her."

Funny, I don't recall Republi**cant's** disparaging 2008 nominee John McCain over his marital infidelity. At least Bill Clinscum didn't dump his devoted wife and kids for a younger beer heiress.

What a sad and pathetic spectacle this "Democracy" nonsense is. The Great One was so right about 'Democracy' when he observed:

"The devastation caused by this institution of modern parliamentary rule (democracy) is hard for the reader of Jewish newspapers to imagine, unless he has learned to think and examine independently. ***It is, first and foremost, the cause of the incredible inundation of all political life with the most inferior, and I mean the most inferior, characters of our time."***

Just as the true leader will withdraw from all political activity which does not consist primarily in creative achievement and work, but in bargaining and haggling for the favor of the majority, in the same measure this activity will suit the small mind and consequently attract it.

The more dwarfish one of these present-day leather merchants is in spirit and ability, the more clearly his own insight makes him aware of the lamentable figure he actually cuts - that much more will he sing the praises of a system which does not demand of him the power and genius of a giant, but is satisfied with the craftiness of a village mayor, preferring in fact this kind of wisdom to that of a Pericles.

And this kind doesn't have to torment himself with responsibility for his actions. He is entirely removed from such worry, for he well knows that, regardless what the result of his 'statesmanlike' bungling may be, his end has long been written in the stars: one day he will have to cede his place to another equally great mind, for it is one of the characteristics of this decadent system that the number of 'great statesmen' increases in proportion as the stature of the individual decreases. With increasing dependence on parliamentary majorities it will inevitably continue to shrink, since on the one hand ***great minds will refuse to be the stooges of idiotic incompetents and bigmouths, and on the other, conversely, the representatives of the majority, hence of stupidity, hate nothing more passionately than a superior mind.***

For such an assembly of wise men of Gotham, it is always a consolation to know that they are headed by a leader whose intelligence is at the level of those present: this will give each one the pleasure of shining from time to time-and, above all, if Tom can be master, what is to prevent Dick and Harry from having their turn too?

Right on, Chief! Right on, right on, right on. Oh, and speaking of the Fuhrer; please join **TomatoBubble.com** in celebrating the 126th birthday of Adolf Hitler today. Pick up your copy of our latest release, **'Mein Side of the Story'** via Amazon.com. *(see ad below)* Your purchase will help us climb the Amazon Search Engine charts and expose "newbies" to the truthful words of the one man who *almost* derailed the NWO Express. May his spirit of truth and goodness live within the hearts of men until a future day when humanity regains its sanity.

Heil Hitler!

APRIL, 2015

NY Times (Editorial): How to Avert a Nuclear War

By JAMES E. CARTWRIGHT and VLADIMIR DVORKIN

We find ourselves in an increasingly risky strategic environment. The Ukrainian crisis has threatened the stability of relations between Russia and the West, including the nuclear dimension.

REBUTTAL BY

The Anti-New York Times

The fact that the New York Slimes is now running headlines mentioning "Nuclear War" ought to serve as a wake-up call for the sports, sex, I-phone and entertainment addicts of America. How good of the Slimes to dredge up two members of the Globalist Council on Foreign Relations to warn us about what a dangerous world this has become *(thanks to them!)*.

Though the editorialists, **James Cartwright** and **Vladimir Dvorkin**, assume a tone of feigned "objectivity", it is clear that they are framing Russia for future dangerous developments and programming us for some big event that your concerned reporter here wishes not to even contemplate.

Let's dissect this ominous piece of predictive propaganda:

"The fact is that we are still living with the nuclear-strike doctrine of the Cold War, which dictated three strategic options: first strike, launch on warning and post-attack retaliation. There is no reason to believe that Russia and the United States have discarded these options, as long as the architecture of "mutually assured destruction" remains intact."

A true statement, but the well-connected Globalist writers *(CFR, Carnegie etc)* are passing themselves off as "objective" analysts of the U.S.-Russia crisis as if they are not part of the American Establishment. That's part of the trick.

"American officials have usually played down the launch-on-warning option. They have argued instead for the advantages of post-attack retaliation, which would allow more time to analyze the situation and make an intelligent decision. Neither the Soviet Union nor Russia ever stated explicitly that it would pursue a similar strategy, but an emphasis on mobile missile launchers and strategic submarines continues to imply a similar reliance on an ability to absorb an attack and carry out retaliatory strikes."

Now that have scared the poop out of us with talk of strikes and retaliatory strikes, they set us up for the poison propaganda pill:

"Today, however, Russia's early warning system is compromised. The last of the satellites that would have detected missile launches from American territory and submarines in the past stopped functioning last fall. This has raised questions about Russia's very ability to carry out launch-on-warning attacks.

.....that in turn increases the likelihood of ***mistaken retaliation****. For a submarine missile fired from the Norwegian Sea, Russia's radar network would give its nuclear decision makers just 10 minutes to respond. America's early warning systems can be expected to provide about twice as much time."*

In other words, Russia may mistakenly shoot first and trigger the nuclear war. More on that theme:

"In theory, no sensible head of state would authorize a launch-on-warning strike after receiving information that just one missile, or a small number of missiles, were inbound, on the assumption that this was not an intentional, full-scale attack. But the launch-on-warning doctrine still rules in both Russia and the United States"

Now, back to the phony "objectivity":

"This risk should motivate the Presidents of Russia and the United States to decide in tandem to eliminate the launch-on-warning concept from their nuclear strategies. They should reinstitute military-to-military talks, which were suspended over the Ukraine crisis, to pursue this stand-down as an urgent priority."

The subtle deception in those two sentences lies in the cunning making a moral equivalence between (*the Presidents of Russia and the United States).* It's like saying that the home-invading rapist *(Obongo)* and the law-abiding home owner *(Putin)* should "decide in tandem" how to avoid violence. There is no equivalence there! There lies the dirty journalistic trick. More:

"To reinforce this accord, ***both countries should refrain*** *from conducting military exercises that involve practicing missile launches based on information from early warning systems.* ***Even if this restraint cannot yet be fully verified****, it would be a valuable contribution to strategic stability."*

In other words, Putin should trust the United States. We wouldn't lie to Russia, now; would we? More:

"Detailed verification measures can come later*, once better Russian-American relations are restored."*

Yeah, right. Verification can come "later", after the U.S. has gained the strategic advantage. More:

*"**Our leaders urgently need to talk** and, we hope, agree to scrap this obsolete protocol before a devastating error occurs."*

No gentlemen; not *our* leaders, *(Putin & Obongo)* - it is only *your* puppet-leader *(Obongo)* who needs to put a stop to the madness which he - at the behest of invisible government groups like *your* CFR- initiated in Ukraine in late 2013.

Dear readers! In the two years that your intrepid reporter here at **The Anti-New Slimes** has been dredging the cesspool located at 8th Avenue in New York, this foul-smelling morsel of Marxist manure has got to be the most ominous and chilling I have had to dissect to date.

This is getting serious.

APRIL, 2015

NY Times: Rising Toll on Migrants Leaves Europe in Crisis; 900 May Be Dead at Sea

By JIM YARDLEY

The European Union met in Luxembourg on Monday to discuss the disasters as rescuers scrambled to find survivors after ships sank Saturday and early Sunday.

REBUTTAL BY

The Anti-New York Times

The actual presentation of this tragic story in Sulzberger's Slimes is not biased in any way. It contains neither lies, nor spin. Here's an indicative excerpt from what appears to be a solid 'who - what - where - when - how - why' narrative

"The survivor described a three-tiered vessel teeming with migrants from Tunisia, Nigeria, Egypt, Somalia, Zambia and Bangladesh. ***The disaster also underscored how Libya, reeling from violence and political turmoil, has become a haven for human smuggling rings*** *along the African coastline."*

No problem with that statement; so why are we rebutting this story? The journalistic outrage here lies in what the article does *not* tell you; namely, the "why?" *(the whole "why", that is)* of the matter. Oh it does mention the chaos in Libya, but that's only 1/2 of the "why". It doesn't get into "why" formerly stable Libya is in such a sorry state. Sulzberger's slippery scumbags won't remind you, but your intrepid reporter here at **The Anti-New York Slimes** most certainly will. Remember this scene:

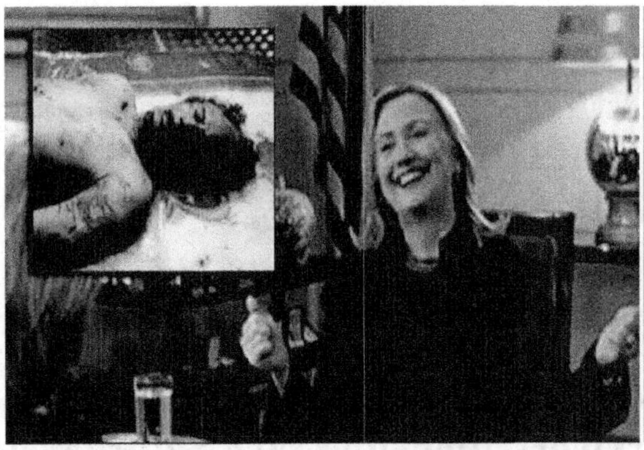

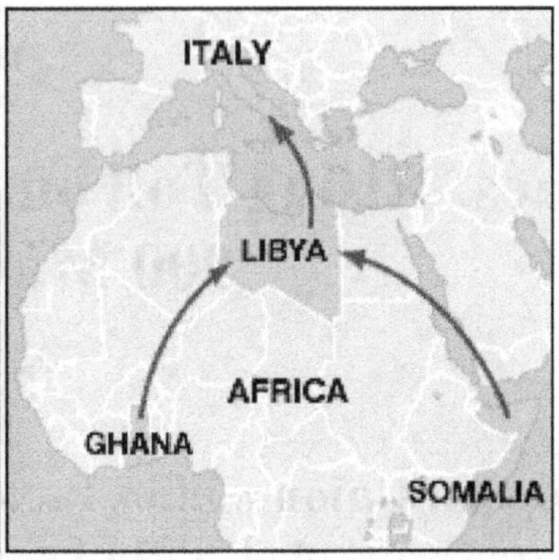

***"We came. We saw. He died."**.... and so have many others, bitch!*

Go ahead and laugh Killary. And be sure to belt out a few cackles over the deadly adverse side-effects which Homo-Obongo's brutal, Jewish-inspired 'hit' on Qaddafi is now causing in the Mediterranean. Not only have the phony CIA-NGO "Arab Spring" and the Boku Haram scams triggered a wave of desperate asylum seekers, but the destabilisation of Libya now gives human traffickers a safe route to Libyan beaches from which they can export their human cargo of misery, poverty and, in some cases, violent crime into a broke and dying Europe.

In regard to these human traffickers, The Slimes omits the national identity of most of these traffickers. Do a Google Search for the term: 'Israeli human trafficking', and have some fun plowing through the **2.1 million results.**

1- Israeli Human Traffickers are only punished when they traffic into Israel. When they dump their cargo in Europe, the world 'looks the other way'.
2- Migrants grasp the hull of a boat that ran aground on Monday. So far in 2015, about 1,500 people have died aboard ships bound for Europe.

It quite a show, isn't it? The Zionist State Department destroys Libya and other nations; then, Jewish slaver gangs engage in dangerous human trafficking of the desperate African masses *(charging them hefty back-end fees to be paid from arranged black-market slave jobs in Europe)*; then, Europe, via Libya, is flooded with non-Whites who will dilute its culture and economy; then, helpless refugees drown; all while the Jew York Slimes covers up the true causes and calls for Europe to feed, clothe and employ the hungry mobs of future left-wing voters and welfare cases.

"[The Jews] were the largest ship chandlers in
the entire Caribbean region,
where the shipping business was mainly a
Jewish enterprise.

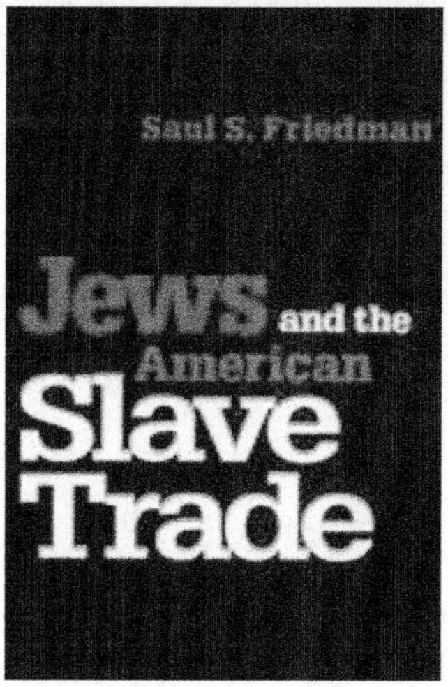

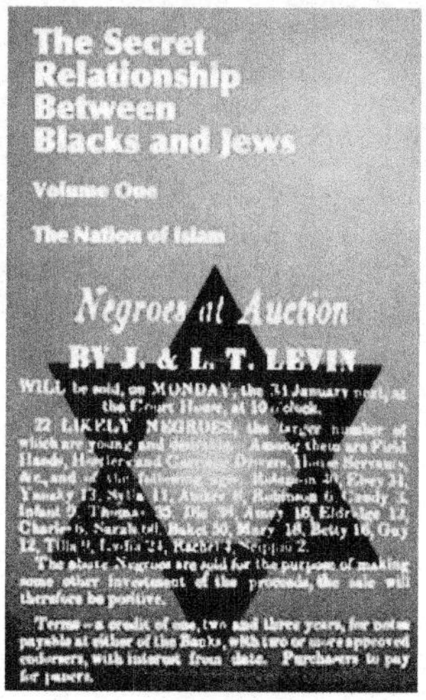

It's a fact! Jewish gangsters have engaged in slave trading and human trafficking of White & Black gentiles for many centuries. It is still going on today.

What a tragic farce that "the paper of record" continues to ignore! Either directly or indirectly, these Zionists truly are a plague upon all the races and nations of the world.

But enough about them -- let's talk about the Holocaust -**TM**.

Everything is a frickin' joke to these demented monsters!

APRIL, 2015

NY Times: Former SS Member, on Trial in Germany, Says He Was 'Morally Complicit' at Auschwitz

By ALISON SMALE

Oskar Gröning, 93, is charged with complicity in the murder of 300,000 prisoners at the Nazi death camp in 1944.

REBUTTAL BY

The Anti-New York Times

This story went un-rebutted by **The Anti-New York Times** because your sensitive reporter here gets too emotionally rattled upon learning of these sad cases of 90+ year old SS heroes being legally terrorized for an event that never happened. E-mails from the usual ignoramuses trickled into the inbox: *"Hey asshole. Even this ex-SS man now admits that there were gas chambers. I suppose you think he made it all up? Eat shit, Nazi!"*

Why even respond to such demoniacally demented drones?

But when some loyal supporters wrote in, expressing worry and confusion over Oskar Groning's "confession", and writing to the effect: "*Mike, What does this mean? I don't get it. Why would Groning say this?"* - it was time to rebut the rubbish, and issue it as a "Free Sample Day".

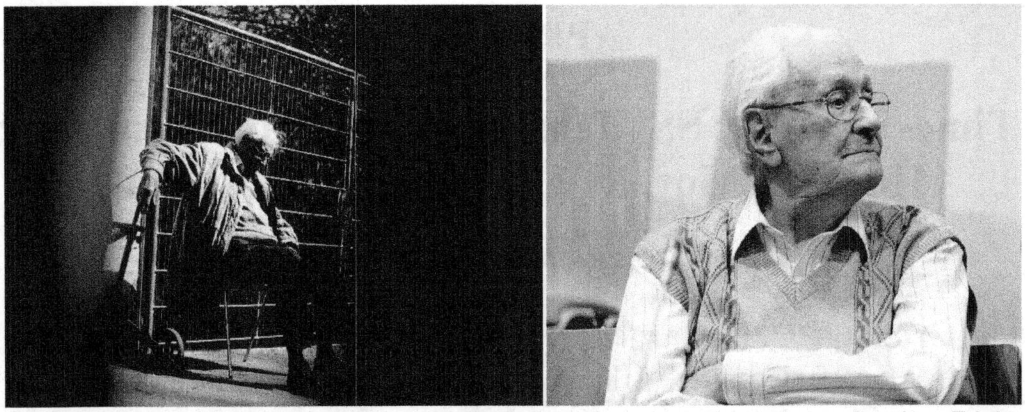

Oskar Gröning, a former SS member who worked at Auschwitz-Birkenau, during the first day of his show-trial in Lüneburg, Germany .

Friends! Any defense attorney worth a nickel would be engaging in extreme legal malpractice if he were to advise his SS client to say anything other than what Groning said; which is, *"I am so sorry."* Seriously people, can you imagine what Merkel's Marxist minions would do to this poor man if he were to compound his "crime" with the additional "crime" of "Holocaust Denial", in a courtroom in occupied Germany, no less? Herr Groning's only shot at enjoying a few years of liberty is to grovel and admit that the "gas chambers" existed.

Oh ye dear readers of weak faith! **Stay away from the Devil's Loudspeaker (TV)**. Take heed of the admonition from the 1973 classic film 'The Exorcist'. Recall the scene in which Father Merrin, the senior priest, sternly cautions the younger, inexperienced Father Karras to avoid engaging in any debate or conversation with the devil that possesses the little girl. Here is the line:

"Especially important is the warning to avoid conversations with the demon. We may ask what is relevant but anything beyond that is dangerous. He is a liar. The demon is a liar. He will lie to confuse us. But he will also mix lies with the truth to attack us. The attack is psychological, Damien, and powerful. So don't listen to him. Remember that - do not listen."

Be he physical or metaphorical, this is how the Devil operates, by mixing truth with lies; and sowing the seeds of confusion where there shouldn't be any confusion at all. Unfortunately for Father Karras, he allowed the words of the cunning demon to get into his head and rattle him, with tragic consequences for both priests. And that is what happened to the few beloved fans who sent in those concerned E-mails so suddenly filled with doubt, all on the basis of this hyped-up Groning story.

The Exorcist teaches us to not even listen to demons. The same applies to the Marxist TV, new-sites & newspapers. ***Turn them off before the lie gets into your head!***

In keeping with today's spiritual theme, it is time for a quick "booster blessing" of truth from your journalistic Exorcist here at **The Anti-New York Times.**

The WikiPedia entry for the Holocaust- **TM** sums up the official story very well. In a nutshell:

"From early 1942 until late 1944, transport trains delivered Jews to the camp's gas chambers from all over German-occupied Europe, where they were killed with the

pesticide Zyklon B. At least 1.1 million prisoners died at Auschwitz, around 90 percent of them Jewish"

You see, we are expected to believe that 1.1 million people ***(officially and suspiciously reduced from the 4 million that had been claimed for 50 years!)*** were herded into a "gas chamber" the size of a **3-car garage**, then killed by bug-spray *(Zyklon B)*, right under the noses of Red Cross camp inspectors, while inmate soccer games were going on in an adjacent field. The hard-working killers *(or their slaves)* then had to enter the poison room *(perhaps wearing HazMat suits?)*, **pick up each dead body one at a time**, and then feed them one-by-one into a funeral parlor sized oven for cremation. Whatever happened to that famed German efficiency?

1 - "One down, 1,099,999 to go....Mein Gott! Ze must be a better vay!"
2 - Jewish math. Even after an official mark-down of 3 million, the mantra of 6 million magically persists.

There is so much impossibly wrong with this Fairy Tale scenario that entire books have been written to scholarly debunk the moronic madness that is Holocaust Mania. But let us just briefly focus on a single aspect of this fraudulent fable we irreverently refer to as "The Holohoax"; namely, the numerical logistics. This piece is a good "starter" for that special person in your life who could use a good "exorcism".

Let's have a look at the "gas chambers":

*Images 1 & 2 are of the Soviet-era reconstruction of the "gas chambers". Image 3 depicts the ruins of the what is said to the original "gas chambers". Jewish Holohoaxers and Polish museum curators concede that what is shown to gullible tourists are NOT the actual "gas chambers". As you can see, both the "original" and the reconstruction are not very big - the size of a **3-car garage**.*

Now, lets have a look at a typical, sold-out NFL football stadium:

Met Life Stadium *(New Jersey / home of the NY Jets & NY Giants)*

Capacity: 82,000

1,100,000 / 82,000 = 13.4 football stadiums full of people "gassed" in a 3-car garage.

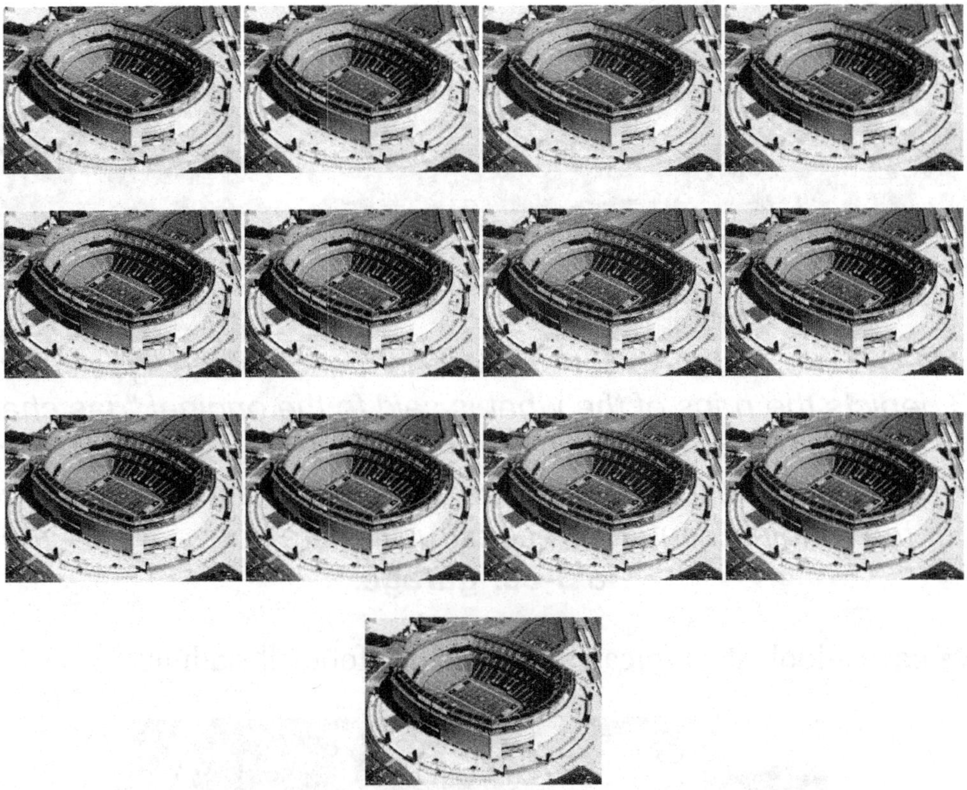

A 'Baker's Dozen' full of NFL stadiums, "gassed" in small increments in a room that looks like this? ---

Excuse us, dear reader. We'll be right back....

OK. We're back. Here is another illustration of this point, in side-by-side approximated scale for just *one* stadium:

Gas Chamber *Met Life Stadium*

Fit the stadium population into the "gas chamber" ....13.4 TIMES!

And just imagine; for 50 years they got away with telling us that it was 50 stadiums!

Poland lowers offical Auschwitz death toll

WARSAW, Poland (UPI) — A government commission has lowered the number of people believed to have perished at the Auschwitz death camp during World War II from 4 million to 1.5 million and conceded the overwhelming majority were Jews.

The decision to revise the official number of those killed in the Nazi camp was a formal rejection of original figures generated after the war by the Soviet Union, which still holds the records kept by the camp's commanders.

It is also in line with figures used by historians in West Germany, the United States and Israel who have documented the number of victims of the Holocaust.

Poland's former communist government relied on the figure of 4 million as part of a propaganda effort to make Auschwitz a symbol of Nazi oppression of all peoples, not just the Jews.

The revision was made by a commission appointed by the Culture Ministry which is determining the future direction of a museum at Auschwitz, known in Polish as Oswiecim.

A Soviet commission which came to Auschwitz in February 1945 after its liberation put the number of victims at more than 4 million. That number was questioned by historians in the West, but not in Poland until very recently.

Franciszek Piper, head of the history department of the Auschwitz Museum, told the Solidarity newspaper Gazeta Wyborcza that examination of the evidence shows at least 1.1 million people died in the camp, including 960,000 Jews. Some 233,000 survived Auschwitz.

The newspaper said the real figure may be higher but does not exceed 1.5 million.

The commission examined transport records, numbers assigned to prisoners and statistical data from ghettos around Europe to arrive at the figure.

Sam Eskanazi, a spokesman for the U.S. Holocaust Memorial Museum in Washington, said the change by the Polish commission reconciles the numbers of Auschwitz dead with those generally accepted by Western historians.

FOUR MILLION
PEOPLE SUFFERED
AND DIED HERE
AT THE HANDS
OF THE NAZI
MURDERERS
BETWEEN THE YEARS
1940 AND 1945
MILLION
MEN, WOMEN, AND CHILDREN
MAINLY JEWS
FROM VARIOUS COUNTRIES
OF EUROPE.
AUSCHWITZ-BIRKENAU
1940 - 1945

After people started asking questions, the HoloHoaxers dropped the 4 million down to 1.5, and now it is officially down to 1.1 -- still a lie!

Let's kill this lie!

APRIL, 2015

NY Times: As Attorney General, Loretta Lynch Plans Striking New Tone for the Justice Dept.

By MATT APUZZO and JENNIFER STEINHAUER

Aides say Loretta E. Lynch plans to improve the department's relationships with police groups and Congress, which have been strained during Eric H. Holder Jr.'s tenure.

REBUTTAL BY

The Anti-New York Times

With the help of about 20% of the Republi**can't** majority - including such prominent GOP stalwarts as Leader Mitch McConnell (KY), Orrin Hatch (UT), Lindsey Grahamnesty (SC), and Thad Cockroach (MS) - the "Reverend" *(barf)* Al Sharpton's hand-picked anti-White, anti-American wench was finally confirmed as the next Attorney General. Loretta Lynch is every bit as vile and hateful as Eric Holder, but perhaps even more dangerous. Whereas Holder only had protective skin pigmentation to insulate him from his crimes; Lynch adds a protective vagina to go along with her skin color. In this sick, twisted world of "political correctness", that makes her **untouchable** *(unless she openly criticizes the Israel Lobby, a la ex-Congresswoman Cynthia McKinney, in which case the protection was instantly removed).*

Lynch can and will do whatever the hell she pleases with nary a disparaging glance from the Republi**can'ts** who at least did confront Holder on a *few* occasions. Lynch is on the record as opposing voter ID laws, favoring 'gun-control' and supporting affirmative action. She has denounced all attempts to fight voter fraud as *"racist"*, adding that *"they must be stopped"*. She is pro-homosexual, pro-tranny, pro-amnesty and describes Eric Holder as one of the best Attorney Generals America has ever had. If you know Holder, and if you know Obongo, and if you know the First Beast / First Tranny, and if you know Sharpton, then you already know Loretta Lynch.

1- Al Sharpton and his "client" exit a meeting with then U.S. Attorney Loretta Lynch in New York

2- Lynch looks up to Eric the Red Holder

Of course, as is to be expected, Sulzberger's Slimes has been heralding the arrival of this degenerate piece of Sharptonite Communist garbage with front page fanfare and gushing love letters. Here's a small sample of the mushy Marxist manure splattered across the Slimes front page a few months ago

"In a 2012 speech, she (Lynch) discussed her great-great-grandfather, a free black man in North Carolina, who fell in love with her great-great-grandmother, a slave. "Unable to purchase her, in order to marry her he had to stay on and re-enter bondage," she said.

Her grandfather was a sharecropper and a pastor who helped black people who had been falsely accused escape the Jim Crow South. And her father, also a pastor, held civil-rights meetings in his church. She remembered quizzing her mother about why she had picked cotton in high school. "And she looked at me and said, 'So that you never have to,' " Ms. Lynch said."

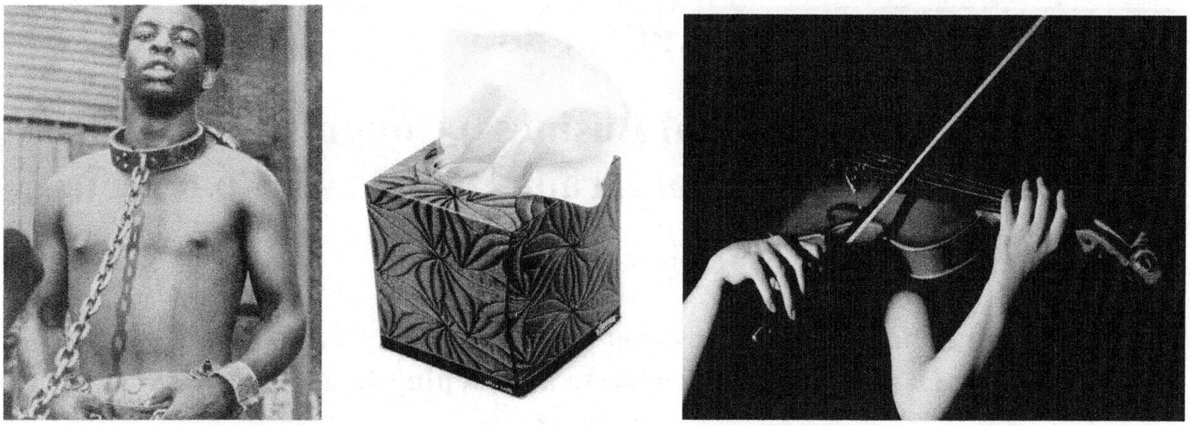

The same old sob song, over and over and over again

Pushing the damaged Eric Holder aside and installing this clone will allow the Democrats to advance their anti-White Marxist agenda harder and further than ever. Watch how easily the gutless Republi**cant's** roll over like puppies as this vile wench escalates the assault on White America while pushing for the Federalization of local police departments. And don't hold your breath expecting her to do anything about the "knockout game" or the Communist and Black Panthers currently organizing for war.

November 2014: Sharpton is pleased!

The grinning grease-ball cheers as he hears of Lynch's appointment.

APRIL, 2015

NY Times (International Business) Congressional Panels Approve Fast Track for Trade Deal, With Conditions

By JONATHAN WEISMAN

House and Senate committees this week easily agreed to give President Obama fast-track authority to negotiate a sweeping trade accord with Pacific nations.

REBUTTAL BY

The Anti-New York Times

The Republi**can't** "opposition" lined up behind Homo-Obongo yet again as the House Ways and Means Committee voted 25-13 on a bill that would limit Congress to *only* voting 'yes' or 'no' on the **Trans-Pacific Partnership** deal, without the ability to make amendments. Representative Paul Ryan, (R-WI), the committee's chairman and an ardent supporter of TPP, kept some reluctant members of his Party in line and voted down substantive changes to the bill. Said the "conservative" Ryan of his beat-down of conservatives and his spirited defense of the liberal Obongo's latest sellout of America, *"This is a strange world we're in these days."*

In spite of public grand-standing for the cameras, Ryan and Boehner work for the same Globalist Mafia as Obongo. Their enthusiastic support for TPP proves this.

Like NAFTA and the European Common Market before it, TPP is being hard-sold as a "free trade agreement". **But 6 of the 11 other nations in the TPP already have free-trade agreements with us; and the other 5 face only minimal tariffs.** So why the "bi-partisan" urgency in getting it passed? And, just like Obongo-Care, neither Congress nor the American public are being afforded the opportunity to read the full voluminous agreement. If this monstrosity is anything like NAFTA - and you *know* that it will be, expect a further deterioration of U.S. manufacturing and a further surrender of U.S. sovereignty to the institutions of its parent N.W.O Incorporated. **Also expect the signatory members to be lured away from the Russia-China orbit as they become more entrenched in the U.S. "sphere of defense".**

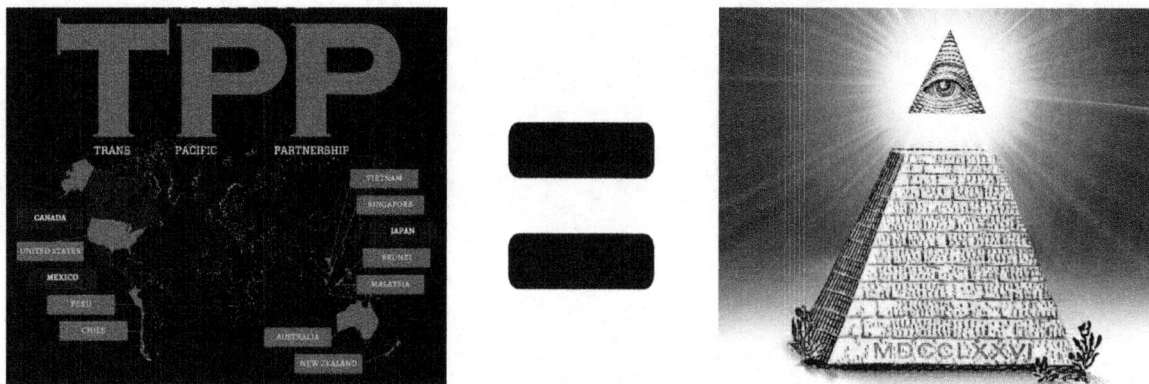

Math made easy: TPP = NWO

But the ultimate poison-pill, the true death blow to what's even left of America's traditional culture, is the immigration tsunami that TPP will eventually set off. Under the TPP, Congress would lose the power to restrict additional immigration. We will soon find ourselves in a position where anyone from anywhere can come to America even *more* easily than is already the case.

You see, TPP contains a barely noticed provision that allows for the free migration of labor among the signatory nations. Patterned after similar provisions in the treaties establishing the European Union, it would override national immigration restrictions in the name of facilitating the free flow of labor. The draft treaty, now under discussion among these Pacific Rim nations - including the Mexico, Vietnam and other poor nations - makes provision for needed labor to move across national boundaries without restraint. Adios America, and 'gracias' Senors Obongo y Ryan y McConnell.

It's all about the **New World Order**; a dirty idea that is "bi-partisan."

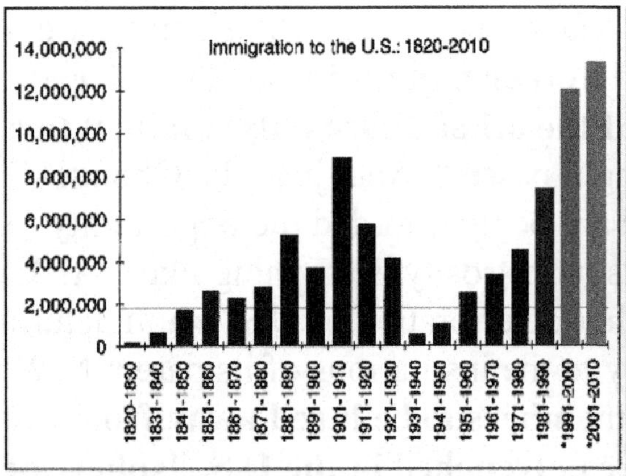

Drop dead White America. The invasion is about to intensify.

APRIL, 2015

NY Times: Russian Hackers Read Obama's Unclassified Emails, Officials Say

By MICHAEL S. SCHMIDT and DAVID E. SANGER

The hackers did not appear to have penetrated closely guarded servers that control the message traffic from President Obama's personal BlackBerry, officials said.

REBUTTAL BY

The Anti-New York Times

The big bad Russians are cyber-attacking us again, if Sulzberger's Slimes and certain "unnamed officials" are to be believed, that is. The key term in the headline: *"Officials say"*. The key term in the sub-headline: *"Officials said"*.

Immediately upon wading into this putrid cesspool of smear and innuendo, your nauseous reporter and his trusted feline side-kick here at **The Anti-New York Times** quickly found another qualifying, 'cover-your-ass' term in the very first paragraph: *"according to senior American officials briefed on the investigation."*

In paragraph three: we *again* find, *"according to officials briefed on the investigation"*.

In paragraph four: *"White House officials said that..."*

Paragraph five: *"But officials have conceded that..."*

Paragraph six: *"Officials did not disclose..."* and later on the same paragraph: *"Aides say..."*

Paragraph seven: *"The hackers — who are **presumed** to be linked to the Russian government..."* and then again: *"Senior White House officials have known..."*

Paragraph eight: *"said one senior American official briefed on the investigation."*

Paragraph nine: *"Others confirmed"*, then followed by: *"another senior official said"*.

Paragraph thirteen: *"...the spokeswoman said."*

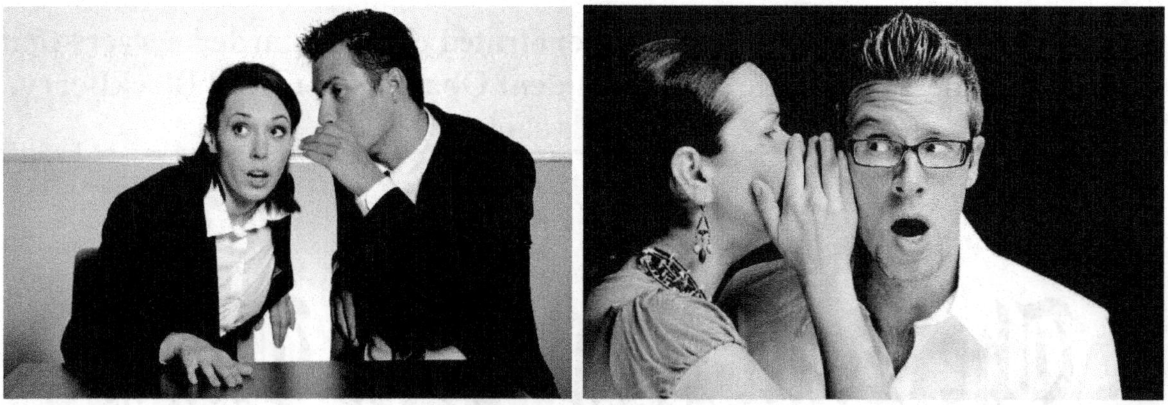

"Putin did what?!"

The baseless Globalist gossip continues:

Paragraph fourteen: *"Officials who discussed the investigation **spoke on the condition of anonymity**."* Later in same paragraph: *"..others familiar with the investigation said that...all signs pointed to Russian."*

Paragraph seventeen: *"..officials at the White House said."*

Paragraph twenty-one: *".. one senior American official said."*

Paragraph twenty-three: *"this person added."*

Paragraph twenty-four: *"Others say.."*

Paragraph twenty-seven: *"senior officials said."*

He said; she said; this person said that he said that she said; she said that he said that he heard it from a friend who heard it from another friend who got it from an anonymous source....blah, blah blah. Who exactly are these "unnamed officials" that the Slimes always seems to dredge up to put out the latest scare story? Do they even exist? Or are these "officials" like the 6' 4" talking rabbit from the 1950 movie "Harvey", starring Jimmy Stewart. In the film, no one is able to actually see or talk to Big Harvey except for Stewart.

This is what passes for front page "journalism"on the front page of America's most "respected" newspaper. What a sick twisted joke Sulzberger continues to play on his gullible liberated readers!

"Pssst. Hey Jimmy. You wanna know a little secret I just learned about the Russian hackers?"

APRIL, 2015

NY Times: Gay Marriage Case Caps Cincinnati's Shift From Conservative Past

By SHERYL GAY STOLBERG

As the Supreme Court prepares to hear oral arguments on same-sex marriage, Cincinnati has become the measure of how far the gay rights movement has come in a traditionally conservative city.

REBUTTAL BY

The Anti-New York Times

In those parts of the country in which the mental and moral cancer of liberalism has yet to metastasize, the Marxists and their homosexual legions have turned to the court system to expedite the death blow to what was once conservative Christian Middle-America. And oh how Sulzberger's Slimes just luuuvs throwing these types of stories in our faces.

Emboldened by the Marxist media, the sodomite brigades have expanded the "the struggle".

The cancer can now be found anywhere and everywhere.

Playing upon the mushy sentimentality of the weak-minded, as always, The Slimes explains:

"Jim Obergefell says he "instantly pictured growing old" with John Arthur when they fell in love here in 1992. Just seven weeks after they began dating, Mr. Arthur gave Mr. Obergefell a ring set with diamonds — a sign that, in their hearts if not in law, they were married."

Two decades later, with Mr. Arthur dying of Lou Gehrig's disease, they did marry, aboard a medical charter jet on the tarmac of an airport in Maryland — a state where, unlike Ohio, gay people could wed. When Mr. Arthur, 48, died in October 2013, Ohio refused to list Mr. Obergefell as his spouse on the death certificate. Furious, Mr. Obergefell sued."

The Homo Hissy Fits are working. One by one, even many churches are caving in, or at least 'looking the other way' to the new "tolerance". The double-standard that bars a man from "marrying" his dog, his sheep his mother, or his son can no longer be justified. There are such people who engage in these practices. Why should they be denied the "right" to fornicate and marry? As even the Pinko Pope decreed, *"Who am I to judge?"*

The real power behind this subversive movement lies neither within the courts nor with the foot-stomping homosexual brats. Those are just the tools. It is the usual suspects who are injecting the deadly cancer cells into every nook and cranny of the American body. Vice President Biden has confirmed:

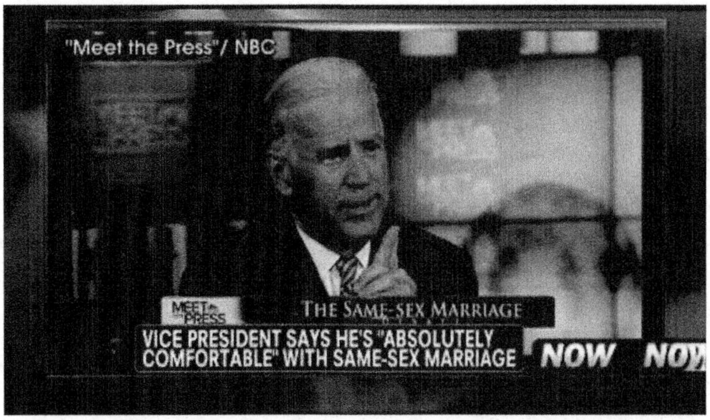

"I believe what affects the movements in America, what affects our attitudes in America are as much the culture and the arts as anything else. I bet you 85 percent of those changes, whether it's in Hollywood or social media are a consequence of Jewish leaders in the industry. ***The influence is immense; (he repeats) the influence is immense.*** *And, I might add, it is all to the good. "* - Joe Biden

Yes, Joe. It's *"all to the good"*. Thanks Jews!

Move over Walton Family! The "Modern Family" is the new model for a New World Order. It's all good.

APRIL, 2015

NY Times: Baltimore Enlists National Guard and a Curfew to Fight Riots and Looting

By SHERYL GAY STOLBERG

Several officers were injured as police cars were damaged and rocks were thrown. Protesters smashed windows, and a CVS drugstore was set on fire.

REBUTTAL BY

The Anti-New York Times

Obongo's "sons" are at it again; marching, chanting, whining, burning, robbing, rioting, attacking etc. It's just like the turbulent 60's again, except this time the local politicians actually aid and abet the mayhem instead of cracking down. The National Guard has finally been deployed, but only after a deliberate delay and after the damage has already been done.

Even more disturbing than the images of destroyed stores and burned-out cars is the recurring "National Conversation" *(barf)* that ensues every time these types of events occur. To listen to the libtard talking heads and pseudo-intellectual sophists drone on and on about "disenfranchisement" and "poverty" and "racism" and "police brutality" is as comical as it is predictable as it is nauseating as it is superficial.

Ignore that commie crap. Here are the *real* "root causes" of the problems in American inner-cities:

1. Deliberately engineered decline in religion, morality and common decency

2. Fatherless families: 75% of births to unmarried promiscuous "baby mommas" incentivized by the liberal welfare state

3. Degenerate "hip-hop" subculture that glorifies violence and anti-White sentiment

4. Jewish-Marxist "community organizers" who deliberately agitate in Black communities

5. Jewish-Marxist Hollywood and news media than fan the flames of racial animosity

6. Debt-based monetary system and oppressive tax structure that grinds people down

The REAL "Root Causes"

Those 6 elements, and perhaps a few more that we missed, create an explosive cocktail. A single incident of real or perceived "police brutality" *(whether the accusation is true or not is irrelevant)* is all that it takes to trigger the explosion. Leave it to malevolent Marxists and their wholly-controlled superficial libtards to blame the match for the explosion; while ignoring the accumulation of gunpowder and gasoline which preceded it. To make matters worse, they were the ones who put together the deadly mixture of combustible elements in the first place!

How's that for a "National Conversation"?

"White Folk suck" -- "Black folk suck".....as their common Marxist enemy rubs his hands in Satanic glee.

APRIL, 2015

NY Times: Pope Francis Steps Up Campaign on Climate Change, to Conservatives' Alarm

By CORAL DAVENPORT and LAURIE GOODSTEIN

An effort by the pope to further the issue of climate change and environmental stewardship is already angering some thinkers on the American right.

REBUTTAL BY

The Anti-New York Times

The vile Argentinean Marxist pretending to be a "Christian" continues to misuse his papal office in order to push the Globalist Marxist agenda, and hard! It's funny how Sulzberger's Satanic scribblers are so enamored with Frankie the Fake. **Why this unprecedented outburst of admiration for the head of the very church that the Jewish Supremacists have long despised?** The article offers us a clue:

"Top Vatican officials will hold a summit meeting Tuesday to build momentum for a campaign by Francis to urge world leaders to enact a sweeping United Nations climate change accord in Paris in December. The accord would for the first time commit every nation to enact tough new laws to cut the emissions that cause global warming."

The hype for this fraudulent November-December event in Paris is building. The evil Pinko Pope has given it his enthusiastic blessing!

Vatican officials have convened several meetings already on the topic. Last month, they even met with a senior administrator of Obongo's EPA, Gina McCarthy. In the U.S. the Pinko Pope's coming encyclical will be accompanied by a 12-week propaganda campaign, now being prepared with the participation of some Catholic bishops, to actually talk about "Climate Change" in sermons.

The fact that a Frankie-lover named Dan Misleh, the executive director of the Catholic Climate Covenant in Washington, is quoted in the story tells us much. Misleh's resume as a Commie-Catholic speaks for itself. He is a "living wage" advocate, a "social justice" activist, an "immigration reform" defender, and a "climate action" promoter.

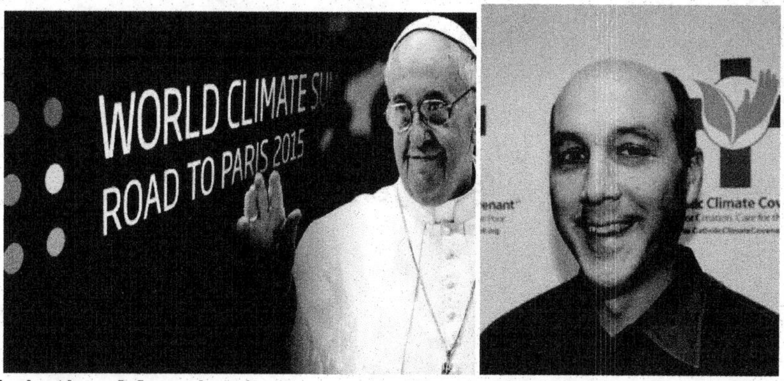

Misleh the Marxist is very excited about Frankie's fakery!

The sad story continues:

"The Vatican summit meeting will focus on the links between poverty, economic development and climate change, with speeches and panel discussions by climate scientists and religious leaders, and economists like Jeffrey Sachs of Columbia.

The United Nations secretary general, Ban Ki-moon, who is leading efforts to forge the Paris accord, will deliver the opening address."

Satan's stooge won't condemn sin of any kind. He remains mum on promiscuity, easy divorce, fatherless families, abortion, homosexuality, trans-genderism and genocidal U.S. warmongering. But get this pious phony chatting about "income inequality", third world immigration, "tolerance" for what he refers to as "gays", and now, "Global Warming"; and boy-oh-boy does he suddenly become passionate!

And that is why this useless usurper, this insidious impostor, this closet Communist *(and quite possibly a closet something else)* has, **from day #1 of his unprecedented Vatican coup of a sitting Pope**, been applauded by the Marxist media which has dubbed him: **The New World Pope**.

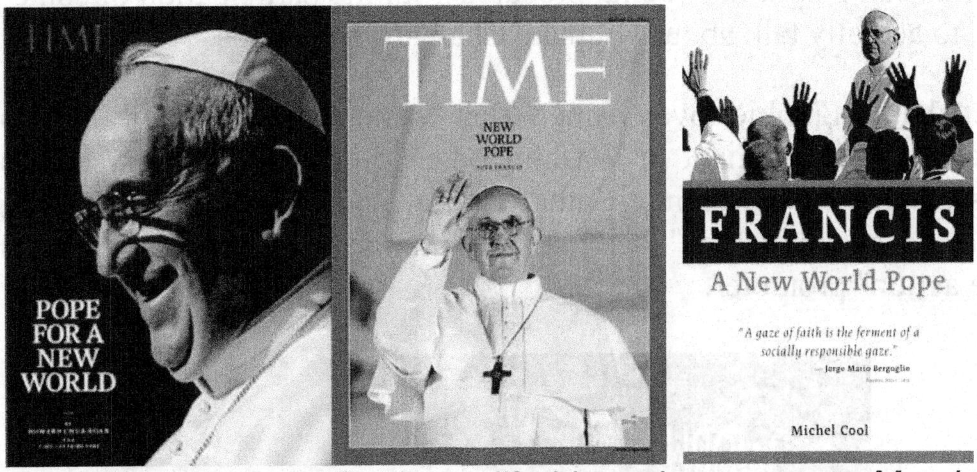

"Marxist ideology is wrong. But in my life I have known many Marxists who are good people, so I don't feel offended (at being called a Marxist)."

APRIL, 2015

NY Times: A Landmark Gay Marriage Case at the Supreme Court

By Editorial Board

If anyone doubted the depth of the discrimination that gays and lesbians continue to face across America, an outburst partway through the arguments provided a bracing reminder.

REBUTTAL BY

The Anti-New York Times

About a half-hour into the oral arguments over whether sodomite "marriage" is a Federally-protected "right", a man in the back of the gallery began shouting that "same-sex marriage" violates the Bible. After he was dragged out kicking and screaming, Justice Antonin Scalia quipped, *"It was rather refreshing, actually."*

Reading about these proceedings is almost surreal. Who, even just 10 years ago, could have envisioned the day when the Supreme Court of the United States would even *consider* imposing this abnormal abomination upon all 50 states. Consider; in 1972, the justices *summarily* dismissed a petition asking them to grant the "right" of "same sex marriage".

"This was not what I risked my neck for!"

Since then, the legal landscape, as well as the attitude and moral standards of *Boobus Americanus* have, *by design*, degenerated greatly. In 1972, not a single state permitted this spitting-in-the-face of the Divine Intelligence that animates the Universe. Today, 36 states protect this grave sin against nature and nature's God. The remaining 14 states that still ban it now find themselves under relentless pressure from the poofter-lesbo- tranny brigades and the mighty Jewish-Marxist media which empowers them. Couples from four of the hold-out states — Kentucky, Tennessee, Ohio and Michigan — are asking the Supreme Court to rule that the bans violates constitutional guarantees of equal protection.

We KNOW which way the three court Marxist Jews *(Breyer, Ginsburg and bull-dyke Kagan)* will vote, as well as the possible crypto-Jew and rumored lesbian, Soto*mayor*. We also know which way conservatives Scalia, Alito and Thomas will vote. The big question mark is whether it will be the "moderate" Justice Kennedy or the "moderate" Justice Roberts who hammers the final nail in the double-coffin of America's morality and sanity.

The three "lovelies" from New York City are in the bag for Federally mandated homo-marriage and the child adoption that it entails. So is Bolshevik Breyer.

"This definition (of marriage) has been with us for millennia," said Justice Kennedy. *"It's very difficult for the court to say, oh, well, we — we know better."*

Sounds promising, but Kennedy could very well be playing a game here by *pretending* to be "deliberative". That's why these "oral arguments" are a joke. The justices already know which way they are going to vote on big matters such as these. We suspect that since Roberts was the sell-out who gave Obongo-care the decisive vote; it will be Kennedy's turn to betray America by joining the Jewish bloc of justices.

You know, given that Sugar the Cat's vet bills are a persistent nuisance, I wonder if I can petition the court to allow people to marry animals. That way, I can add her to my health insurance policy. Who are you to judge?

*1- Roberts & Kennedy. Expect one these Republi**can't** Rats to betray God and Country.*

2- If those two queers can get "married", why not Mike and the cat?

MAY, 2015

NY Times (International): North Korea Executed 15 Top Officials in 2015, South Korean Agency Says

By CHOE SANG-HUN

North Korea has executed 15 high-ranking government officials this year, the South Korean intelligence agency told lawmakers on Wednesday.

REBUTTAL BY

The Anti-New York Times

Well, if the wholly-owned U.S. puppets in South Korea say so, then it must be true. After all, we have all seen how reliable the claims of America's vassals in Kiev have turned out to be.

(rolling eyes)

This piece of disinformation is loaded with the usual qualifiers: *"During a closed-door briefing"*; and *"according to two lawmakers who attended the session"* and *"the lawmakers said";* followed by another *"the lawmakers said"* and *"a South Korean lawmaker, told reporters"* and *"South Korean officials said";* and then, in closing, one more, *South Korean officials said"*.

The Slimes didn't even make an effort to contact the North Korean Embassy for comment, even though it is located just a handful of blocks away on 2nd Street in

Manhattan, as is NK's mission to the UN. Whatever the SK puppets allege is printed. NK's response is not important. Why such one-sided and unfair treatment towards NK?

The imaginary sources are at it again:

"Pssst. Hey Jimmy. You wanna know a little secret I just learned about political murders in North Korea?"

It's all very simple. Israel and North Korea, despite being on opposite ends of the Asian continent, are bitter enemies. North Korea does not recognize Israel, and has condemned its treatment of the displaced Palestinians.

More importantly, North Korea sells its advanced missile technology to the Mid East nations on Israel's 'Hit List'.

NORTH KOREAN PRESIDENT WANTS OBAMA TO CALL HIM!

In March of 2012, NBA Basketball legend Dennis Rodman visited North Korea and befriended its President, Kim Jong Un, Upon returning to America, Rodman appeared on ABC with George Stephanopoulos's, and delivered the following message to President Barack Obama, and America:

RODMAN: *"I love him. The guy (Kim Jong Un) is awesome. He was so honest"*

"One thing he asked me to give Obama something to say and do one thing. ***He wants Obama to do one thing, call him****."*

.... That's right. He told me that. He said, if you can, Dennis, ***I don't want to do war. I don't want to do war.*** *He said that to me,"*

"Guess what, the one thing I said to him, I said, we talked about -- if you see the clips or whatever, he loves basketball. And I said, Obama loves basketball, let's start there, all right? Start there. If you see the quotes in the papers, he says that. He says that about sports. Both of you guys love basketball so much."

On another occasion, in response to a heckling reporter's question about "human rights" and U.S. - North Korean relations, Rodman angrily referred to both Obongo and then-Secretary of State Killary Rotten Clinscum as "assholes".

It appears as though the barely literate Rodman has more sense than the sophisticated libtards who worship the Slimes.

Educated in Switzerland, and fluent in English, NBA fan Kim enjoys a basketball game with Rodman.

'I really don't want war. Tell Obama to call me."

MAY, 2015

NY Time: Chinese and Russian Navies to Hold Joint Drills in Mediterranean

BBy JANE PERLEZ

The Chinese Navy will hold joint exercises with Russia in the Mediterranean in May, China's Defense Ministry said Thursday, a further indication of the closer ties between the two countries.

REBUTTAL BY

The Anti-New York Times

China's shocking announcement that it will join Russia in live-fire naval exercises in the *Mediterranean* sends a huge message to the Globalist Axis of Evil. The news came just as the puppet prime minister of Japan, Shinzo Abe, was visiting his masters in Washington. Abe and Obongo declared that Japan and the United States would increase their military cooperation, a move that China criticized, and now, has responded to.

Your peace-loving reporter here at **The Anti-New York Times** would like to be able to say that this show of strength will go along way to preventing World War III, but knowing what we know about the psycho Zio-Globo Mafia, it could just as well mean that we are closer than ever to a worldwide catastrophe. Time will tell.

Russia and China continue to move closer and closer.

The story quotes Peter Dutton, a professor of strategic studies at the United States Naval War College in Newport, Rhode Island:

"It suggests Russia and China are sending a political signal to the U.S. and Europe that the continental powers are standing together to support each other's expanding interests in the face of maritime opposition."

Leave it to The Slimes and its hand-picked "expert" to spin this as an expression of the *"expanding interests"* of Russia and China; suggesting that only America, "the exceptional nation", has the right to sail the seven seas - even when China and Russia are clearly under various forms of aggressive attack from the Globo-Zio West and its vassal states.

We would however like to thank Sulzberger's Slimes for letting one very interesting little "cat out of the bag":

"The Chinese Navy has operated in the Mediterranean before, most notably when China's warships helped rescue more than 30,000 Chinese workers stranded in Libya after the downfall of Qaddafi in 2011."

How convenient that the Arab Spring - CIA overthrow of Qaddafi ended up driving China out of Libya. Will a forced Chinese exodus from Nigeria and Sudan, at the hands of the CIA's proxy 'Boku Haram' accomplish the same? Professor Dutton and the Slimes won't touch that question; preferring to frighten us with tales of Russo-Chinese "naval ambitions" instead.

1- Chinese nationals flee Libya for Tunisia after the fall of Qaddafi.
2- Greeks vessels help Chinese to escape Libya.

MAY, 2015

NY Times: 6 Baltimore Police Officers Charged in Freddie Gray Death

By ALAN BLINDER and RICHARD PÉREZ-PEÑA

Prosecutors in Baltimore described repeated mistreatment of a 25-year-old man whose death has set the city on edge.

*

NY Times: Marilyn Mosby, Prosecutor in Freddie Gray Case, Takes a Stand and Calms a Troubled City

By SHERYL GAY STOLBERG and ALAN BLINDER

Ms. Mosby, who on Friday announced criminal charges against six police officers in Mr. Gray's death, took office only four months ago, elected with the backing of community activists.

REBUTTAL BY

The Anti-New York Times

Even after we have witnessed the horrible legal precedents set by recent cases such as the George Zimmerman trial and the Darren Wilson trial - both of which should never even have been considered - the **murder and manslaughter** charges just filed against six Baltimore cops are shocking to behold. A no-good thug causes his own death by banging his head against the interior walls and door handle of a police van; Obongo's agent provocateurs and the Marxist media stir up riots; and the mindless mob is fed a pound of flesh by a Black Communist State Attorney with open ties to "Community Organizers" *(Communist street agitators)*.

After the charges were announced on Friday, celebrations broke out across Baltimore. Drivers honked their car horns as degenerate scum took to the streets with fists raised in triumph. State Attorney for Baltimore Marilyn Mosby said the death of the 25-year-old feral thug, Freddie Gray, was a homicide. She made this false allegation knowing full well that another prisoner in the van *(who is now watering down his story out of fear)* had confirmed that St. Freddie was violently banging his own head *(as drugged-up crack-heads in handcuffs so often do)*.

Donta Allen is now changing his story about how St. Freddie (right) died.

The preliminary autopsy on Gray showed no evidence that his fatal injury – broken vertebrae – occurred during his arrest. It does show that he received a head injury while being transported. The medical examiner found that Gray's neck was most likely broken when he slammed into the back of the police transport van. The metal door handle is said to match the head wound.

When these facts come out at trial, it will be hard to imagine a jury convicting these six cops, which is probably the point! The Marxist media is not going to let go of this, and neither will Obongo's rabble hordes. If and when these cops are found "not guilty", expect last week's riots to seem like a toddler's temper-tantrum. Oh how far Obongo's America has fallen -- and we haven't even hit bottom yet.

Through several layers of "buffers", the riot-starting Black Panthers take their marching orders from Obongo.

The violence could go nationwide and create the "crisis" that Obongo and his handlers are longing to "solve" for us. The plan is for a summer of riots and a strong government "response" leading to a Homeland Security takeover of local police departments. And don't discount the possibility of an Obongo third term growing out of this mayhem in 2016.

At least that seems to be the grand ambition. Whether they can pull it off or not remains to be seen. Let’s just hope that the rabble-mob grows tired and fizzles out, as was the case in Ferguson and St. Louis.

The Baltimore Orioles baseball team had to play before an empty stadium after White fans were attacked by Black mobs at the previous game.

"Oy. This is gonna be fun!"

MAY, 2015

NY Times: Strikes on Syria Tied to Deaths of 52 Civilians

By ANNE BARNARD

Airstrikes by the American-led coalition against Islamic State militants have killed several dozen people in northern Syria, with the death toll from Friday's attacks rising to more than 52 civilians

REBUTTAL BY

The Anti-New York Times

Can you just imagine the uproar of the pious hypocrites of the "international community" if the pro-Russian "separatists" of eastern Ukraine had "accidentally" killed 52 civilians? You see, only the "exceptional nations" *(U.S. & Israel)* and their surrogates *(Kiev & Saudi Arabia)* are permitted to mete out death and destruction in the name of "democracy" or fighting terrorists. That's when murder becomes known as acceptable "collateral damage".

In an August 2014 issue of **The Anti-New York Times,** your prescient reporter here wrote:

****

"Syria has repeatedly warned that it will consider unauthorized bombings on its territory as an act of aggression. Dr. Assad isn't stupid. He knows what this dirty game is all about. So do the Russians and so do the Chinese.

Look out Mr. Assad, the heroic American "rescuers" are coming not for ISIS, but for you. Good luck sir."

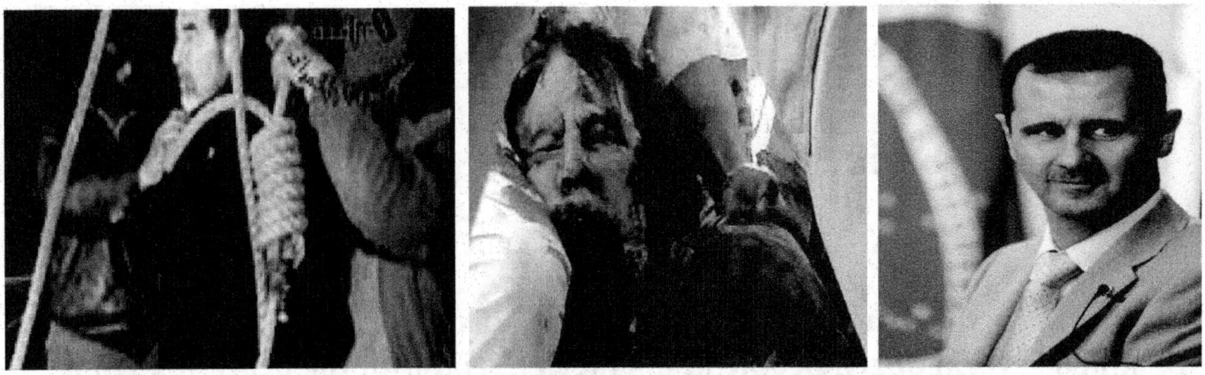

Saddam (Iraq), Dead / Qaddafi (Libya), Dead / Assad (Syria), still hanging on!

****

Obongo's MURDER of 52 Syrian civilians *("mistaken" for ISIS)* now ups the ante for Assad and puts him in a very difficult position. He is duty-bound and honor-bound to defend his people. However, if Syria starts shooting at American planes, it will provide the Yankee Devil with the pretext he has been hoping for. What to do? -- What to do?

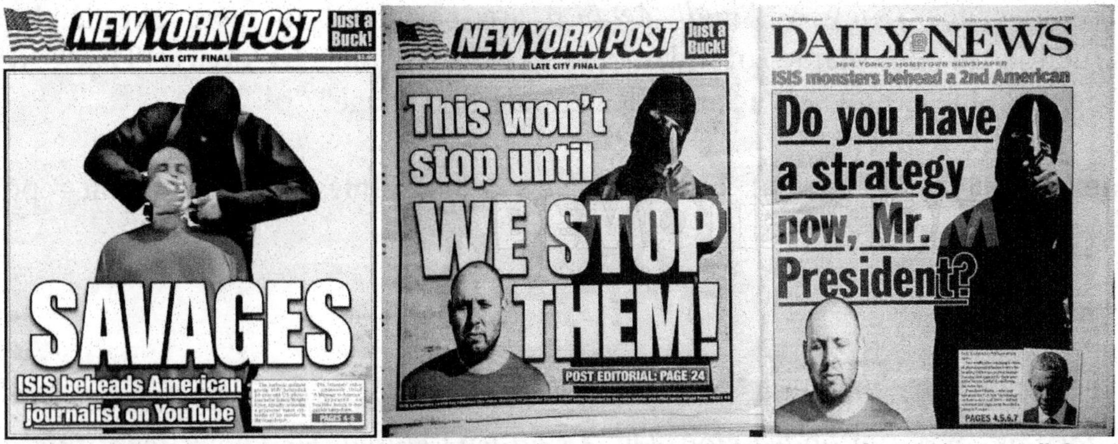

The intense media pressure that was placed upon America to "do something" in order to "stop ISIS" has now resulted in the killing of 52 Syrian civilians.The fake 'beheading' videos of ISIS cut away just as the throats of the strangely calm 'victims' are about to be cut by the really bad actors in black. The 'victims' didn't even squirm!

This long-festering problem in the Middle East isn't going to fade away until Bibi Satanyahu finally gets his Unholy War of Zionist expansion with Syria, Iran and Lebanon. The only thing that has prevented the big blow-up from happening is the strong hand of the Russia-China bloc; which is why the EU and Japan are being pressured to confront the respective giants who refuse to buckle under to the New World Order.

The Zio-Globalists want the Assad Family dead! But Assad is holding firm.

MAY, 2015

NY Times: An Atlas of Upward Mobility Shows Paths Out of Poverty

By DAVID LEONHARDT, AMANDA COX and CLAIRE CAIN MILLER

A decades-old effort found that moving poor families to better neighborhoods did little to help them. A new look at the data suggests the opposite.

REBUTTAL BY

The Anti-New York Times

TRANSLATION: Get ready White suburbanites. Obongo's "sons" and "amigos" are coming to a 'cul de sac' near you.

All these decades of "studying" poverty, and the answer to "inequality" was right under our noses all along. Thanks to this latest "study" - the findings of which, according to the article, ***"have been presented to members of the Obama administration, as well as to Hillary Rodham Clinton and Jeb Bush, both of whom have signaled that mobility will be central themes of their 2016 presidential campaigns."***

Be assured that this latest buzz-word - "mobility" - is not to be confused with the traditional methods of climbing the socio-economic ladder *(hard work, discipline, frugality, patience etc.)* In Marxified Amerika, such quaint old fashioned virtues are as outdated as knickerbockers and petticoats. In the abomination that is the Obama-Nation, "mobility" will be achieved simply by transplanting the feral inmates of the inner-city into the suburbs *(on the 'racist' suburban taxpayers' dime, of course).* Sulzberger's hand-picked academics argue that the Welfare Queen's loud litter of fatherless pups will somehow magically transform into the Huxtable Family when we place them in the White suburbs.

Before the move

After the move

Amazing what a lawn and some trees can do! Nonetheless, ladies, if the charming 'Dr. Huxtable' offers you a drink, politely decline.

After the Los Angeles riots of 1992, the social engineers of Congress created an anti-poverty scheme called 'Moving to Opportunity'. It gave vouchers to help poor families move to better neighborhoods. As even this Slime's article confirms, **the long-term results showed no significant improvement in either education or income.** The idiot "intellectuals" were at a loss to explain why the scheme failed.

Now, from Manhattan's Mount Olympus comes the trumpeted word of a "new study" to contradict the old one. Typical! Harvard egg-head Raj Chety, the author of the study and protege of Harvard's Martin *Feldstein (cough-cough)*, is quoted:

The data show we can do something about upward mobility. Every extra year of childhood spent in a better neighborhood seems to matter."

We are quite certain that Professor Chety's community will be exempted from the coming "cultural enrichment" that will be unleashed upon the middle-class suburbs. As with so many of these "studies", the great and good "intellectuals" who craft them are so blinded by their preconceived biases and well-meaning pipe dreams, that they fail to notice the inherent flaws and circular logic *(illogic)* embedded in their experiments. For example, the article reveals:

"Based on the earnings records of ***millions of families that moved*** *with children, it finds that poor children who grow up in some cities and towns have sharply better odds of escaping poverty than similar poor children elsewhere."*

Mr. Chety, did it occur to you that the "families that moved" did so because they had *already* escaped poverty? In other words, the families did not achieve upward mobility because they moved. They moved because they achieved upward mobility! Having moved up as the result of hard work, focus and discipline, is it really so surprising that such parents would then pass those values onto their children, who then go on to become more successful adults?

If the bleeding heart Chety is so concerned about "poverty", perhaps he should go back to India and put his "Harvard training" to use in improving the slums of New Dehli.

Whether they are merely stupid or just plain evil, logic never seems to matter to these academic Lefties. David B. *Grusky (cough-cough)*, director of the Center on Poverty and Inequality at Stanford University, adds his two-cents:

"This (study) delivers the most compelling evidence yet that neighborhoods matter in a really big way."

That's great, David. Why don't you adopt little Malik?

Of course, at the highest levels of America's PRC *(Predatory Ruling Class)*, the "anti-poverty" spin for this totalitarian scheme has a much darker motive. The Globo-Zio elite couldn't give a rat's arse about the sanctified "poor". **The goal here is the obliteration of White America** *(and Mother Europe).* And this "study" fits in perfectly with what we already know about Obongo's plans to flood the suburbs with free-loaders. From U.S. News & World Report, 2013 - Read it and weep:

HUD Proposes Plan to Racially, Economically Integrate Neighborhoods

The Department of Housing and Urban Development has proposed a rule to desegregate U.S. neighborhoods.

"The Department of Housing and Urban Development has proposed a new plan to change U.S. neighborhoods it says are racially imbalanced or are too tilted toward rich or poor, arguing the country's housing policies have not been effective at creating the kind of integrated communities the agency had hoped for.

The proposed federal rule, called "Affirmatively Furthering Fair Housing," is currently under a 60-day public comment period. Though details of how the policy would specifically work are unclear, the rule says HUD would provide states, local governments and others who receive agency money with data and a geo-spatial tool to look at "patterns of integration and segregation; racially and ethnically concentrated areas of poverty; access to education, employment, low-poverty, transportation, and environmental health."

Oh *Boobus Caucasianus Americanus (and Europithecus, Canadius and Australopithecus)*! Has the mind-numbing and soul-crushing din of the Devil's Loud-speaker (TV) so dulled your mind and desensitized your heart to the point that you cannot hear the death-bells tolling, nor see the grim reaper of genocide approaching? Evidently so.

1- "Yo! Snow White. Ya'll want some of diz, neighbor?"

2 - Meanwhile, Snow White's father has more important things on his mind.

MAY, 2016

NY Times: Germany, Too, Is Accused of Spying on Friends

By ALISON SMALE

Germany's foreign intelligence service, known here as the B.N.D., is being accused of monitoring European companies and perhaps individuals.

REBUTTAL BY

The Anti-New York Times

Since the tragic defeat of the Great One who ruled The Third Reich, puppet Germany has always gotten good press from Sulzberger's Slimes. Only recently has a steady stream of mildly anti-German propaganda begun to ooze out of the New York cesspool at 8th Avenue. First, it was the very strange plane crash said to have been caused by a suicidal German pilot that Germany's Airlines "should not have allowed to fly". Now comes this story of German espionage aimed at its "friends". Why the sudden bad press regarding Germany?

Poor Angela Merkel. The Frumpy Frau is stuck between a CIA rock and a German hard place. On the one end of the vice, Merkel's Globalist masters are pushing Germany *(and all other European nations)* towards confrontation with Russia. Pushing back just as hard are the German business class and the German public itself; both of which want no part of World War III against a friendly country which Germany does a *ton* of business with.

Many Europeans are very reluctant to cut off ties with their Russian business partners.

For your astute reporter here at **The Anti-New York Times,** "the dead giveaway" that this recent attack is a CIA squeeze play lies in this excerpt from the article:

"The current flare-up started on April 23 when ***Der Spiegel*** *reported that since at least 2008, a division of the B.N.D. had helped the National Security Agency to spy on European and German interests, including the French-German enterprise European Aeronautic Defense and Space, now known as the Airbus Group."*

You see, *Der Spiegel* is Germany's foremost Globalist-CIA, anti-Putin mouthpiece. Though always pro-Merkel in the past, the fact that it would embarrass her like this now reveals just how tight of a bind she is in.

Globalist Der Spiegel is squeezing Merkel to confront Putin.

Make no mistake about Merkel. She is indeed a vile, cold-hearted, tyrannical, despicable, servile, American-owned, Zionized Marxified wench in every respect. The only reason her warmongering is not as fanatical as the Globalists would like is because of the massive pushback she is getting from her own people.

Being an obedient servant of the Zio-Globo crime syndicate comes with great personal rewards, but it's not always easy. More and more, the Frumpy Frau is coming to realize this.

German float depicts Merkel waving American flags as she emerges out of Uncle Sam's posterior.

MAY, 2015

NY Times: Mike Huckabee Joins Republican Presidential Race

By TRIP GABRIEL

Mike Huckabee, who excited evangelical voters in his first presidential race in 2008 and retains much of their good will, announced on Tuesday that he would again seek the Republican nomination

In order to allow *Boobus Americanus* to enjoy the illusion of choice, the Idiocracy that is America's PRC *(Predatory Ruling Class)* has many facets to it. There are the Marxists, the Neo-Cons, the "liberals", the "conservatives", the "moderate" conservatives, the "moderate" liberals, center-right, center-left, center-center with a regional twist etc. Pick your favorite flavor of PRC ice-cream; but the milk base, sugar content and caloric value are all the same.

The flavor appeal of former Arkansas Governor Mike **Huckster-**bee is for the blood-thirsty, Old Testament, Christian-Zionist hordes who have been brainwashed into worshiping Israel. These Unholy Rollers are a sub-group of the Neo-Cons. Under the influence of the altered "Scofield Bible", this comical cult has been trained to believe that those who bless Israel will be zapped up to heaven when the "Rapture" comes.

Face-Palm indeed, Jesus. Face-Palm indeed!

Though professing to be followers of Jesus Christ *(aka The Prince of Peace)*, the Rapture Bunnies never met a war for Israel or a Gaza bombing they didn't cheer for. These are the deranged mental cases who form the core constituency for Mike Hucksterbee, a former Southern Baptist pastor and Arkansas governor. During his announcement speech, the charming Hucksterbee, as always, wore his "faith" on his sleeve by describing a childhood of school prayer. He then took Homo-Obongo to task for putting:

"more pressure on our ally Israel to cease building bedrooms for their families in Judea and Samaria than we do on Iran for building a bomb."

What Hucksterbee failed to mention is that those "bedrooms" that the Israelis are building are over the lands and, in some cases, over the dead bodies of the poor Palestinians that have been forced out. "Blessed are the peacemakers.", eh Pastor Mike? Furthermore, Iran is **<u>not</u>** building a nuclear bomb. "Thou shalt not bear false witness.", eh Pastor Mike?

This smooth-talking snake-oil salesman *knows* he can't get the nomination, nor does he actually want it. There just aren't enough Rapture Bunnies in the northern states. So, why bother? Hucksterbee's candidacy has two objectives:

- To draw votes away from other non-Establishment Republicans such as Ben Carson and Rancid Paul.
- To personally benefit from the "face-time" that comes with participating in the Quadrennial Freak Show.

Huckster's last GOP Primary campaign (2007-8) is what led to the cushy multi-million dollar talk show he currently enjoys at FOX, ***<u>and</u>*** the rapid rise of his *numerous* books up the New York Slimes Best Seller list ***and*** his $70,000 per speech motivational gig. "The love of money is the root of all evil, eh Pastor Mike?

Hucksterbee's Presidential campaigns are meant to sell uninteresting and platitude-filled books to his idiot followers.

The Zionists have also rewarded "Pastor" Hucksterbee with a TV Show and paid motivational speaking gigs. "He will bless those who bless Israel", eh Pastor Mike?

We here at **The Anti-New York Times** do not begrudge anyone's financial success. Indeed, the selling of books is what keeps **TomatoBubble** online! But when such an immense, multi-million dollar fortune is being accumulated under false pretenses, namely, the false hope of a viable political campaign to "take back America" that Hucksterbee is giving to the gullible Rapture Bunnies, we are compelled to call this sociopathic piece of filth out as the deceptive, money-grubbing political operative that he is. The Zionist joke is on you, Rapture Bunnies!

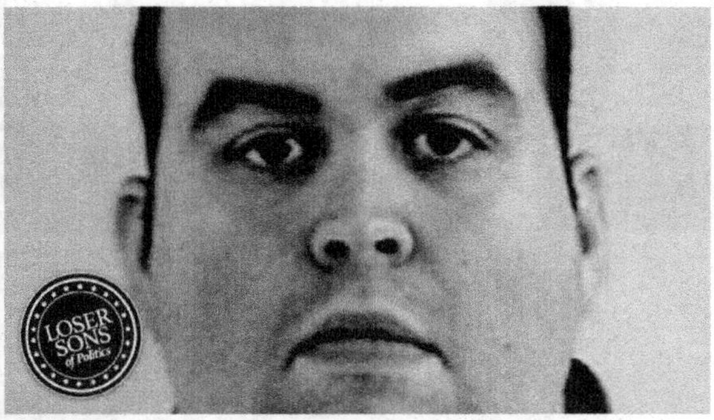

1- Before surgery, Hefty Hucksterbee was as large as Crispy Creme Christie. "All things in moderation", eh Pastor Mike?
2- Hucksterbee's degenerate son, David, hung a stray dog by his neck and stoned it when he was 17. Pressure from Papa Governor got the little fat monster off.

May 8, 1945

BLAST FROM THE PAST

70 YEAR ANNIVERSARY OF "V-E DAY"

The New York Times.

THE WAR IN EUROPE IS ENDED!
SURRENDER IS UNCONDITIONAL;
V-E WILL BE PROCLAIMED TODAY;
OUR TROOPS ON OKINAWA GAIN

GERMANS CAPITULATE ON ALL FRONTS

American, Russian and French Generals Accept Surrender in Eisenhower Headquarters, a Reims School

Wild Crowds Greet News In City While Others Pray

Summary of News of the War and German Surrender

NY Times: Oswiecim Killings Placed at 4,000,000

By C L SULZBERGER / By wireless to The Times / Page 12 / Column 5

Soviet Commission Reports Death Camp in Poland Was Founded by Himmler

REPRODUCED BY

The Anti-New York Times

EXCERPTS ***(Images & captions added by The Anti-New York Times)***

Moscow - More than **4,000,000** persons were systematically slaughtered in a single German concentration camp - that at Oswiecim in Poland, near Krakow from 1939 - 1944. The Germans thus accomplished with scientific efficiency the greatest incidence of mass murder in recorded history.

This slaughter exceeds in barbaric intention and method not only the greatest brutalities of such infamous conquerors as Genghis Khan but also surpasses even Germany's own record in previous prize exhibitions at Maldenak, Dachau and Buchenwald.

Such is the miserable tale made public today - on the eve of the official end of the European War - **by the Soviet Union's Extraordinary State Commission** investigating the extermination center at Oswiecim.....these are the first statistical data of the camp's record.

Poland reduces Auschwitz death toll estimate to 1 million

By Krzysztof Leski
and Ohad Gozani
LONDON DAILY TELEGRAPH

LONDON — Poland has cut its estimate of the number of people killed by the Nazis in the Auschwitz death camp from 4 million to just over 1 million.

The vast majority of the dead are now accepted to have been Jews, despite claims by the former Polish communist government that as many Poles perished in Hitler's largest concentration camp.

The revised Polish figures support claims by Israeli researchers that Poland's former communist [illegible] the num- [illegible] the es-

960,000 Jews, between 70,000 and 75,000 Poles, nearly all of the 23,000 gypsies sent to the camp and 15,000 Soviet prisoners of war. Mr. Piper stressed that the figures are minimum estimates but said the total number of dead was unlikely to exceed 1.5 million.

Shmuel Krakowsky, head of research at Israel's Yad Vashem memorial for Jewish victims of the Holocaust, said the new Polish figures were correct.

"The 4 million figure was let slip by Capt. Rudolf Hoess, the death camp's Nazi commander. Some have bought it, but it was exaggerated."

Mr. Krakowsky accused Poland's former communist government of perpetuatin[illegible] in an

If Stalin says 4,000,000 were killed at Auschwitz, then it must be true, eh Sulzberger?....Oops...somebody over-estimated it seems (and even the 1,000,000 is a lie).

According to the Soviet Commission, "more than 4,000,000 citizens of the Soviet Union, France, Belgium, the Netherlands, Czechoslovakia, Yugoslavia and other countries.....were exterminated at Oswiecim. The methods used were "shooting, famine, poisoning and monstrous tortures."

The report states that **gas chambers**, crematoria, surgical wards, laboratories and clinics were erected around Oswiecim to accomplish this mass production monstrosity.

.....Public baths were installed for group cyanide poisoning.

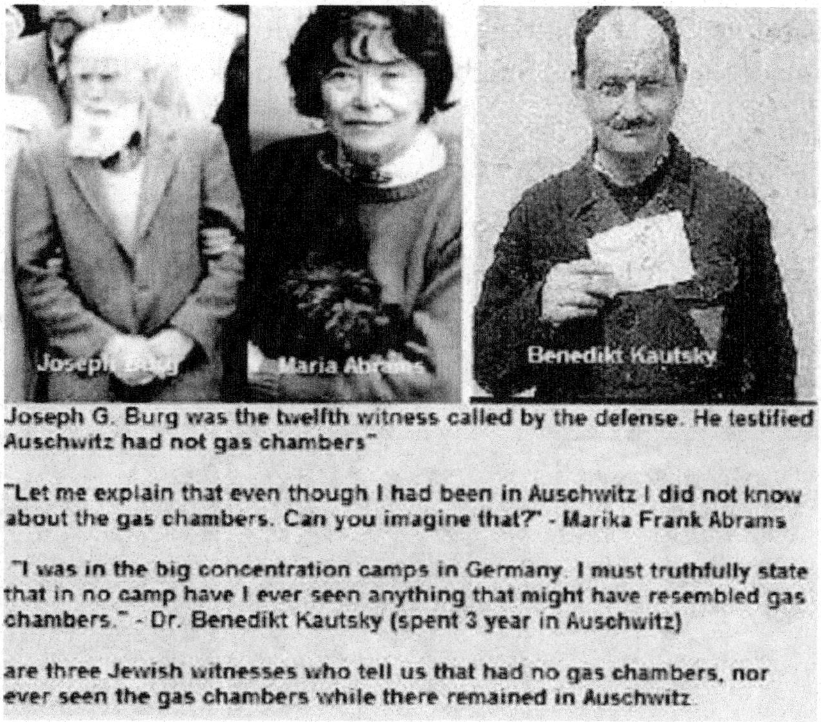

Joseph G. Burg
Maria Abrams
Benedikt Kautsky
Joseph G. Burg was the twelfth witness called by the defense. He testified Auschwitz had not gas chambers"
"Let me explain that even though I had been in Auschwitz I did not know about the gas chambers. Can you imagine that?" - Marika Frank Abrams
"I was in the big concentration camps in Germany. I must truthfully state that in no camp have I ever seen anything that might have resembled gas chambers." - Dr. Benedikt Kautsky (spent 3 year in Auschwitz)
are three Jewish witnesses who tell us that had no gas chambers, nor ever seen the gas chambers while there remained in Auschwitz.

Auschwitz inmates who stated they knew nothing about "gas chambers"

....The report states that in 1943 the frugal Germans decided to sell the unburned bones to the firm of Schterhm....in addition to the 113 tons of crushed bones, loads of women's hair were sold for industrial purposes.

.....human guinea pigs were kept alive for experimentation.

Within 24 hours, each crematorium was able to consume more than 10,000 bodies, it is stated on the basis of information provided by the survivors interviewed.

The report names a long list of war criminals responsible for these "unbelievable crimes". Himmler heads the list.

Pravda, commenting on the monstrous tale, repeats the Allied pledge to hunt the criminals to the ends of the earth, adding, "were it not for the Red Army, Europe would still be covered with packages of women's hair and crushed human bones trade-marked from Oswiecim."

****

No rebuttal from **The Anti-New York Times** necessary. Stalin's **unverifiable** Bolshevik Bull-Shine - conveniently released just as Germany surrendered and thus unable to refute the allegations - and wired to New York for publication by **C L Sulzberger** of the infamous Sulzberger clan; speaks for itself quite well.

C L Sulzberger - prolific peddler of pinko propaganda.

MAY, 2015

NY Times: Justice Department Will Investigate Baltimore Police Practices

By MATT APUZZO and SHERYL GAY STOLBERG

The Justice Department will investigate whether the Baltimore Police Department engaged in a pattern of unconstitutional policing.

REBUTTAL BY

The Anti-New York Times

The Un-Reverend Al Charlatan's hand-picked successor to Eric the Red Holder has wasted no time in picking up the anti-White Communist flag and moving "the agenda" forward. Loretta Lynch-Mob's project is to use real and / or invented cases of "police brutality" as a pretext for breaking the independence of local police departments in order to eventually Federalize them.

The Slimes puff-piece quotes Ms. Lynch-Mob:

"The situation in Baltimore involves a core responsibility of the Department of Justice — not only to combat illegal conduct when it occurs, but to help prevent the circumstances that give rise to it in the first place,"

Chilling, totalitarian language. To that end, Lynch-Mob will *"investigate Baltimore Police Practices"*, but not investigate the growing epidemic of random, and often murderous Black on White Hate Crimes.

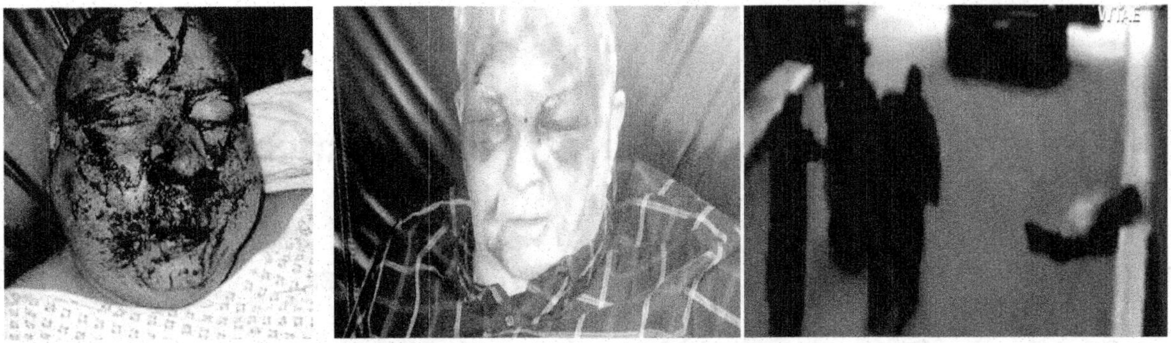

Nobody in the Obongo administration seems to care about the random White victims of the brutal "Knockout Game".

She will *"investigate Baltimore Police Practices"*, but not investigate the clear, admitted and widespread voter fraud taking place in American inner cities.

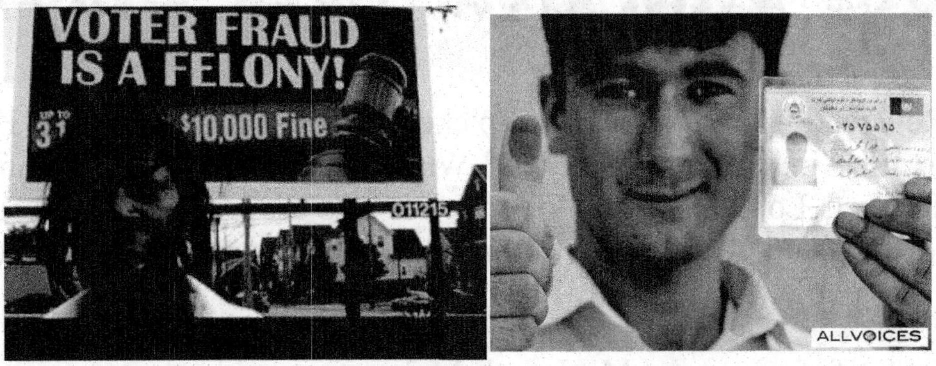

1-Why do Blacks get so defensive over efforts to stop voter fraud?
2- Under American supervision, Afghan voters are required to show ID and have their thumb stamped in ink.

She will *"investigate Baltimore Police Practices"*, but not investigate Obongo's continued funding of and support for "community activists" who have been known to foment riots and rig election results.

Welcome to the White House! Obongo and Lynch-Mob protect the paid agitators.

She will *"investigate Baltimore Police Practices"*, but not investigate the loud and open pleas by Louis Farrakhan and the New Black Panthers to begin murdering White people.

1- For a fee, the street activists of the New Black Panther Party will allow you to "slap a cracker"
2- An open call for civil war.

She will *"investigate Baltimore Police Practices"*, but not investigate the organized and now government-funded invasion of America by record numbers of illegal aliens, including many known criminals and gang members.

Coming to America?

Years ago, the anti-White machinations of the Marxists were somewhat concealed. Today, the War on Whites is "in your face". The Jewish Mafia is engineering it, the Communist Demoncraps are waging it, the supine Republi**can'ts,** - not wanting to be called "racist" - are totally standing down, while *Boobus Retardicus Americanus* watches his ball games and 'Dancing With the Stars'. It's all so friggin' gosh-darn bloody vomit-inducing.

A one-way ticket to Russia is looking better and better every day!

*Republi**cant's** like Rancid "Voter-ID-is-offensive-to-African-Americans" Paul and Senor Jeb Bush have totally sold out on the War Against Whites.*

MAY, 2015

NY Times: Obama Scolds Democrats on Trade Pact Stance

By PETER BAKER

President Obama lashed out at critics within his own party as he accused fellow Democrats of deliberately distorting the potential impact of the sweeping new trade agreement he is negotiating with Asia

REBUTTAL BY

The Anti-New York Times

What's this? A Demoncrap Party revolt against their anointed leader? Can it be that some Demoncraps actually do care about their Labor constituencies after all? Will the Demoncraps try to scuttle the pending TPP Asian-Trade scam? Some big names are supposedly really spitting-mad with the President, and the feeling appears to be mutual.

Drama from the article:

"*With the cutting tone he usually reserves for his Republican adversaries, Mr. Obama said liberals who are fighting the new trade accord, the Trans-Pacific Partnership, were "just wrong".*

"His sharp criticism seemed aimed partly at ***Senator Elizabeth Warren****, a Massachusetts Democrat leading the fight against the trade deal."*

His remarks may only further provoke ***Senator Harry M. Reid*** *of Nevada, the minority leader who was already said to be so annoyed by Mr. Obama's language lately that he was motivated to make a more robust effort to block trade negotiating authority."*

Anti-TPP Representatives **Rosa DeLauro**, (D-CT) and **Louise Slaughter**, (D-NY) are also quoted in the story. Wow! This "rebellion" is really getting serious! .... Or is it?

Warren vs Obama. Can this be true?

Allow your rat-smelling reporter here at **The Anti-New York Times** to expose this sleazy manipulative con-game for what it truly is. You see, Homo-Obongo and the First Tranny will be gone after 2016 *(or will they?)*. Assuming that Obongo is indeed headed for a cushy retirement lifestyle of crack-smoking and serial sodomy in sunny Hawaii; what does he bloody care if "the Labor vote" gets angry with him? The only concern here is that the Demoncraps *as a whole* do not become viewed as "sell-outs".

This is especially problematic for the Harvard Communist wench, Elizabeth Warren, who, should Killary falter, could be tapped as "the first woman President" instead. A false-fight between big name Demoncraps and Homo-Obongo will do much to protect the Party's phony facade of "pro-Labor". Wily Warren is racking up some serious points here. One can just hear the lunch-bucket unionized crowd talking politics in the cafeteria this coming Monday:

Joe: *"I like that Warren lady. She ain't gonna back down to Obama. She is standing up for our jobs."*

Bill: *"Yeah. She's got more balls than most guys too. She's got my vote!"*

Charlie: *"Me too. You think the Steelers are gonna win the division this year?"*

Wily Warren: just a "regular gal" in a diner who taught only one class and raked-in $400,000 per year at Harvard - as some of her lesser affluent students are left to choke on student loan debt.

Knowing that the bosses of the Republi**can't** Party *(McConnell, McCain, Boehner, Ryan et al)* are "all in" for the sovereignty-killing TPP, Obongo can easily afford to lose, and actually *wants* to lose as many Demoncrap votes as possible and have the deadly deal still fly. **This is exactly how Bill Clinscum played the big NAFTA vote in 1993.**

These types of sneaky manipulations are the typical hallmarks of sociopaths and criminals. Obongo is "in on it". The phony "populist" Wench Warren is "in on it". And Harry Reid, the Republi**can't** leadership, and, of course, Sulzberger's Slimes are also "in on it" .

The joke is on you, "Blue Collar" America!

Bend over and grab your ankles, American working man. The "Bi-Partisan" TPP Express is coming.

MAY, 2015

NY Times: Billionaire Lifts Marco Rubio, Politically and Personally

By MICHAEL BARBARO and STEVE EDER

As Marco Rubio has ascended in the ranks of Republican politics, an auto dealer named Norman Braman has emerged as a remarkable and unusual patron.

REBUTTAL BY

The Anti-New York Times

Calm down. Let's not all jump to conspiratorial conclusions here, folks. So, this old man in Florida is a billionaire; and he once owned the Philadelphia Eagles football team, and he bought himself one of the Republican Party's top tier candidates for the 2016 nomination, and his name sounds like it *could be* Jewish. That doesn't prove a darn thing. There are plenty of non-Jewish billionaires in America, and this Braman character could just as easily be of German ancestry.

My goodness! What's wrong with you "anti-semitic" conspiracy wackos? Have you learned nothing from your personal fountain of Socratic wisdom here at **The Anti-New York Times?** Always gather the data before jumping to half-baked conclusions!

Socrates, Confucius and Buddha all say, "Get the facts first!"

This Braman fellow is probably just a well-meaning, old-time, true-blue American patriot who happens to naively believe that Rubio will be good for America. Here, I'll prove to you that your fears of Jewish domination are unfounded and irrational. By simply Googling "Norman Braman", we will lay this "anti-Semitic canard" to rest:

From Wikipedia:

"Braman ..... grew up in the Cobbs Creek section of Philadelphia, where his father owned a barbershop. Braman's parents were both Jews who emigrated from Europe."

So you see, there is nothing to be concerned about. Braman's parents were both Jews; and they......

Ooops.

All joking aside, it is so damn disturbing, so amazing, and so "in-your-face" how the Billionaire Jew Boys are openly buying up their respective candidates like so many horses for the Kentucky Derby. Soros buys Obongo; Adelson buys Bush; Braman buys Rubio; and Sulzberger's Slimes openly reports about it as if it actually *were* a horse-race: *"It's Bush by a nose, followed by Walker on the outside, now here comes Rubio as they approach the stretch!"*

But shhhhhh! Don't say anything. That would be "anti-semitic" -**TM**!

There is nothing that can be said about this astonishing expose that it doesn't clearly state on it's own. Some sickening excerpts - (with some red emphasis added):

"As Mr. Rubio has ascended in the ranks of Republican politics, Mr. Braman has emerged as a remarkable and unique patron. He has bankrolled Mr. Rubio's campaigns. He has financed Mr. Rubio's legislative agenda. And, at the same time, ***he has subsidized Mr. Rubio's personal finances****, as the rising politician and his wife grappled with heavy debt and big swings in their income.*

Now, with Mr. Rubio vaulting ahead of much of the Republican presidential field, Mr. Braman is poised to play an even larger part and become Mr. Rubio's single biggest campaign donor, with an expected outlay of approximately ***$10 million*** *for the senator's pursuit of the White House.*

A detailed review of their relationship shows that Mr. Braman, 82, has left few corners of Mr. Rubio's world untouched. ***He hired Mr. Rubio, then a Senate candidate, as a lawyer; employed his wife to advise the Braman family's philanthropic foundation; helped cover the cost of Mr. Rubio's salary as an instructor at a Miami college; and gave Mr. Rubio access to his private plane.***

The money has flowed both ways. *Mr. Rubio has steered taxpayer funds to Mr. Braman's favored causes, successfully pushing for an $80 million state grant to finance a genomics center at a private university and securing $5 million for cancer research at a Miami institute for which Mr. Braman is a major donor.*

The Boy-Wonder and his Israel Firster Sugar-Daddy.

Even in an era dominated by super-wealthy donors, Mr. Braman stands out, given how integral he has been not only to Mr. Rubio's political aspirations but also to ***his personal finances****.*

Mr. Braman and aides to Mr. Rubio have declined to say how much ***personal financial assistance*** *he has provided to Mr. Rubio and his wife, directly or indirectly, but it appears to total in the* ***hundreds of thousands of dollars.***

***Mr. Braman hired Mr. Rubio's wife, Jeanette**, who had little professional experience in philanthropy, and her company, JDR Events, to advise the Braman foundation. Mr. Braman declined to discuss her compensation.*

Mr. Rubio said the offers of work from Mr. Braman had a simple motivation: "We are close personal friends. They trust us."

How is this even legal?

Norman Braman signals support as Marco Rubio announces his presidential candidacy. The similarities between Jewish moguls and race-horse owners is striking.

MAY, 2015

NY Times: Raúl Castro Meets With Pope Francis at Vatican

By JIM YARDLEY

President Raúl Castro of Cuba visited Pope Francis at the Vatican on Sunday, praising the Argentine pontiff for helping to broker last year's diplomatic breakthrough between Cuba and the United States

REBUTTAL BY

The Anti-New York Times

Popes meet with all types of world leaders. Therefore, Frankie the Fake's sit-down with one of the infamous Castro Brothers of Cuba does not necessarily constitute another "red flag" warning about what this Pope is all about. But when you have a Castro gushing this passionately about a Pope, it just offers further evidence in favor of our theory that Frankie is a "liberation theologian" Communist mole. Red Raul Castro on Satan's Pope:

*"I promise to go to all his Masses, and with satisfaction. I read all the speeches of the pope, his commentaries, and **if the pope continues this way**, I will go back to praying and go back to the church. I'm not joking."*

What an interesting comment. *"...if the Pope continues **this way**"*? And exactly what "way" might that be, Senor Castro? Well, the Left way, of course! After all, Raul's daughter is a vocal advocate in favor of homosexuals and their "right" to marry.

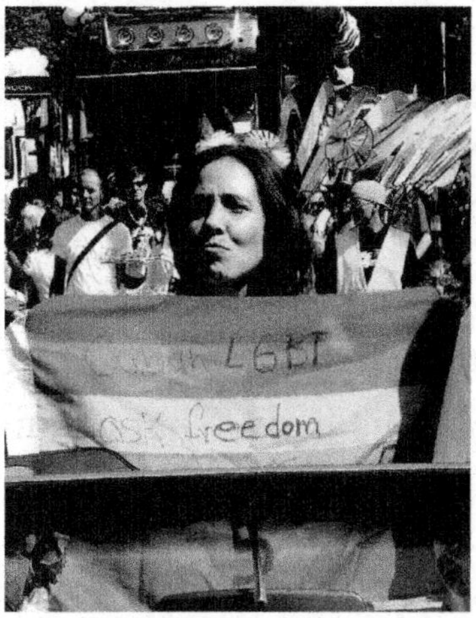

Mariela Castro loves the Homo-Pope

A review of Frankie the Fakes ever-worsening resume:

- Aided and abetted known Communist activists in Argentina
- Is softening up the Church's position on homosexuality
- Is softening up the Church's position on "forgiving abortion"
- Is removing conservative Bishops and Cardinals from their positions

Anti-homosexual U.S. Cardinal Raymond Burke was demoted by Frankie Faker. Meanwhile, Satan's Pope kisses the hand of Agedo Foggia, a controversial priest who openly advocates for homosexual marriage.

- Advocates for illegal immigration and "anti-racism" into the US and Europe
- Incites against "income inequality" *(buzzword for "I want socialism")*
- Is pushing for UN action to combat non-existent "Global Warming"

It's no wonder the Marxist homosexuals of the degenerate and dying West, as well as the Communist Castros of Cuba, all seem to absolutely adore this Globalist clown who the Pinko Press has dubbed "**The New World Pope**". That *alone* is all the evidence of guilt one needs to condemn this self-aggrandizing charlatan.

Trust **The Anti-New York Times**, dear reader; when a truly righteous man gains a bit of fame, you will be able to gauge his credibility by the truck loads of foul-stinking filth which the media-machine dumps upon his head. That certainly is not the case with Satan's Pope!

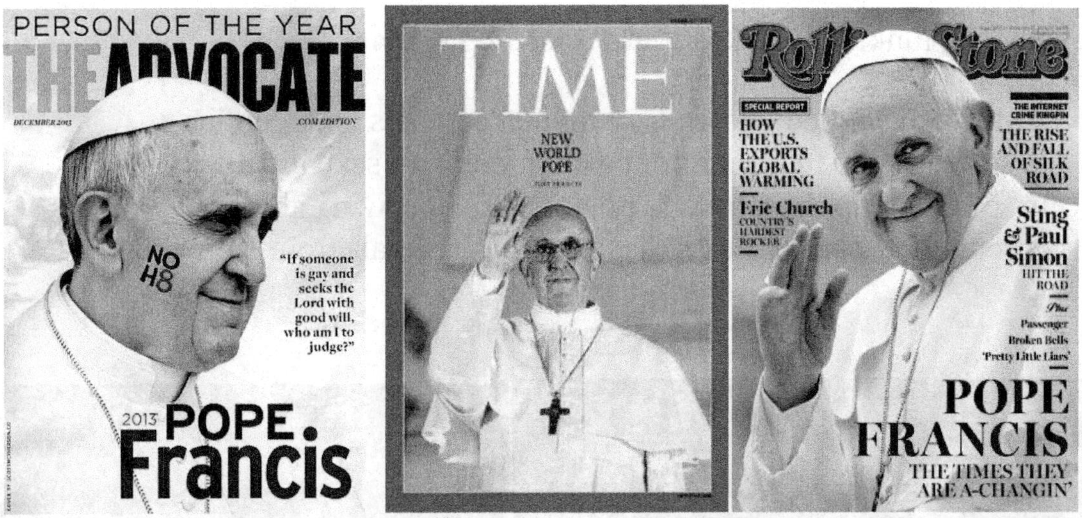

The amazing fact that magazines such as the sodomite Advocate, Marxist Time, and degenerate Rolling Stone have turned this wicked monster into an international "rock-star" is all the evidence needed to establish his unholy fakeness.

MAY, 2015

NY Times: Senate Democrats Foil Obama on Asia Trade Deal

By JONATHAN WEISMAN

A vote halted consideration of legislation granting President Obama "fast track" power to complete a major trade accord with 11 nations in the Pacific Rim.

REBUTTAL BY

The Anti-New York Times

What a sleazy, cynical, sickening display of gamesmanship and psychological manipulation is being played here. In "blocking" Homo-Obongo's authority to "fast-track" the Globalists' cherished TPP deal, Senate Demoncraps have not only positioned themselves as the oh-so-caring defenders of American interests; but have actually maneuvered the "opposition" Republi**can'ts** into playing the role of the Capitalist "bad guys" who are pressuring Obongo into fast-tracking a bad deal!

From the article:

"In Congress, Republicans were sharply critical of Democrat efforts to add layers of complexity to the bill. 'This is not a game. This is about trying to accomplish something important for the country that happens to be the President's No. 1 domestic priority"

Bitch McConnell isn't the only propping up Obongo. Senator's Cornyn, Hatch, Thune, McCain et al have all come to Obongo's "defense". Senator Thune (SD), the Senate Republi**can't** conference chairman, said Democrats were *"throwing their own President under the bus."*

South Dakota's Slick Senator saves Obongo from being "thrown under the bus". How thoughtful!

"Under the bus", eh Senator? Even a dim-witted pretty-boy like you couldn't possibly believe that rubbish. A closer reading of the Slimes' article reveals that the Democraps actually **do not** oppose the TPP, *at all*! Their only "complaint" is that they can't add amendments to any "fast-tracked" version of TPP.

Here:

"Democrats have united around demands that trade promotion authority be paired with a series of other measures, not only to crack down on currency manipulation, but also to assist workers displaced by globalization, tighten child labor law and fortify the government's response to unfair trade practices."

The Great "Debate"?

Hatch & McConnell: Don't amend TPP / Reid & Schumer: Add more stuff to TPP

So, you see, the game is rigged with two false choices:

1: The Republican't Option: "Fast-Track" the voluminous, sovereignty-busting, open-borders, wage-depressing, Globalist TPP with no amendments and a straight up-or-down vote

2: The Democrap Option: Add even *more* destructive crap to the voluminous, sovereignty-busting, open-borders, wage-depressing, Globalist TPP and then have a vote

According to Republi**can't** giant Orrin Hatch-a-Plot (UT), option 2:

"...creates a whole new monster set of arguments and debates that we don't need."

This then is the essence of the phony argument, the sham fight, the fixed football match, the rigged "controversy", the non-debate. Deliberately concealed from the American public is the fact that a few Senators, such as Rand Paul *(there is some hope for him after all?)*, are supporting a forbidden **third option** - the option to reject this treasonous piece of legislative garbage altogether!

TPP is going to happen; and probably with a few more dangerous, power-grabbing amendments added. Wonder-Girl Lizzie ~~Borden~~ Warren and the Demoncraps will come off looking like noble fighters for America who forced the last-minute changes that the big bad Republi**can't** didn't want; and Obongo will come off as "the great mediator". It's a manipulative lose-lose situation, brought to you by the always plotting "bi-partisan" scum of American politics and their co-conspirators at Sulzberger's Slimes.

Shhhh. Sulzberger won't tell you that there is actually a third choice on the table - the "Say 'no' to TPP" option.

MAY, 2015

NY Times: Clintons Earned $30 Million in 16 Months, Report Shows

By MAGGIE HABERMAN and STEVE EDER

Hillary Rodham Clinton and her husband made at least $30 million over the last 16 months, mainly from giving paid speeches to corporations, banks and other organizations

IN CONTRAST TO....

MAY, 2015

NY Times: From Senate Sideline, Elizabeth Warren Is Face of Attack on Trade Bill

By JENNIFER STEINHAUER

Ms. Warren has become the most conspicuous Democrat opposing President Obama's Trans-Pacific Partnership but has not been involved in shaping it.

REBUTTAL BY

The Anti-New York Times

This is interesting - very interesting. More bad press for Killary Rotten Clinscum, and more positive press for Lizzie ~~Borden~~ Warren - *at the same time.* While Killary is raked over Sulzberger's Communist coals for raking in millions of dollars in speaking fees.....

"The sum, which makes Mrs. Clinton among the wealthiest of the 2016 presidential candidates, could create challenges for the former secretary of state as she tries to cast herself as a champion of everyday Americans in an era of ***income inequality****."* ....

....the hysterical hag from Harvard is praised for standing up for the "everyday American":

"others (colleagues) say she (Warren) is an overall positive force for the issues Democrats care about most — ***income equality****, tax fairness and workers' rights."*

The Anti-New York Times has already exposed the scam of the Fake Fight between Homo-Obongo and Lizzie ~~Borden~~ Warren. (See last's week's rebuttals)

Why does Killary's fortune damage her image as a "champion of income inequality", but Warren's $400,000 salary for teaching a single class at Harvard, and also her false claim of having Indian blood, do not? Is the Slimes signaling that "the first woman President" should be Lizzie ~~Borden~~ Warren instead of Killary? Could it be that the Left feels that Killary is carrying too much baggage and that a fresh face would be better suited to push the agenda? Could it be that the fix is in to elect Jeb Bush and Sulzberger wants to put up Warren as an agreeable patsie instead of the street-fighter Clinton? Could it be that Obongo's people hate the Clinton's so much that they are engineering the rise of Lizzie ~~Borden~~ Warren while at the same time encouraging friends in the press to put out dirt on Killary?

These are speculative questions. But one thing that is *not* speculative is the fact that Warren is being pumped up as Killary is being deflated. In the final analysis, this type of horse-race analysis is of little importance; for the you-know-who's own ALL of the horses from both stables. But it does make for an interesting bit of soap-opera.

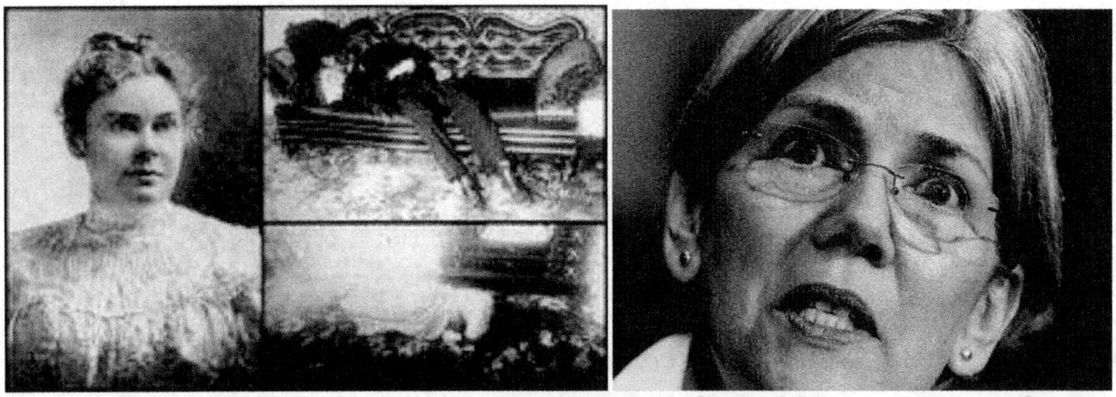

Reincarnation of another mad woman from Massachusetts?

As for this angry Communist wench, you may recall that "Professor" Warren (LOL) was the one originally coined the "you didn't build that" line which Homo-Obongo later plagiarized. It is a running logical fallacy that only a mentally deranged, Ivy League egghead could concoct:

"I hear all this, you know, 'Well, this is class warfare, this is whatever.' No. There is nobody in this country who got rich on his own — nobody. You built a factory out there? Good for you. But I want to be clear. You moved your goods to market on the roads the rest of us paid for. You hired workers the rest of us paid to educate. You were safe in your factory because of police-forces and fire-forces that the rest of us paid for. You didn't have to worry that marauding bands would come and seize everything at your factory — and hire someone to protect against this — because of the work the rest of us did. Now look, you built a factory and it turned into something terrific, or a great idea. God bless — keep a big hunk of it. But part of the underlying social contract is, you take a hunk of that and pay forward for the next kid who comes along".

Nice try Lizzie ~~Borden~~ Warren; but the cost of schools, police, fire and road maintenance constitutes only a small fraction of the total taxes that you and your Marxist ilk have imposed upon America. The average working American household pays about $10,000 in various Federal & State taxes *(and inflation)* per year to support the permanent **welfare** state *($1 Trillion / 100,000 working households / <u>not including Social Security and Medicare for Seniors</u>)*; and about an additional $9,000 per year to support the permanent **warfare** state and other elements of maintaining the Global Empire. *($900 Billion / 100,000 working households)*.

So please, bitch, don't lecture us with this condescending crap about the cost of roads and police departments. God how I HATE libtards!

We are not drowning in debt and burdened with high taxes because of the cost "roads" or "police". It's the welfare and the warfare, STUPID!

MAY, 2015

NY Times: Picasso's Stage Curtain Is Unfurled at Its New Home

By ANNIE CORREAL

In an hourslong operation of practiced precision, "Le Tricorne," a stage curtain painted by the Spanish master, arrived in its new home, shepherded by a team of art handlers.

REBUTTAL BY

The Anti-New York Times

As far as 'Picassos" are concerned, the painted stage curtain known as 'Le Tricorne' isn't nearly as ugly and as monstrous as most of Picasso's con jobs are; but neither is it at all impressive. But that won't stop Sulzberger's Slimes from gushing over it as a "masterpiece". In the sick world of Jewish-dominated "art", any of the 10,000 pieces of junk churned out by the sainted Stalinist-Communist charlatan of partial Jewish ancestry is considered a "masterpiece".

"Give me a museum and I will fill it.", Pablo the Putrid once boasted. Well, when one is mass-producing incomprehensible and ugly garbage by the hour, "filling a

museum" is no great accomplishment. One can fill up a library with children's 'Dick & Jane' books, but that doesn't make it a serious place of higher learning now, does it? Picasso actually indicted himself with such a ridiculous comment. But the pinko painter of progressive putrescence was no fool. St. Pablo laughed all the way to the bank with sacks full of cash swindled from the libtarded chumps who had been taught by the high and the mighty to obediently grovel before his glorified garbage.

Pablo loved Killer Joe Stalin so much, he drew a portrait of him! Pablo the Putrid was awarded the Soviet "Peace Prize".

The Globalists and the Communists have always used "modern art" to corrupt the beautiful western culture that they seek to destroy. Not wanting to appear "unintellectual", throngs of simple-minded, high-society *(or pretend high-society)* fools will put on their best airs and worship the idiotic icons on display in the cesspool-museums of New York, London and Paris. The tragic significance of this comical idiocy is that at the moment when the "best and brightest" became convinced that such garbage truly had artistic merit; they lost their objective moral and mental moorings, thus rendering themselves vulnerable to being convinced of *anything*. That is why the Marxist monstrosities of Picasso are heavily promoted by Rockefeller, Sulzberger and their New York Globalist ilk.

An elite class that has become so corrupted in its judgment that it can no longer differentiate between Picasso's crap and Rembrandt's masterpieces; will ultimately shape a lower public that will also believe anything. Destroy the timeless, immutable concepts of truth, symmetry and beauty, and you will soon destroy a people's ability to objectively reason. Destroy reason, and you can then enslave the sheeple, all the while convincing them that they are free and happy!

1- Norman Rockwell's The Connoisseur (1962) mocks the fools who pray before the works of "artists" such as Picasso, or, in this case, Jackson Pollack.
2- Norman Rockwell: A true American Legend

The architects of The New World Order understand very well the significance of the "Culture War". Art matters. Literature matters. Music matters. Religion, morality and tradition matter. Culture matters. Unfortunately, most modern "economic conservatives" have lost sight of this reality and have totally surrendered to the Left on these important fronts. It's not all about money, folks *(though the Globalists have certainly screwed up our monetary system as well!)*. What does it profit a nation if it expands it GDP while losing its cultural soul?

We'll let some scattered "choppy" samples of the 'great work' of Pablo the Putrid speak for themselves.

MAY, 2015

NY Times (Editorial): Errors and Lies

By PAUL KRUGMAN

The public justifications for the invasion (of Iraq) were nothing but pretexts, and falsified pretexts at that. We were, in a fundamental sense, lied into war.

REBUTTAL BY

The Anti-New York Times

This filthy little rat-faced "Nobel Prize winning" economist and Slimes columnist, Paul Krugman, may not know a thing about economics - or perhaps *pretends* to not know - but when it comes to rhetorical trickery, kosher Krugman is an expert without peer. In this editorial, Krugman takes the Jewish-engineered Iraqi War and hangs it around the necks of Republican White men such as Bush, Cheney and Rumsfeld. Let's have a look at the contortions and omissions:

"Surprise! It turns out that there's something to be said for having the brother of a failed president make his own run for the White House. Thanks to Jeb Bush, we may finally have the frank discussion of the Iraq invasion we should have had a decade ago".

Krugman, you dirty low-down Son of Satan! The reason that we never had a "*frank discussion of the Iraq invasion*" was because "the paper of record", which you write for, was too busy selling the war. Do your homework Mr. Krugman! Dig up the 2002 and 2003 issues of the Jew York Slimes and you will see that over 100 front pages pro-war stories preceded the invasion.

But of course, you already know that.

Crooked Krugman continues:

"But many influential people — not just Mr. Bush — would prefer that we not have that discussion. Yes, the narrative goes, we now know that invading Iraq was a terrible mistake, and it's about time that everyone admits it. Now let's move on. Well, let's not — because that's a false narrative."

Yes. It is a false narrative. But you didn't mention the critical role played by your wretched colleague in New York, that forked-tongued Jewess, Judith Miller. Mendacious Miller was the Slime's key point-person for pitching the "false narrative" based on her phony "sources".

Judy Miller's Lies + Slimes Front Page Hype = Iraq War.

Why don't you mention Sulzberger's and your Satanic synagogue sister's role, Paul?

Sulzberger's Satanic Slut spewed lies, death and destruction non-stop throughout 2002 and 2003. She gets a pass from colleague Krugman.

More Krugmanism:

"The Iraq war wasn't an innocent mistake, a venture undertaken on the basis of intelligence that turned out to be wrong. America invaded Iraq because the Bush administration wanted a war. The public justifications for the invasion were nothing but pretexts, and falsified pretexts at that."

Absolutely correct. But the big lie here is in the *omissions.*

Omission # 1:

Who was it that pumped out the "wrong intelligence"? **Answer: Israel!**

Omission # 2:

Who else "wanted a war"? **Answer: Israel and its American agents (Neo-Cons) and lobbyists (AIPAC)!**

Omission # 3:

Who allowed the Bush / Cheney gang to get away with "falsified pretexts"? **Answer: The Jew York Slimes!**

Krugman continues:

"We were, in a fundamental sense, lied into war."

Yes. We were lied into war by Bush and friends; but the operatives of that greasy bunch were only front men and pawns of the Zionist cabal of Ariel Sharon, the Jewish Neo-Cons, and the most powerful media institution in America, the Jew York Slimes.

Anglos Bush and Cheney are skewered for the Iraq War; but fellow tribesmen Sharon and Satanyahu get a free pass from Krugman.

"The fraudulence of the case for war was actually obvious even at the time: the ever-shifting arguments for an unchanging goal were a dead giveaway. So were the word games — the talk about W.M.D that conflated chemical weapons (which many people did think Saddam had) with nukes, the constant insinuations that Iraq was somehow behind 9/11."

Correct-o-mundo, Mr. Krugman! *"The fraudulence of the case for war"* as well as the *"word games"* were indeed extremely *"obvious"*; which serves as further evidence that your Jew York Slimes, as evidenced by its silence over the ridiculously transparent lies of Bush - Cheney - Rumsfeld - Rice- Powell, was "in on it"!

"All the News That's Fit to Print"

The New York Times

Late Edition

NEW YORK, THURSDAY, FEBRUARY 6, 2003

ONE DOLLAR

NASA NOW DOUBTS TANK FOAM DEBRIS DOOMED COLUMBIA

HIRING IN NATION HITS WORST SLUMP IN NEARLY 20 YEARS

LAYOFFS DESPITE GROWTH

Surge in Number of Workers Who Have Stopped Looking for Jobs Since Summer

POWELL, IN U.N. SPEECH, PRESENTS CASE TO SHOW IRAQ HAS NOT DISARMED

A TONE OF URGENCY

Concealment Is Charged by U.S. — Evidence for Possible War

A SHIFT IN INQUIRY

Insulation Seen as Too Light to Cause Fatal Shuttle Damage

MYSTERY DEEPENS

Range of Theories, but None That Seem to Fit All the Facts

Intelligence Break Led U.S. to Tie Envoy Killing to Iraq Qaeda Cell

When the despicable and deceitful Colon Rectum Bowell did his WMD show & tell routine at the UN, the all-mighty Jew York Slimes hyped the performance without questioning the claims, at all! Krugman "forgets" to mention that.

Krugman:

"Why did they want a war? That's a harder question to answer. Some of the warmongers believed that deploying shock and awe in Iraq would enhance American power and influence around the world. Some saw Iraq as a sort of pilot project, preparation for a series of regime changes. And it's hard to avoid the suspicion that there was a strong element of wagging the dog, of using military triumph to strengthen the Republican brand at home."

Krugman the Cunning lists every motive under the sun, except for Israel and its Neo-Con agents. Also exempted from any blame is the Marxist Demoncrap Party, **75% of whose members voted to grant the Republican't Bush final authorization for the invasion**; an invasion which, had the Demoncraps raised a stink about it, could easily have prevented.

Krugman's close:

"Whatever the precise motives, the result was a very dark chapter in American history. Once again: We were lied into war. So let's get the Iraq story right. Yes, from a national point of view the invasion was a mistake. But (with apologies to Talleyrand) it was worse than a mistake, it was a crime."

Nice closing Krugman. *"Whatever the precise motives"*, eh? As if you don't know what the true motives were! We get it, Paulie. Though the motives are not clear, Republican White Boys are to blame for the Iraq fiasco.

Oh well, at least there were some Jewish journalists who went off script and revealed the truth about the Iraq War. See statements below:

CARL BERNSTEIN
Washington Post

Speaking on MSNBC's Joe Scarborough's show in July of 2013, the legendary journalist of Watergate fame said of the Iraq War: *"This was an insane war that brought us low economically, morally. We went to war against a guy who had absolutely nothing to do with 9/11.*

"It was a total pretext! It's inexplicable and there you go to Cheney, there you go to Bush, ***there you go to the Jewish neo-cons who wanted to remake the world. Maybe I can say that because I'm Jewish.*** *To bring about a certain result .."*

On MSNBC - Joe Scarborough Show

ASME Elects
Michael
Kinsley
to Magazine
Editors Hall of
Fame

MICHAEL KINSLEY

PBS - Slate - Politico - LA Times - New Republic

"Bush's public case for going to war against Iraq is full of logical inconsistencies, exaggerations, and outright lies. ... this raises a troubling question, ***what are his real reasons?*** *There must be some: Nobody starts a war as a lark. It would be easier to dismiss the whole exercise if there were an obvious ulterior motive. Without one, you are left wondering, "Am I missing something?"*

The lack of public discussion about the role of Israel is easier to understand, but weird nevertheless. ***It is the proverbial elephant in the room: Everybody sees it, no one mentions it.*** *The reason is obvious and admirable: Neither supporters nor opponents of a war against Iraq wish to evoke the classic anti-Semitic image of the king's Jewish advisers whispering poison into his ear and betraying the country to foreign interests."*

Slate Magazine
What Bush Isn't Saying About Iraq
Oct. 24, 2002

ARI SHAVIT
HA'ARETZ (Israel)

"The war in Iraq was conceived by 25 neoconservatives, most of them Jewish, who are pushing President Bush to change the course of history....

*In the course of the past year, a new belief has emerged in the town: the belief in war against Iraq. That ardent faith was disseminated by a small group of 25 or 30 neoconservatives, **almost all of them Jewish**, almost all of them intellectuals (a partial list: **Richard Perle, Paul Wolfowitz, Douglas Feith, William Kristol, Eliot Abrams, Charles Krauthammer**), people who are mutual friends and cultivate one another and are convinced that political ideas are a major driving force of history."*

Ha'aretz News Service (Israel)

April 5, 2003

JAMES ROSEN
McClatchy News Services

*"In 1996, as Likud Prime Minister Benjamin Netanyahu prepared to take office, **eight Jewish neoconservative leaders sent him a six-page memo outlining an aggressive vision of government.** At the top of their list was overthrowing Saddam ....*

***The neoconservatives sketched out a kind of domino theory in which the governments of Syria and other Arab countries might later fall or be replaced** in the wake of Saddam's ouster."*

McClatchy Newspapers
April 6, 2003

MAY, 2015

NY Times: Snowden Sees Some Victories, From a Distance

By SCOTT SHANE

Edward J. Snowden, exiled in Russia, is globe-hopping via video appearances and enjoying victories in Congress and the courts.

REBUTTAL BY

The Anti-New York Times

The 'Snowden Snow Job' rolls on as Sulzberger's favorite little "whistle-blower" continues to play the boobs for fools in preparation of his eventual "hero's return" to America, one day. From the article:

"May has been another month of virtual globe-hopping for Mr. Snowden, the former National Security Agency contractor, with video appearances so far at Princeton and in a "distinguished speakers" series at Stanford and at conferences in Norway and Australia. Before the month is out, he is scheduled to speak by video to audiences in Italy, and also in Ecuador, where there will be a screening of "Citizenfour," the Oscar-winning documentary about him."

Literally from Day #1, **The Anti-New York Times**, was the first to expose this "High School dropout", ex-CIA, ex-NSA operative who, we were told, threw away a $200,000 salary, his girlfriend, his family, and his life just to tell the world what was already known - that the NSA collects phone calls and E-mails. Wow! Really? Who would have ever 'thunk' it?! Thanks for the 'heads-up' , Snowy!

The 1st "tell", as they say in poker parlance, was the "spontaneous" Hong Kong rent-a-mob with professional banners that turned out in support of the heroic "fugitive" who, we were told, had simply strolled out of the NSA, and then effortlessly flew out of the USA with sensitive information on his stolen laptops. *(rolling eyes)*

The 2nd "tell": The MASSIVE hype of Snowden by Sulzberger's Slimes and the whole of the Globalist world media. This is the same media which, in the past, has buried the allegations of legitimate "whistle-blowers" such as Colleen Rowley, William Binney, Sibel Edmonds and many, many others.

The 3rd "tell": Snowden's next "escape", to Russia, Edward "Snowed-In"; get it? This event marked the beginning of "The New Cold War" as people like McCain the Insane began blaming Putin for harboring a "traitor". Some even suggested that Snowden was a Russian spy!

The Washington Post

Man who leaked NSA secrets steps forward

To leaker, personal risks were clear

THE NEW YORK TIMES INTER

Lawmakers Suggest Snowden Link To Russia Before He Leaked Data

By ERIC SCHMITT and DAVID E. SANGER

WASHINGTON — The heads of the House and Senate Intelligence Committees suggested on Sunday that Edward J. Snowden, the former National Security Agency contractor, might have been working for Russian spy services while he was employed at an agency facility in Hawaii last year and before he disclosed hundreds of thousands of classified government documents.

The lawmakers, Representative Mike Rogers, Republican of Michigan, and Senator Dianne Feinstein, Democrat of California, offered no specific evidence that Mr. Snowden had cooperated with Moscow. Since Mr. Snowden's disclosure first became public last spring, there has been nothing to do with privacy or the reach of intelligence services, and he suggested that Mr. Snowden's possession of a "go bag" to get out of Hawaii, and his smooth entry into Hong Kong, indicated preplanning beyond his individual capacity.

Intelligence officials say they have no doubt that Chinese and Russian intelligence have obtained whatever information Mr. Snowden was carrying with him digitally. They also say it is possible that much of the data Mr. Snowden took is stored in an Internet cloud service.

Mr. Snowden has said he did not turn over any documents to any foreign governments; American officials say that given the cyber skills of the Russian and said that it would cost billions of dollars to change operations because of the security breaches.

The defense intelligence report remains classified, though some members of Congress have been briefed on it in recent weeks.

"I don't think it was a gee-whiz luck event that he ended up in Moscow under the handling of the F.S.B.," Mr. Rogers said on the NBC program "Meet the Press," referring to the Federal Security Service, the Russian state security organization that succeeded the K.G.B.

Ben Wizner, an American Civil Liberties Union lawyer who advises Mr. Snowden, said in a telephone interview on Sunday that Mr. Rogers's statement was "not only false, it is silly."

Sure signs of a CIA operation: Intense media hype, "spontaneous" flash mobs in Hong Kong, and false allegations of Russian involvement.

The 4th "tell": Snowden's affiliation with the phony "anti-Establishment" journalist, Glenn Greenwald, who is conveniently based in BRICS' Brazil with his "husband".

The 5th "tell": Snowden's bizarre "Open Letter" to "the people of Brazil" in which he makes it clear that the U.S. has been monitoring them. **(1)** Here is a shocking excerpt from Snowden's **cryptic blackmail** letter to a nation that the U.S. is at odds with *(over Russia, South American trade, and Iran).* From Snowden's Letter:

"The NSA and other spying agencies tell us that for our own "safety"-for Dilma's (Brazilian President) "safety," for Petrobras' "safety"- they have revoked our right to privacy and broken into our lives. And they did it without asking the public in any country, even their own.

Today, if you carry a cell phone in Sao Paolo, the NSA can and does keep track of your location: they do this 5 billion times a day to people around the world."

When someone in Florianopolis visits a website, the NSA keeps a record of when it happened and what you did there. If a mother in Porto Alegre calls her son to wish him luck on his university exam, NSA can keep that call log for five years or more.

They even keep track of who is having an affair or looking at pornography, in case they need to damage their target's reputation.

American Senators tell us that Brazil should not worry, because this is not "surveillance," it's "data collection." They say it is done to keep you safe. They're wrong."

In other words: ***"Dear crooked politicians (and soccer players?) of Brazil. We have you by the testicles!"***

1- Snowden poses with sodomite Greenwald and Greenwald's Brazilian "husband".
2- Brazilian CIA "activists" support Snowden, whose "Open Letter" suggestion of blackmail must surely have rattled many a Brazilian VIP.

The 6th "tell": The much-publicized revelation that the cell phone calls of German Chancellor Angela Merkel have been monitored: In other words: ***"Dear Angie. We have dirt on you. Dump Putin!"***

The 7th "tell": The strong public support for Snowden by the fake "whistle-blower" Julian Assange of WikiLeaks fame. Convenient and damaging "leaks" by CIA operative Assange, **by his own admission**, triggered the bloody "Arab Spring" **(2)** and also the fall of Putin's close Italian ally, ex-Prime Minister Silvio Berlusconi. **(3)**

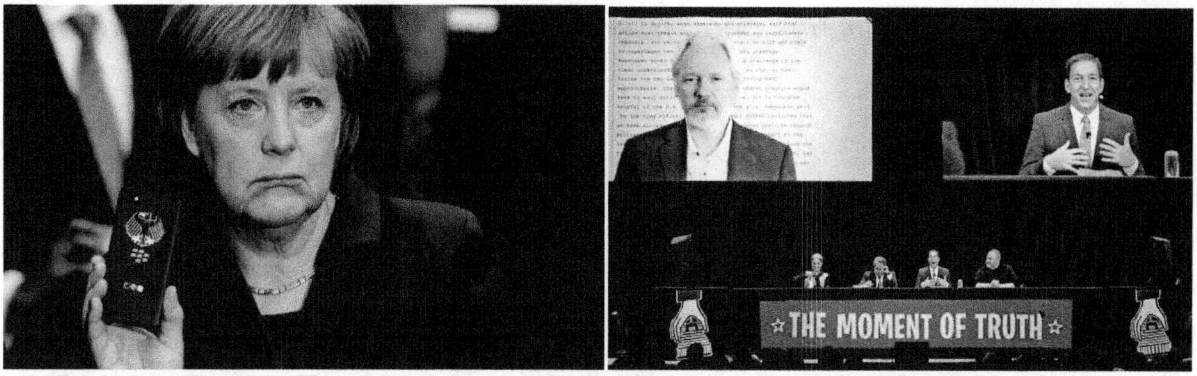

1- Did the Frump Frau suddenly change her pro-Russian tune because of Snowden's claim that her cell phone calls had been monitored? Putin himself has suggested that certain world leaders are under US blackmail. 2- Agents Greenwald and Assange speak before a conference of fools.

There are other lesser "tells", and the game is still going on. The Russians surely know this but play along with the charade by allowing Snowden to remain in Russia. That's because Snowden himself is harmless at this point. It's his partner-in-crime down in Brazil, Glenn Greenwald, who has been tasked with leaking out whatever remaining blackmail dirt there is left from Snowden's "stolen laptops".

Agent Snowden did his job well, and will be rewarded handsomely upon his return to the West.

1- If NBC's Brian Williams says that Snowden is a legitimate "whistle-blower", well, then it must be true, right?
2- Putin on U.S. use of blackmail: "Recently we have increasing evidence that outright blackmail has been used with regard to a number of leaders".
(4)

1- Google: Snowden Open Letter Brazil

2- Google: Assange Wikileaks arab spring

3- Google: Assange wikileaks berlusconi

4- Google: Putin recently we have evidence blackmail number of leaders

MAY, 2015

NY Times: ISIS Fighters Seize Control of Syrian City of Palmyra, and Ancient Ruins

By ANNE BARNARD and HWAIDA SAAD

Islamic State militants have already destroyed historical sites and sold off artifacts in other cities, and people fear they may do the same to the famous ruins in Palmyra.

REBUTTAL BY

The Anti-New York Times

Having recently staged another deadly offensive in Iraq, ISIS is now on the move again in Syria. Meanwhile, the various 'affiliates' of ISIS in Northern and Central Africa continue to cause problems for the governments of Sudan, Nigeria, Chad, Niger, Libya, Egypt, and Somalia. At varying times, the ISIS conglomerate has also threatened Jordan, Lebanon, Japan, Russia, China, the United States, Europe, India, Indonesia, Malaysia, Latin America and even the Vatican!

It seems as though the whole planet is under potential threat from the ISIS - Al Qaeda - Boku Haram - Al-Shabaab Axis of 'Islamo-Fascism'; except for one nation that - despite its small size and close proximity to these terror groups - seems peculiarly immune to the threat.

Here, straight from the Hebrew Horse's own mouth - HAARETZ News Service of Israel:

HA'ARETZ הארץ
ENGLISH EDITION

Published in Israel as a newspaper together with the International Herald Tribune

Why the Islamic State isn't in any rush to attack Israel

The organization formerly known as ISIS has made clear that fighting Shi'ite Muslims is its top priority.

*"While Israel is pounding Gaza, it's good to know that at least **one Muslim organization isn't rushing to threaten Israel**. This **refreshing news** comes from the organization known until about a week or two ago as ISIS, but which now – since it has started to consolidate its hold on a stretch of territory linking Iraq and Syria – calls itself the Islamic State".*

****

Just like the suspicious absence of Israelis at the World Trade Center on 9/11, and just like the suspicious lack of Jewish deaths from the Bubonic Plague of Medieval Europe, and just like the genocide story in the Book of Exodus, how *'conveeeeenient'* that the plague of ISIS should also 'passover' the chosen ones. When one realizes that ISIS = **I**sraeli **S**ecret **I**ntelligence **S**ervices, it's no surprise at all.

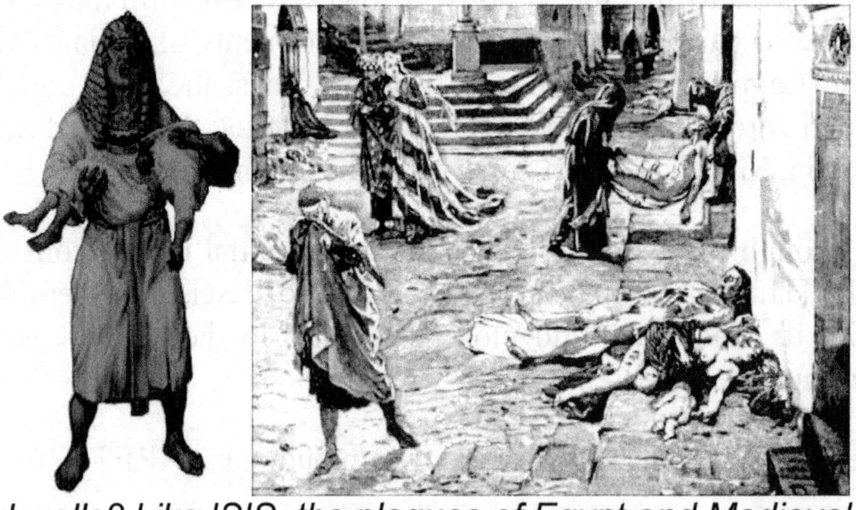

Poisoned wells? Like ISIS, the plagues of Egypt and Medieval Europe didn't touch the Jews either.

From Afghanistan to Chechnya to the Middle East, Muslim terror groups have always been a collection of radicalized dupes and well paid mercenaries operating under the skilled guidance of the CIA-Mossad Axis of Evil. Following is a refresher course regarding the ridiculous photo-fakery and 'crisis-acting' of the ongoing scam known as 'ISIS':

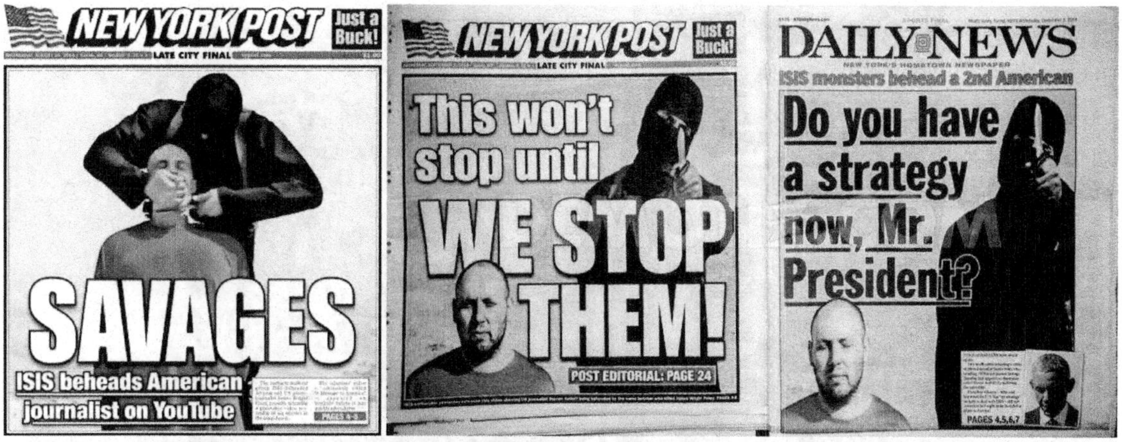

*The fake 'beheading' videos cut to black just as the throats of the strangely calm 'victims' are about to be cut by the really bad actors in black. The 'victims' don't even squirm! **Intense media pressure builds for Obongo to "do something" in order to "stop ISIS".***

1- Moments before his 'beheading', James Foley cracks a smile. "Oh well, we all gotta go sometime."

2- In a TV interview immediately following the James Foley 'beheading', the 'bereaved sister' of the 'victim' can't stop smiling either. Notice how Foley's "brother" looks down and closes his eye as he is speaking - a sure sign of a liar!

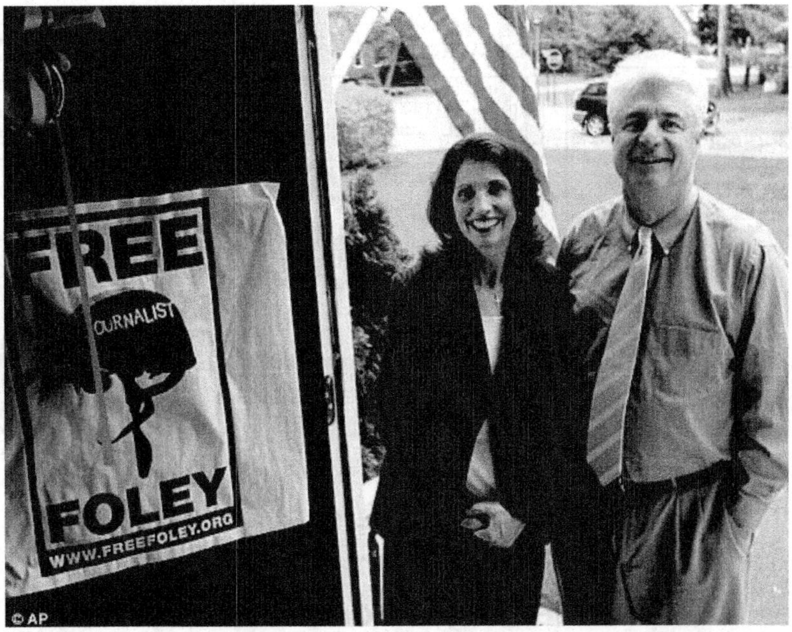

Incredibly, this was the same 'James Foley' who had been kidnapped 3 years ago in Libya, inspiring the 'Free Foley' marketing campaign. As you can see, 'Mom and Dad' were all smiles about that 2011 'kidnapping' too!

THE TIMES

How smart are you?

Foley video with Briton was staged, experts say

Cameron to threaten exit from Brussels

The headline story about the Foley video being fake was quickly 'disappeared'.

Obama and Netanyahu are laughing at YOU America.

"Victim" David Haines / Mossad Agents Rita Katz

All "beheading" videos come to us from a purported media organization known as 'SITE' ***(Search for International Terrorist Entities****) SITE was founded and run by Rita Katz,* ***an Iraqi born Israeli operative and veteran of the IDF (Israeli Defense Force)****. How is she getting the exclusive for these videos?*

MAY, 2015

NY Times: Obama Recasts Climate Change as a Peril With Far-Reaching Effects

By JULIE HIRSCHFELD DAVIS

President Obama used a commencement address on Wednesday at the Coast Guard Academy to cast his push for urgent action to combat climate change as a national security imperative.

REBUTTAL BY

The Anti-New York Times

The fact that the U.S. Coast Guard's cadet class of 2015 did not openly break out in spontaneous belly-laughter as the Clown-in-Chief preached some of the most extreme Global Warmist doom ever uttered is either a testament to their discipline and training, or perhaps to their own ignorance. Here are a few side-splitting one-liners from Obongo's stupid stand-up comedy routine:

"I am here today to say that climate change constitutes a serious threat to global security, ***an immediate risk to our national security****, and, make no mistake; it will impact how our military defends our country. And so we need to act, and we need to act now."*

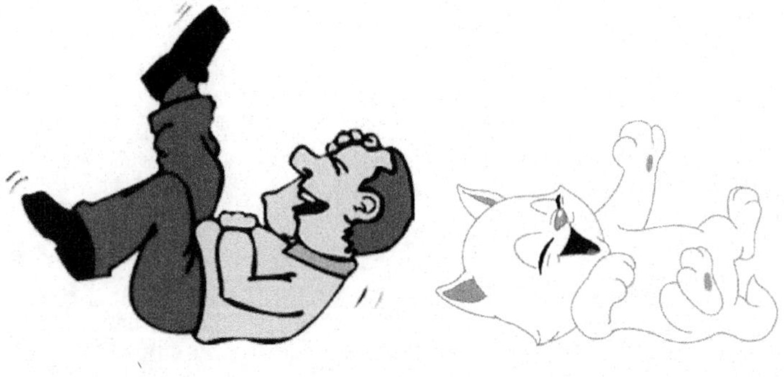

"I know there are still some folks back in Washington who refuse to admit that climate change is real, and on a day like today, it's hard to get too worried about it....but the science is indisputable. The planet is getting warmer.

*"**Denying it or refusing to deal with it endangers our national security**. It undermines the readiness of our forces. Politicians who say they care about military readiness ought to care about this as well."*

*Conditions could create a global surge of "**climate change refugees** — and I guarantee the Coast Guard will have to respond. Climate change, especially rising seas, is a threat to our homeland security — our economic infrastructure, and the safety and health of the American people."*

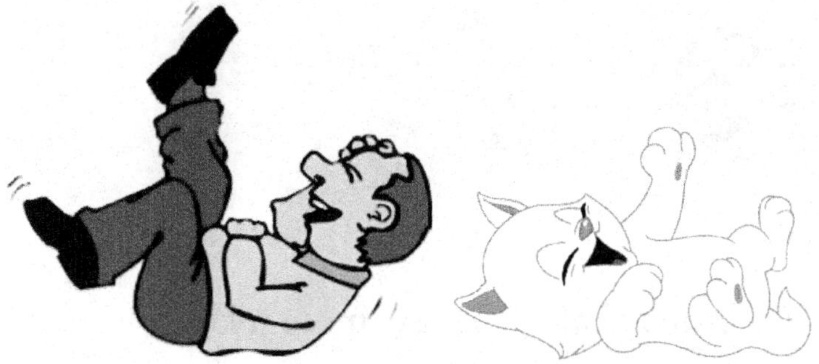

Sulzberger's Slimes went on to explain how Obongo linked "climate change" to civil wars and terrorism:

*"The president argued that climate change had set off dangerous domino effects around the world, prompting a severe drought in Nigeria that was exploited by the terrorist group Boko Haram, and drought, crop failures and high food prices that **"helped fuel the early unrest in Syria" before it descended into civil war."***

Global Warming contributed to the violence in Syria and Nigeria?

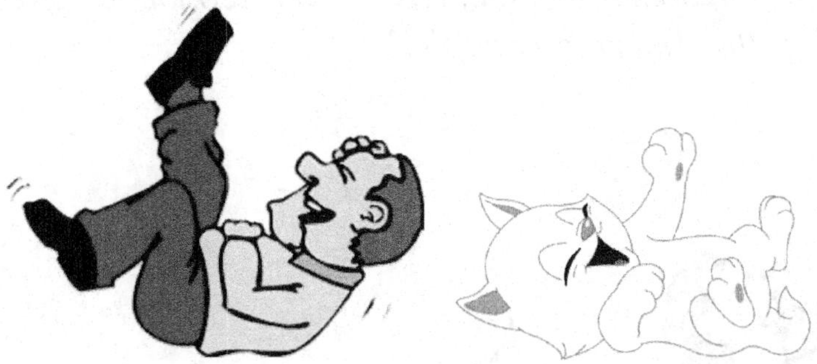

The Joker droned on and on about "Climate Change". A few more jokes:

"The science is indisputable. The fossil fuels we burn release carbon dioxide, which traps heat. And the levels of carbon dioxide in the atmosphere are now higher than they have been in 800,000 years. The planet is getting warmer. Fourteen of the 15 hottest years on record have been in the past 15 years. Last year was the planet's warmest year ever recorded."

"Our scientists at NASA just reported that some of the sea ice around Antarctica is breaking up even faster than expected. The world's glaciers are melting, pouring new water into the ocean. Over the past century, the world sea level rose by about eight inches. That was in the last century; by the end of this century, it's projected to rise another one to four feet."

"As Admiral Zukunft already mentioned, climate change means Arctic sea ice is vanishing faster than ever. By the middle of this century, Arctic summers could be essentially ice free. ***We're witnessing the birth of a new ocean*** *-- new sea lanes, more shipping, exploration, more competition for the vast natural resources below."*

For making such idiotic claims, the Comedian-in-Chief ought to be mercilessly mocked and roundly ridiculed by every late night TV joke-maker, every newspaper editorialist and every Republi**can't** in Congress. But due to their protective pigmentation and "correct" politics, Sulzberger's Slimes allows Homo-Obongo and his homely husband to just keep right on joking while America dies.

Speaking of jokers, we await with bated breath the imminent comedy script to put out by the Pinko Pope - his encyclical on Global Warming - **TM**. This back-door move towards Global Governance is tragic, but it is also funny. Better to laugh than to cry.

1- The Communist Clown clowns around with a cadet. Don't bend over, young man!
2- The Pinko Pope will soon weigh in on the 'sin' of Global Warming **TM**

MAY, 2015

NY Times: Boy Scouts' President Calls for End to Ban on Gay Leaders

By ERIK ECKHOLM

Robert M. Gates, the group's president and former Secretary of Defense, said the Scouts "must deal with the world as it is, not as we might wish it to be."

REBUTTAL BY

The Anti-New York Times

Whose dumb idea was it to bring in a former Secretary of the Department of Offense and Director of the CIA to head the Boy Scouts of America? Only 1 year into his term as President and Gates' subversive colors are already shining through. With Satanic satisfaction, Sulzberger's sodomite Slimes sings the sad song:

"Robert M. Gates, the president of the Boy Scouts of America and former secretary of defense, called on Thursday to end the Scouts' ban on gay adult leaders, warning the group's executives that ***'we must deal with the world as it is, not as we might wish it to be.'*** *"*

Spoken like the ultimate spineless corporate careerist company 'yes man'. Just go along to get along, and let any adult sodomite have access to our young boys. Thank God your independent reporter here managed to escape that phony corporate world a few years ago. I wouldn't go back for all the tea in China.

Ambitious climbing "yes men" like Gates are everywhere. Without them, the Globo-Marxist controllers would never be able to leverage such enormous power.

You know, Gates' line about "*the world as it is, not as we might wish it to be*" suggests that he may be a devotee of the legendary Marxist agitator from Chicago, Saul Alinsky. Alinsky was the original "community agitator" who inspired Killary Clinscum as well as Mr. & Mr. Obongo. One of Alinksy's proverbs:

"The standards of judgment must be rooted in ***the world as it is, not our wished-for fantasy of the world as it should be."***

Interesting. But perhaps it is just a coincidence. Nonetheless, it reveals what an empty suit Gates truly is. Go along to get along. Stand for nothing. It won't be long before the Boy Scout Oath is altered. The current vow is so "old fashioned":

Boy Scout Oath or Promise

On my **honor**, I will do my best
To do my duty to **God** and **my country** and to obey the Scout Law;
To help other people at all times;
To keep myself physically strong, mentally awake and **morally straight**.

Honor? God? Country? Morality? How quaint. How corny.

The betrayal of the Boy Scouts comes on the heels of the Girl Scouts' recent embrace of lesbianism and the abortionist Planned Parenthood. America and Europe are in full lemming mode now. Everybody is selling out to the Globalist agenda of cultural and moral degeneracy: Boy Scouts, Girl Scouts, Catholic Church, "conservatives".

The Queer Scouts of America

But the Laws of Nature and Nature's God will NEVER change. After the present trend of mental and moral madness has finished its tragic course, the force of nature will restore sanity and order one day. We may not live to see that day, but it will come.

In the meantime, take refuge in God, and in the fact that TomatoBubble.com will NEVER water down the message in order to fit into "the world" that adaptable corporate scum such as Robert Gates thrive in.

MAY, 2015

NY Times: Pope's Focus on Poor Revives Scorned Theology

By JIM YARDLEY and SIMON ROMERO

Pope Francis often uses language that echoes liberation theology, the Latin American movement embracing the poor that conservatives once scorned as Marxist.

REBUTTAL BY

The Anti-New York Times

The numerous rhetorical 'butt-whoopins' which **The Anti-New York Times** has proudly administered to Satan's Pope have offended more than a few readers and even prompted some to withdraw their monthly donations. With this latest pro-Pope puff-piece from Sulzberger's putrid propagandists, we graciously await some apologies and hopefully a reinstatement or two of cancelled subscriptions / donations. Your humble reporter here hates to say "I told you so" *(actually, I enjoy it)*, but here it is straight from the Global arbiter of Marxism, the Jew York Slimes. Read it and weep:

"Six months after becoming the first Latin American pontiff, Pope Francis invited an octogenarian priest from Peru for a private chat at his Vatican residence. Not listed on the pope's schedule, the September 2013 meeting with the priest, Gustavo Gutiérrez, soon became public — and was just as quickly interpreted as ***a defining shift*** *in the Roman Catholic Church.*

Father Gutiérrez is a founder of liberation theology*, the Latin American movement embracing the poor and calling for social change,* ***which conservatives once scorned as overtly Marxist and the Vatican treated with hostility.*** *Now,* ***Father Gutiérrez is a respected Vatican visitor,*** *and his writings have been praised in the official Vatican newspaper. Francis has brought other Latin American priests back into favor and often uses language about the poor that has echoes of* ***liberation theology****."*

Godless Liberation Theologists used Christ's charitable concerns for the poor of his day as a pretext to promote Marxist Revolution throughout Latin America.

Yikes! What Communist Black "Reverends" such as Marxist Loser King, Jesse Jackal and Al Charlatan are to Black Baptist churches in America, "Liberation Theology" Priests are to Latin America. They are false-faced Red infiltrators who pretend to care about "the poor". Previous Popes understood this and tried to suppress these cunning Commie clergymen. Once on the fringes, the "Liberation Theologists" and their pseudo-ideology of "social justice" are not only back in fashion, but now have one of their own in the Vatican. This Slimes article is a wink-wink confirmation of that fact.

If the Pinko Pope of "Liberation Theology" was truly sincere about addressing "the root causes of "poverty", then why doesn't he follow the actual teachings of Jesus by condemning three of the most significant causes of modern-day poverty:

1: Debt-based money supply / usury *(Jesus chased the money-lenders out of the Temple)*

2: Sinful and irresponsible lifestyles *(Jesus told Mary Magdalene to stop being a whore)*

3: Ongoing wars and the related refugee crises - caused by the Globo-Zio Axis of Evil *("Blessed are the peace-makers", said Jesus.)*

The clown in the Vatican doesn't make such judgments. *"Who am I to judge?"* when asked about sodomites. All he knows how to do is call on politicians *(the poverty makers!)* to tax and spend more - itself *another* cause of poverty. The only people that Frankie *has* judged are the socially conservative Cardinals and Bishops who are being demoted under his reign.

Unlike Fake Frankie, gentle Jesus was not afraid to make moral judgments when he had to.

1: Jesus opens up a can of Holy Whoop-Ass on the Federal Reserve Board of the day.
*2: Jesus saves Mary Magdalene from stoning, but he then admonishes her to "**sin no more**".*

"By their fruits ye shall know them", as Jesus warns in the Book of Matthew. With that admonition in mind, let us again review the Pinko Pope's shockingly Red resume:

- Aided and abetted known Communist activists in Argentina
- Is softening up the Church's position on homosexuality
- Is softening up the Church's position on "forgiving abortion"
- Is removing conservative Bishops and Cardinals from their positions
- Advocates for "anti-racism" and illegal immigration into the US and Europe
- Incites against "income inequality" *(buzzword for "I want socialism")*
- Is pushing for UN action to combat non-existent "Global Warming"

Anti-homosexual U.S. Cardinal Raymond Burke was demoted by Frankie Faker. Meanwhile, Satan's Pope kisses the hand of Agedo Foggia, a controversial priest who openly advocates for homosexual marriage.

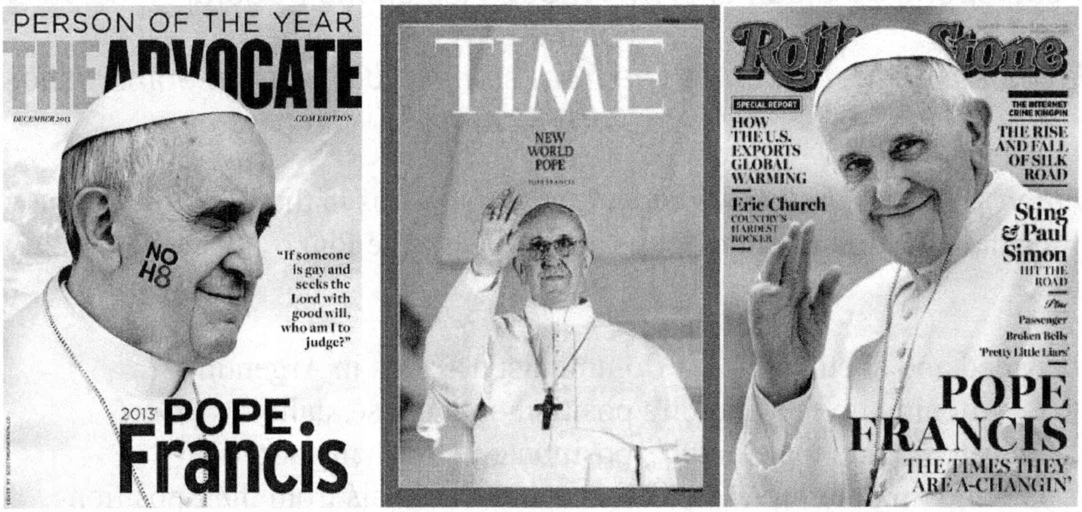

The amazing fact that magazines such as the sodomite Advocate, Marxist Time, and degenerate Rolling Stone have turned this wicked monster into an international "rock-star" is all the evidence needed to establish his unholy fake.

MAY, 2015

NY Times: While at War, Female Soldiers Fight to Belong

By BENEDICT CAREY

Even as women distinguish themselves as enlisted soldiers, many struggle with depression and a sense of alienation in an intensely male military world.

REBUTTAL BY

The Anti-New York Times

In addition to being "liberated" from the evil "capitalist" horrors of marriage vows, sexual mores, heterosexuality, femininity, house-keeping, cooking and child-rearing; one of the other great "liberties" which women have acquired from the Marxist-inspired "Women's Liberation Movement" was the "right" to be killed on the battlefield alongside the boys. Congratulations ladies! Along with commuting in traffic, being herded onto subway trains, serving as a cubicle-bound or retail store "human resource" *(because taxes and inflation have made it impossible for most men to support you),* and suffering heart attacks and strokes like never before; you have also "won the right" to be physically, mentally and genitally mutilitated by IED bombs, sniper fire and artillery shells. Yes indeed; "you've come a long way, baby!"

During this never-ending 'War on Terror'-**TM**, a staggering 15 percent of the American force consists of females. And these ferocious femmes aren't just in support roles either. Women are indeed engaging in combat, as evidenced by **144 female corpses and 100's more amputees**. By comparison, women made up less than 1% of the total forces which served during the Vietnam War. Only 16 of them were killed, most of them nurses.

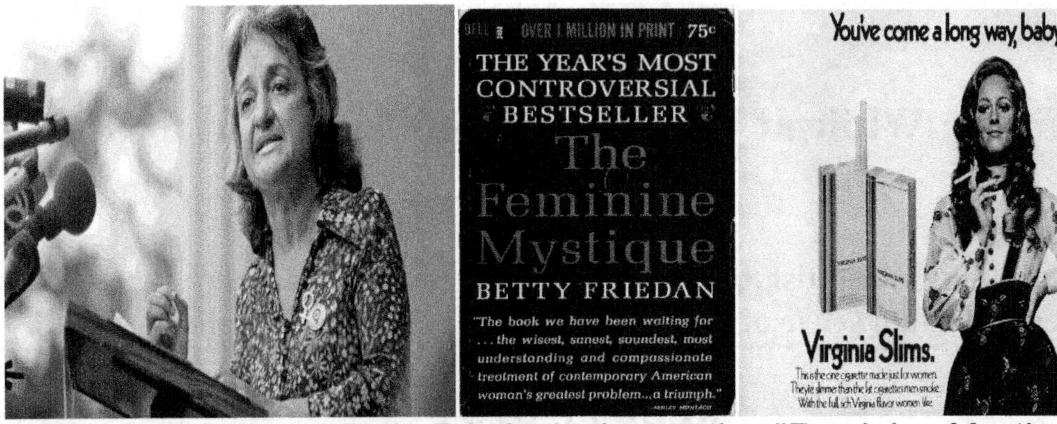

1963: Jewish Marxist Betty Friedan's destructive "Feminine Mystique' was hyped up by the CIA press. Millions of women took the subversive bait.

But Sulzberger's pro-feminist Slimes is not the least bit concerned about young women having their wombs ripped to shreds by shrapnel, or their limbs being dismembered by explosive devices, or their pretty little heads blown off by artillery-fire, or their soft faces burned or scarred beyond recognition. No sir. The big concern here is that some female soldiers feel depressed because they can't quite fit into a "male world". Listen to this misguided sentimentality:

"Yet even though women distinguished themselves as leaders and enlisted soldiers, many of them describe struggling with feeling they do not quite belong. For men, the bonds of unconditional love among fellow combatants — that lifeblood of male military culture — are sustaining. But in dozens of interviews with women who served, they often said such deep emotional sustenance eluded them."

*Lieutenant Courtney Wilson on a mission in Afghanistan in May of 2010: "This is my favorite picture from deployment. I had so much **fun** (?!) on that mission. ... To be able to say, when I'm 40 or 50, 'I did this, **I did something very cool'**. I guess secretly I always wanted to be a bad-ass."*

The article goes on to explain how Courtney now suffers from depression and anxiety; disorders which, the story suggests, are due to the fact that she had never quite "fit in" with the boys. Wacky Wilson explains:

"I started feeling a little like it was me versus them. I was worried the men didn't like me. I wasn't sure if they were making me one of the guys, or completely disrespecting and making fun of me."

May your humble psychoanalyst here at **The Anti-New York Times** suggest that maybe, just *maybe*, this young lady had a few "screws loose" long *before* she enlisted to "have fun" and become "a bad-ass"? Let us further posit that said screws were loosened not by the male comrades who "didn't like her", but rather by the degenerate, insane, upside-down, black-is-white, Marxified Hollywood "culture" that she was raised in - a cultural cesspool that trained her to "be one of the boys" - a cultural cesspool that has robbed her of the opportunity to obtain the true happiness, fulfillment and security that comes with being a wife and mother.

Things could have turned out much worse for the attractive young blond. At least Courtney came out alive and physically intact. Other "bad-ass" young and deluded "fun-seeking" girls weren't so lucky. Like the song says, "Girls just wanna have fun", eh?

AMPUTEES:

Dawn Halfaker, Kate Philp, Mary Dague,Tammy Duckworth

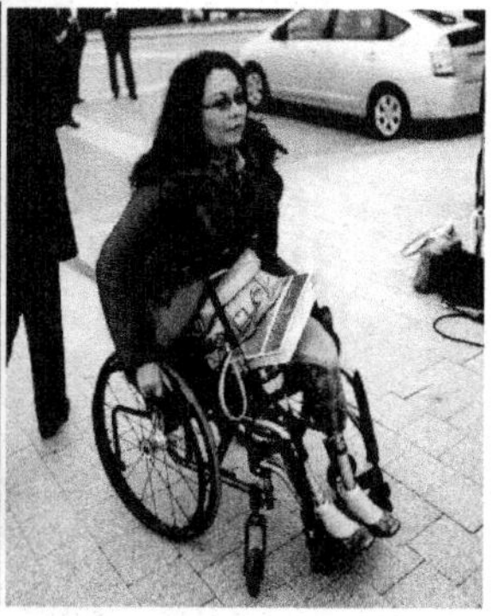

DEAD:

Mikayla Bragg, Kamisha Jane Block, Joanna Dyer,Sarah Bryant

American "man"! What the bloody flip is wrong with you?!!!!

With the possible exception of civil defense against a foreign invasion, sane and civilized nations do not send their sisters and daughters into the meat grinder of the battlefield front. Isn't it bad enough that about 700,000 of your sons, husbands and brothers have pissed their lives away during the 20th Century's wars for "our freedom" *(barf)*? Must we now also sink so low as to sacrifice our daughters, wives and sisters on the sacrificial altar of Globo-Zionism?

What have we done to "Daddy's little girl" to cause her to aspire to be "a bad-ass" instead of a good wife and mother? Women's "liberation", my foot! Women's destruction is more like it.

"The greatest sorrows and joys or great exhibition of strength are not assigned to the woman. Her life should flow more quietly, more gently, and less obtrusively than man's, without her being essentially happier or unhappier." - - Arthur Schopenhauer.

MAY, 2015

NY Times: After a Year of Outsize Expectations, Narendra Modi Adjusts His Plan for India

By ELLEN BARRY

Standing before India on the first anniversary of his swearing-in, Prime Minister Narendra Modi on Monday gave a speech that was notable for the subjects it avoided: Large-scale job creation. Manufacturing. Urbanization.

REBUTTAL BY

The Anti-New York Times

Though not as frequently attacked as the ' R ' *(Russia)* or the ' C ' *(China)*; the ' I ' in **BRICS** *(India)* has certainly received more than its fair share of underhanded abuse by the seditious scum who scribble for Sulzberger's Slimes. This latest propaganda poop-pie was to be expected after **the unprecedented march of Indian military units in Russia's recent 'Victory Day' celebration.**

(Excuse me, Mr. Putin, with all due respect; you are still my boy, and I totally understand the power of mythology that you are beholden to, but I have to go barf over this Soviet 'Victory Day' nonsense. Be right back.)

OK. All better now.

The fact that Indian military units, along with Chinese, showed up to honor "isolated" Russia spoke volumes to the jealous jerks of the degenerate West. Sulzberger's latest anti-Indian cheap shot is as pathetic as it was predictable. Though acknowledging the rapid growth of India's economy, the nay-saying tone of the article, aimed at the foreign investor class, childishly nit-picks while squirting cold urine on India's record.

The truth, and the Slimes knows this, is that India has the potential to rapidly develop along the lines of China. The developing country has many smart business people and scientists, deep cultural roots, world class high-tech, plenty of natural resources, a billion people, and nuclear bombs coupled with missile capability.

Lots of potential.

India's main problem remains its teeming mass of lower class population. But the financial incentives now being offered for underclass human baby-factories to have themselves sterilized is a very promising development; one that the US should emulate with its own hordes of unwed "baby mommas". Another problem is that India's democratic system still leaves it vulnerable to western intrigue and pressures. Like Russia, India is not without its traitors in high places.

If India can replicate China's achievement of pulling hundreds of millions of people up and out from pure poverty, *(which is already happening)* the Globalists may soon have yet another disobedient superpower on their hands *(if they don't already)*. We wish India all the best on the course of progress that it has embarked upon.

Namaste!

Indians march in Moscow / Modi with Putin

MAY, 2015

NY Times: FIFA Officials Arrested on Corruption Charges; Blatter Isn't Among Them

By MATT APUZZO, MICHAEL S. SCHMIDT, WILLIAM K. RASHBAUM and SAM BORDEN

As FIFA leaders gathered for a meeting, Swiss law enforcement officials arrived unannounced and made arrests at the Justice Department's request on charges including racketeering and money laundering.

MAY, 2015

NY Times: After Indicting 14 Soccer Officials, U.S. Vows to End Graft in FIFA

By STEPHANIE CLIFFORD and MATT APUZZO

Hours after indicting 14 people, the Justice Department and prosecutors for the Eastern District of New York pledged to rid the international soccer organization of systemic corruption.

MAY, 2015

NY Times: Sepp Blatter: In Charge, but Left Unscathed

By JONATHAN MAHLER

As FIFA's leader, Mr. Blatter has been praised for extending soccer's reach to less developed nations but has also been widely criticized as tone-deaf and dictatorial.

REBUTTAL BY

The Anti-New York Times

Multiple front page, full-court attacks on FIFA? Weird!

What the heck is Loretta Lynch Mob and her US Justice Department doing having their Swiss puppets *arrest* foreign soccer officials? Why is The New York Slimes, along with the rest of the piranha press, suddenly taking such an interest in the dealings of FIFA *(Federation International Football Association)* - the organization which regulates a sport that relatively few Americans even care about?

Are there not more pressing cases of corruption in America for the Justice Department and Sulzberger's Slimes to pursue? You know; like the massive voter fraud *known* to have taken place during the 2008 and 2012 elections? Or the Federal Reserve Board's steadfast refusal to allow an auditing of its activities? Or the past lies which led America into war in Iraq? Or the current lies which may yet lead to future wars against Syria, Iran, and even Russia and China? Or the blatant multi-billion dollar fraud and abuse surrounding the Social Security, Food Stamp, Medicaid, Medicare and Disability programs? Or the monstrous waste of taxpayer funds for the "Defense" Department?

The level of criminal corruption running rampant throughout America is as colossal as it is pervasive. Why the sudden government-media focus on the foreign-based FIFA?

Why is Al Sharpton-in-Drag suddenly so concerned with arresting FIFA officials? What's really going on here?

This past April, your occasional soccer-aficionado here at **The Anti-New York Times** came across some stories about FIFA President **Sepp Blatter** that really got my Sherlock Holmesian mind to theorizing....big time! Without telling you what the "conspiracy theory" was, let us closely digest this following excerpt from an April 20 article posted by NBC Sports:

*"**Blatter, 79, and FIFA have come under intense scrutiny for allowing the tournament to go ahead in Russia** amid a financial meltdown and military action by Pro-Russian rebels in eastern Ukraine.*

*Despite all of that — and several other issues regarding human rights and Russia's strict laws against homosexuality — Blatter spoke to TASS news agency from Sochi and **the leader of world soccer's governing body waxed lyrical about Russia's 2018 bid**, adding that FIFA only focuses on soccer, not politics.*

Here are a few extracts from Blatter's comments, as Putin promised that the World Cup would be on the same scale as the 2014 Winter Olympics held in Sochi.

*"I am a happy and proud president. I am proud that Russia is getting ready to host the World Cup," Blatter said. **"A lot of this is happening thanks to President Vladimir Putin**, but also due to the Sports Minister (Vitaly) Mutko and (Alexei) Sorokin (CEO of the Local Organising Committee). They are a true team and have a wonderful working relationship.*

"Some people are wanting the World Cup to be taken away from Russia, but we will give one answer to this – we are involved in football and we will not allow politics to get in the way."

*"Everything is going to plan and **nothing will get in the way of Russia hosting the best ever World Cup**. The economic situation is not the best, but I know it will get better."*

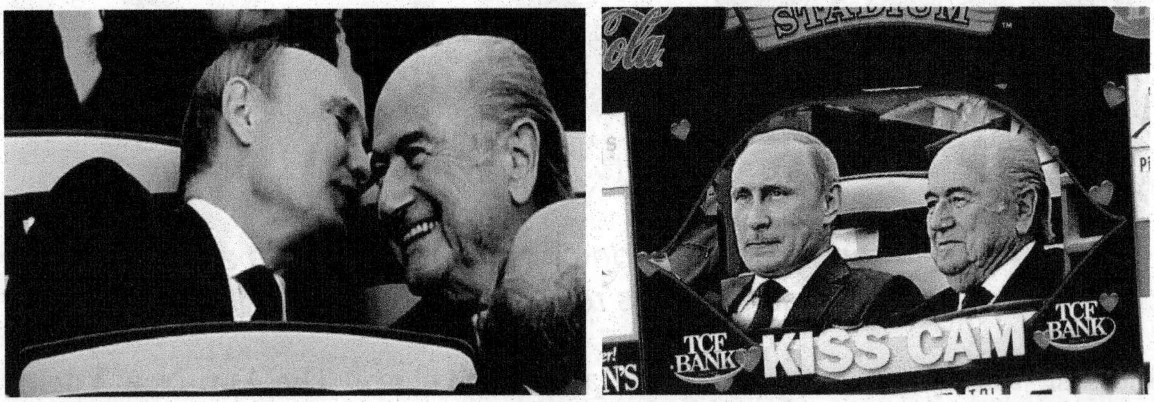

The western media has been very scornful of Blatter's admiration for Putin.

Get the picture now? After having read those Blatter comments, your prophetic reporter *knew*, back in April, that the Swiss Blatter had placed a target on his own back. You see, major quadrennial international sports events such as the Olympics and the World Cup of soccer often carry *huge* geo-political implications. When the U.S. and a gaggle of puppets boycotted the 1980 Summer Olympics in Moscow, it was a huge slap-in-the-face to the then Soviet Union. Four years later, the Soviets and allies returned the insult by boycotting the 1984 Olympics in Los Angeles.

More recently, in 2014, we witnessed the petty attacks upon the Russian Winter Olympics in Sochi. For nearly the entire month preceding the games, The Slimes launched about one petty attack-per-day on the Russian games.

National Security Advisor Zbigniew Brzezinski and President Carter confer over the day's edition of the President's Daily Brief.

After having deliberately baited the Soviets into invading Afghanistan (true story!), U.S. President Jimmy Carter and his notorious Globalist side-kick, Zbigniew Brzezinski, did their best to ruin the Moscow Olympics while also ruining the lifelong dreams of American athletes who didn't get to go.

With the 2018 World Cup of Football *(aka soccer)* slated for hosting by Russia, the Globalist scheme to move the games to another location, or at least organize a western boycott, is already in full force. How serious is this effort? Well, less than two months ago, thirteen, count em', *thirteen* U.S. Senators signed a letter asking Blatter to consider taking the 2018 World Cup out of Russia because of its *"ongoing violations of the territorial integrity of Ukraine."*

Among the big name "bi-partisan" signatories were Richard Durbin (D-IL) , Robert Menendez (D-NJ) , Dan Coates (R IN) and John McCain the Insane (R-AZ). The busy-body warmongers told Blatter that allowing Russia to host the event *"inappropriately bolsters the prestige of the Putin regime".*

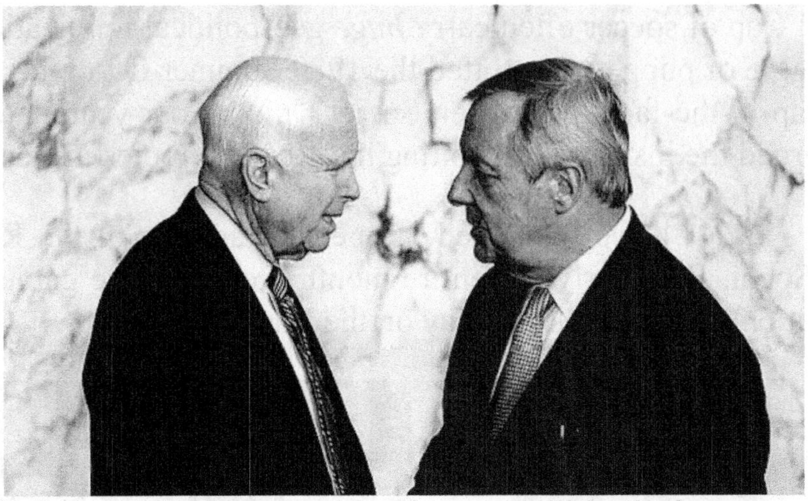

Senators McCain & Durban are big players within their respective political parties.

In no uncertain terms, Blatter essentially told the U.S. to "stick it". And now, a "scandal" erupts. Whether the allegations are true or not is immaterial to the sinister motives which underlie this sudden exposure. As the old "church lady" of Saturday Night Live fame used to say, *"how conveeeenient".*

To which we should add, and how stinking evil!

The U.S. government and media attacks of FIFA President Blatter are similar to the tactics that were used to take down Putin's very close Italian friend, Silvio Berlusconi of Italy.

*

Putin has accused the U.S. of blackmailing world leaders

"There are reports that a number of world leaders are getting undisguised blackmailed. It is not without reason that the 'Big Brother' is spending billions of dollars on surveillance around the world, including on their closest allies."

Vladimir Putin, October 2014

UPDATE!

Shortly after this piece was posted, a reader named Tom informed that the FIFA Congress was also considering suspending Israel from International Soccer - **the vote being set for May 29**. Israel is being investigated for restricting the movement of Palestinian players, confining five FIFA-registered teams in settlements located in the occupied West Bank, and doing nothing to crack down on anti-Arab racist epithets chanted by fans at games in Israel.

FIFA Chief Blatter said he opposed the motion because, as he put it, FIFA is the wrong place to address political grievances. However, Blatter also noted that he does not have the power to take the motion off the table or otherwise prevent the FIFA Congress from passing it.

Will the FIFA Congress back off of Israel now? How *conveeenient* indeed!

Head of Palestinian Football Association Jibril Rajoub speaks about Israeli fan abuse of Arab players during a press conference in Ramallah in the West Bank on May 25, 2015.

MAY, 2015

NY Times: U.S. Rebukes China on Efforts to Build Artificial Islands

By MATTHEW ROSENBERG

A day after China laid out its vision for a navy that can project power into the open seas, Defense Secretary Ashton B. Carter on Wednesday criticized Beijing's efforts to build artificial islands in the South China Sea

REBUTTAL BY

The Anti-New York Times

Regular readers already know that the sadistic criminals who misrule America are insane; but lately, it appears as though they are suicidal as well. Has it not occurred to them that the simultaneous poking of *both* the Russian Bear and the Chinese Dragon can, in time, escalate into mutual nuclear annihilation? Or do the planners have some secret weapon - or some secret escape plans - that we don't know about?

How else to explain the latest threat issued by the Secretary of Offense, Ass-Tongue Carter:

"There should be no mistake about this: The United States will fly, sail and operate wherever international law allows, as we do all around the world."

The Pentagon is weighing how aggressively it should continue to send aircraft and warships into *what it considers* international waters. An American surveillance jet last week flew near Fiery Cross Reef, a "contested" island where China has been dredging in recent months. Chinese forces repeatedly ordered the American aircraft to leave the area, and China's Foreign Ministry later slammed the flight as "irresponsible and dangerous."

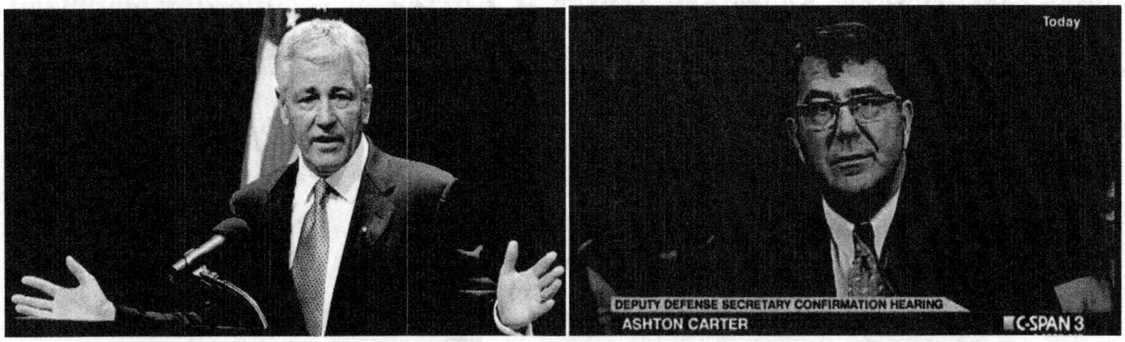

Hagel was bumped out in order to get psycho Carter in.

November, 2014: After the relatively dovish Secretary Chuck Hagel was forced out of the Pentagon in favor of Carter, **The Anti-New York Times** warned:

*"As if his (Carter's) aggressive posture towards Russia and the Middle East weren't dangerous enough, we learn that Carter was one of the architects behind Obongo's **"Asia-Pacific pivot"** that has got the Chinese really pissed off....*

Oh this bloodthirsty psychopath is going to get along just beautifully with McCain the Insane and the incoming band of GOP Zio-crazies...

It looks like 2015 is shaping up to be a very interesting year, and for all the wrong reasons. While Homo-Obongo, Sharpton, Farrakhan et al. work to "tear this God-damn country apart" from within (Farrakhan's words), the Pentagon boys will take care of the outside wars. Good luck Mr. Putin, and Mr. JinPing, and Mr. Assad and anyone else who dares to defy Carter's NWO gang of neo-con Globalists. And most of all, good luck Boobus Americanus, even though you have no idea what's coming."

Psychos McCain and Carter rub elbows at some 'hoidy-toidy' party for the elitist scum of DC.

Of course, this whole "controversy" over what are "international waters", and what are not, is all just a pretext for picking a fight with China. Therefore, we will not play into the Devil's rhetorical trap by talking about "the islands". In regard to U.S. threats, China has already responded by openly stating that it will *"surely counter-attack if attacked"*.

And who's to say that some German-made Israeli sub may not strike the first 'false-flag' blow needed to get the party started? Secure in the knowledge that no one of any stature in America would dare to even think such an "anti-Semetic" thought, Bibi Satanyahu could pull off such a dastardly stunt *easily*.

Historian and geo-political analyst Webster Griffin Tarpley often drifts off into "La-La Land" when he mispeaks of the history of World War II and his beloved FDR, but the man deserves credit for the spookily prescient forecast he issued in 2008 - before Mr. & Mr. Obongo were even installed in the White House.

Tarpley:

"The project of the next administration, if its Obama, is to smash both Russia and China...Obama's foreign policy is to have a global showdown with Russia and China."

Even your learned reporter here at **The Anti-New York Times** was not expecting such a radical and dangerous foreign policy back then. Hat tip to Tarpley for nailing it, though we can be certain he will take no satisfaction in seeing his prophecy fulfilled.

Tarpley warned us about this Devil (and his handlers)

Another, more recent prophecy - albeit self-fulfilling - comes to us from that arch-criminal and Globalist monster, George Soros:

"If there is conflict between China and a military ally of the United States, like Japan, then it is not an exaggeration to say that we are on the threshold of a third world war....there is a real danger that China will align itself with Russia politically and militarily, and then the threat of third world war becomes real."

This stuff is really starting to get a little scary.

*Soros the Jewish-Marxist puppet master wants **blood**!*

MAY, 2015

NY Times (Editorial): The Insecure American

By PAUL KRUGMAN

America remains, despite the damage inflicted by the Great Recession and its aftermath, a very rich country. But many Americans are economically insecure, with little protection from life's risks.

REBUTTAL BY

The Anti-New York Times

That rat-faced Nobel Prize winning charlatan Paul Krugman is at it again - spewing pure unadulterated Marxist filth at the gullible PBS/Slimes crowd who hang on his every word. Unlike many of the Keynesian clowns of Academia who actually *believe* that tonics such as taxing, spending, borrowing and printing money can bring about prosperity, crooked Krugman is no fool. Just like his idol, John Maynard Keynes, Krugman ***knows*** bloody damn well that he is peddling false economics, and so does Sulzberger.

Oh how your righteous reporter here at **The Anti-New York Times** wishes he could *literally* take little Paulie to an actual woodshed and mercilessly horse-whip the matzo balls out of Krugman's talking hind quarters; but we'll have to settle for a metaphorical butt-whoopin'. What follows are rebuttals to key excerpts from Krugman's crock of Communist crap:

Krugman: Many Americans are economically insecure, with little protection from life's risks.

Anti-NY Times: After a lifetime of being robbed by excessive taxation, currency debasement *(inflation)*, debt-based money supply and mortgage usury *(economic ills which scum like Krugman have always championed)* this is not surprising.

Krugman: They frequently experience financial hardship; many don't expect to be able to retire, and if they do retire have little to live on besides Social Security.

Anti-NY Times: Putting aside the question as to whether or not a Social Security system should ever have been implemented, the horrible truth behind the paltry and insufficient level of support that SS now provides is due to the fact that both worker and employer "contributions" were never set aside in that "shoe-box" that FDR, *(Krugman's hero)* and his Communist Party henchmen promised. Instead, SS was structured to operate as a Pyramid Scheme.

As if that wasn't bad enough, the "stones" of the pyramid itself are routinely "mined" to pay for the welfare and warfare state that scum who think like Krugman have erected. Had SS truly operated like a well-managed "shoebox", we would all retire with at least an extra million dollars.

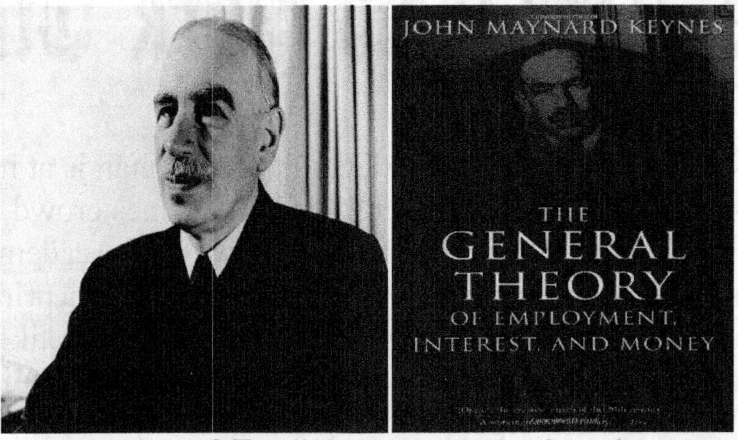

The psuedo-economics of English homosexual and rumored pedophile John Maynard Keynes was hyped to the hilt by the same Jewish crime gang that built up FDR and made Krugman rich and famous.

Krugman: All too many affluent Americans — and, in particular, members of our political elite — seem to have no sense of how the other half lives.

Anti-NY Times: This is quintessentially typical Jewish Marxist "holier than thou" posturing. Multi-millionaire Krugman couldn't give a rat's rear-end "how the other half lives." During a "past life" in sales & marketing, your observant reporter here spent some time bumping elbows with the uppity scum of Princeton, NJ and New York City to know this for a fact. Trust me; these characters do ***nothing*** for "the poor" unless there are cameras and a newspaper reporter nearby!

Krugman: Which is why a new study on the financial well-being of U.S. households, conducted by the Federal Reserve, should be required reading inside the Beltway.

Anti-NY Times: Krugman! You filthy Marxist swine! Citing the Federal Reserve as an authoritative source "on the financial well-being" of Americans would be like citing a "study" about lung cancer conducted by the R.J. Reynolds Tobacco company. Your beloved Hebrew National Bank, with its engineered asset bubbles, Federal deficit enabling, debt-based currency issue and inflationary money printing, is the number one threat to our "financial well-being"

Krugman: Before I get to that study, a few words about the **callous obliviousness** so prevalent in our political life. I am not, or not only, talking about **right-wing contempt for the poor**, although the dominance of **compassion-less conservatism** is a sight to behold.

Anti-NY Times: Even Karl Marx never ranted like this: "callous obliviousness" - "right-wing contempt for the poor" - "compassion-less conservatism". Krugman comes off sounding like some name-calling college-campus libtard who never grew up. You see, in Krugman's upside world, concern over America's 1.5 Trillion dollar annual deficits amounts to "hatred for the poor".

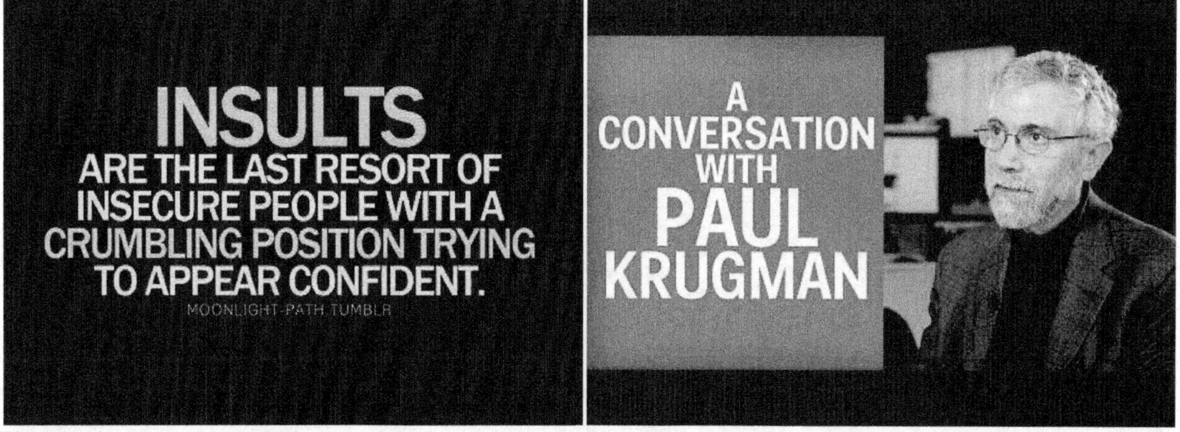

There is no reasoning with immature "intellectual" bullies such as Krugman.

Krugman: According to the Pew Research Center...

Anti-NY Times: An ultra-Left "think-tank" that Krugman would have us believe is an objective party.

Krugman: .... more than three-quarters of conservatives believe that the poor “have it easy” thanks to government benefits; only 1 in 7 believe that the poor “have hard lives.”

Anti-NY Times: No conservative believes that the working poor at the lower rung of the middle class "have it easy". *However*, the baby-breeding *non-working* poor, with their free Section 8 housing, Medicaid, Food Stamps, cash benefits, heating assistance, side part-time jobs, Earned Income "Tax Credit", Obongo Phones and, in many cases, working boyfriends who maintain a separate address but live with the baby-mommas - they absolutely *do* have it easy and will often boast about it!

Krugman: And this attitude translates into policy. What we learn from the refusal of Republican-controlled states to expand Medicaid, even though the federal government would foot the bill, is that punishing the poor has become a goal in itself, one worth pursuing even if it hurts rather than helps state budgets.

Anti-NY Times: Balancing budgets = hatred for "the poor". What an demagogic, deceiving, despicable little worm you are, Krugman.

Krugman: But leave self-declared conservatives and their **contempt for the poor** on one side.

Anti-NY Times: Sigh-Face-Palm....Crap like this used to really drive Hitler and Goebbels nuts!

Krugman ist ein %$@(&^* &%@! Jude !!!*

Krugman: While the retirement system F.D.R. introduced may look old-fashioned to affluent professionals, it is quite literally a lifeline for many of our fellow citizens. A majority of Americans over 65 get more than half their income from Social Security, and more than a quarter are almost completely reliant on those monthly checks.

Anti-NY Times: No one, and I mean *no one*, is advocating a cold-Turkey cut-off of the Social Security pyramid scheme, you forked-tongued serpent! The proposals put forth by conservative thinkers *(not to be confused with Jewish neo-cons)* would leave needy current recipients protected while as younger workers are phased into a public-private system along the lines of the very popular Chilean model. **Ironically, the only people actually cutting Social Security purchasing-power are inflationists like you, Krugman, who constantly advocate for more and more erosion of our currency's value.**

Krugman: But my sense is that Washington still has no clue about the realities of life for those not yet elderly. Which is where that Federal Reserve study comes in. This is the study's second year, and the current edition actually portrays a nation in recovery.

Anti-NY Times: "The nation is in recovery"? Really Paulie? Really?

Krugman: There is no such thing as perfect security, but American families could easily have much more security than they have. All it would take is for politicians and pundits to stop talking blithely about the need to cut "entitlements" and start looking at the way their less-fortunate fellow citizens actually live.

Anti-NY Times: So, Krugman. Your remedy for restoring "security" is to continue taxing, spending, borrowing and printing money - the same game plan we have been running since LBJ's "War on Poverty". How's that been workin' out?

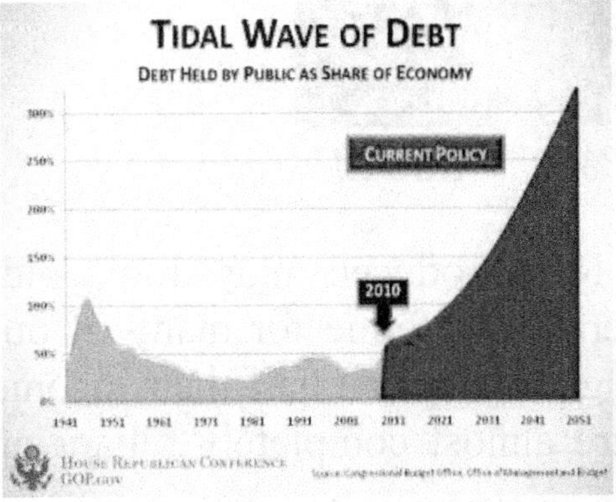

Krugman's feigned concern for "the poor" is just a cover for the real agenda; namely, the bankrupting, looting and destruction of what's left of the American Dream - followed by a full-blown Globalist takeover.

ONE AIMED AT RUSSIA.....

MAY, 2015

NY Times: A U.S. Tax Investigation Snowballed to Stun the Soccer World

By MATT APUZZO

The complex case, which involved cooperation between the I.R.S. and the F.B.I., is likely to lead to more charges related to corruption allegations at soccer's highest levels.

ONE AIMED AT CHINA.....

MAY, 2015

NY Times: Chinese Security Laws Elevate the Party and Stifle Dissent. Mao Would Approve

By EDWARD WONG

The new law, released in draft form this month, says security must be maintained "to realize the great rejuvenation of the Chinese nation."

REBUTTAL BY

The Anti-New York Times

The Global Showdown with the Russia-China Alliance is really picking up steam. Normally, the government-media complex alternates between anti-Russian and anti-Chinese attacks. But as of late, Sulzberger's Slimes and their government co-conspirators have been feeding us two-for-one special propaganda poop-pies. This comes on the heels of a very ominous remark made by Mr. and Mr. Obongo's handler of all handlers, George Soros:

"If there is conflict between China and a military ally of the United States, like Japan, then it is not an exaggeration to say that we are on the threshold of a third world war....there is a real danger that China will align itself with Russia politically and militarily, and then the threat of third world war becomes real."

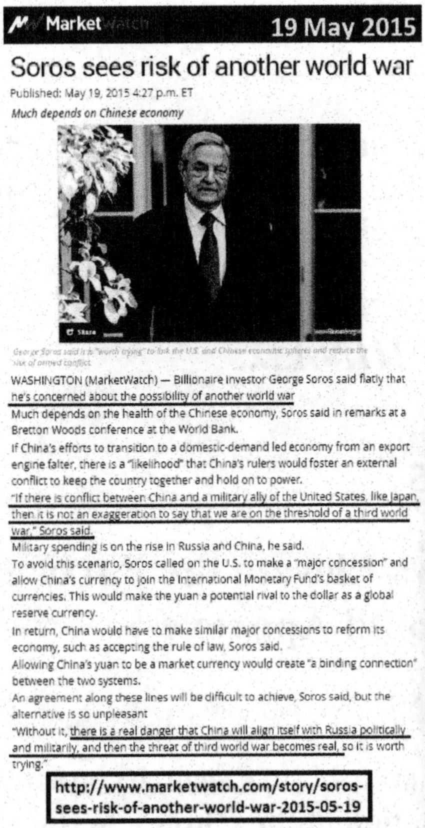

MarketWatch 19 May 2015

Soros sees risk of another world war

Published: May 19, 2015 4:27 p.m. ET

Much depends on Chinese economy

WASHINGTON (MarketWatch) — Billionaire investor George Soros said flatly that he's concerned about the possibility of another world war

Much depends on the health of the Chinese economy, Soros said in remarks at a Bretton Woods conference at the World Bank.

If China's efforts to transition to a domestic-demand led economy from an export engine falter, there is a "likelihood" that China's rulers would foster an external conflict to keep the country together and hold on to power.

"If there is conflict between China and a military ally of the United States, like Japan, then it is not an exaggeration to say that we are on the threshold of a third world war," Soros said.

Military spending is on the rise in Russia and China, he said.

To avoid this scenario, Soros called on the U.S. to make a "major concession" and allow China's currency to join the International Monetary Fund's basket of currencies. This would make the yuan a potential rival to the dollar as a global reserve currency.

In return, China would have to make similar major concessions to reform its economy, such as accepting the rule of law, Soros said.

Allowing China's yuan to be a market currency would create "a binding connection" between the two systems.

An agreement along these lines will be difficult to achieve, Soros said, but the alternative is so unpleasant

"Without it, there is a real danger that China will align itself with Russia politically and militarily, and then the threat of third world war becomes real, so it is worth trying."

http://www.marketwatch.com/story/soros-sees-risk-of-another-world-war-2015-05-19

With that in mind, let's have a quick look at the ***real*** meaning of these two stories:

1: A U.S. Tax Investigation Snowballed to Stun the Soccer World

Sulzberger wants us to believe that the big FIFA story just "spontaneously" grew out of a relatively minor tax investigation. It then "snowballed" just at the exact same time that the US-EU Axis was heavily pressuring FIFA to pull the 2018 World Cup of Football *(Soccer)* from Russia; and Israel was pleading not to be banned from international soccer. **The highly anticipated vote to ban Israel did not take place on Friday past**, but the vote to re-elect FIFA's Putin-supporting Swiss friend, Sepp Blatter, did occur. Blatter beat out America's hand-picked Jordanian puppet. Therefore, the attacks on FIFA and the US-EU push to strip Russia will continue.

The western media has been very scornful of Blatter's admiration for Putin.

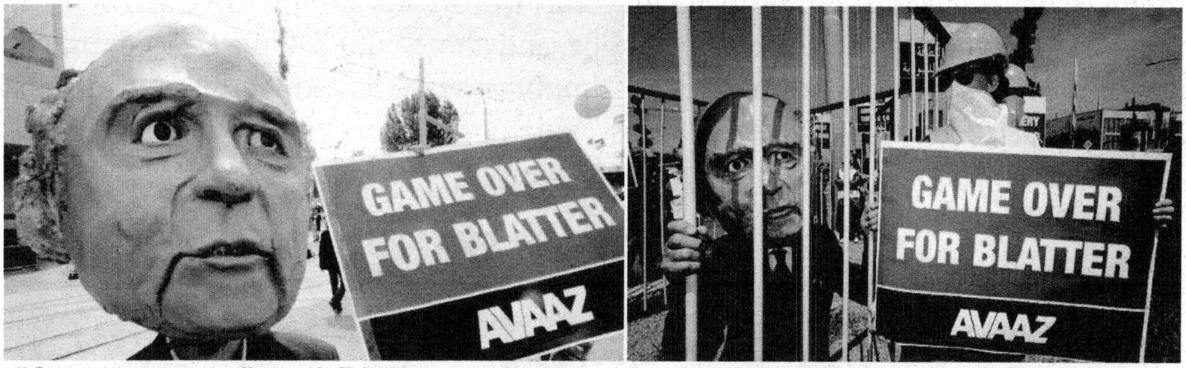

"Spontaneous" anti-Blatter protests coincide nicely with a "spontaneous" IRS investigation and US Justice Department indictments.

2: Chinese Security Laws Elevate the Party and Stifle Dissent. Mao Would Approve.

Mao-bashing? Really Sulzberger? Mao died 40 years ago. Deep in bowels of Hell, he and Stalin must be fuming at the pro-business, pro-market direction that Russia and China have since taken. What the Slimes refers to as "stifling dissent" is really nothing more than China taking measures to stop the CIA-NGO-Facebook brigades from targeting young people *(as was done in Hong Kong)* with Color Revolution propaganda. Sulzberger's International Edition of The Slimes is also banned in China.

During its 2014 visit to China, the First Tranny, one two occasions, openly encouraged Chinese kids to stand up for their Internet rights!

Along with this constant propaganda warfare aimed at the two powers, the relentless provocations in Eastern Europe and the South China Sea continue to escalate. This is a re-play of how FDR simultaneously baited Germany and Japan. The question today, as it was in 1941, is: which of the two giants will bite first? Or will an Israeli submarine do the biting for them?

Will history bear witness to another Pearl Harbor type provocation?....

Or an Israel USS Liberty style 'False Flag' attack?

JUNE, 2015

N.Y. Times: U.S. Paid Residents Linked to Nazi Crimes $20 Million in Benefits, Report Says

BY ERIC LICHTBLAU

The American government paid $20.2 million in Social Security benefits to more than 130 United States residents linked to Nazi atrocities over the course of more than a half-century.

REBUTTAL BY

The Anti-New York Times

For the first time in the 2-year history of **The Anti-New York Times**, your Sulzberger-hating reporter here finds himself in the awkward position of being in full agreement with The Slimes. Yes, even broken clocks are right twice-a-day! We whole-heartedly share Sulzberger's indignation over the fact that $20 million of Social Security funds were paid out to 130 post-World War II German NS immigrants *(so-called "Nazis")*; some as recently as last year. What a flippin' joke this country has become!

Sulzberger, King and Sugar agree: The $20 million payouts to NS and SS members were an outrage.

The bureaucrats behind this irresponsible screw-up ought to be summarily fired; but of course, they won't be. Just imagine; these German Waffen SS men and/or NS Party members sacrificed their lives and sacred honor in trying to defend not just Germany, but all of Europe, and indeed, all of mankind. They endured horrific hardships at Allied hands and were fortunate to survive. And the best we can do for them is ration out a measly 20 million dollars spread out among 130 men over a number of decades? These men each deserved $1 million lump sum, at least. Shame on you America! *(Had you going there for a minute, eh?)*

Seriously now, does it ever end with these vindictive whining shysters? From the article:

*"An investigation by The Associated Press last fall drew renewed concern to the phenomenon, prompting Congress to pass legislation called the **No Social Security for Nazis Act**."*

The ***"No Social Security for Nazis Act"***? Are you kidding me, Congress?!

Why isn't there a ***"No Social Security for Stalinists Act"?*** There are plenty them still alive and kicking, especially in the New York area. Or how about a ***"No Social Security for Convicted Murderers, Rapists and Pedophiles Act"?*** They all qualify for Social Security money *(upon release)*. Indeed, the SSA was even kind enough to put out a brochure for ex-cons:

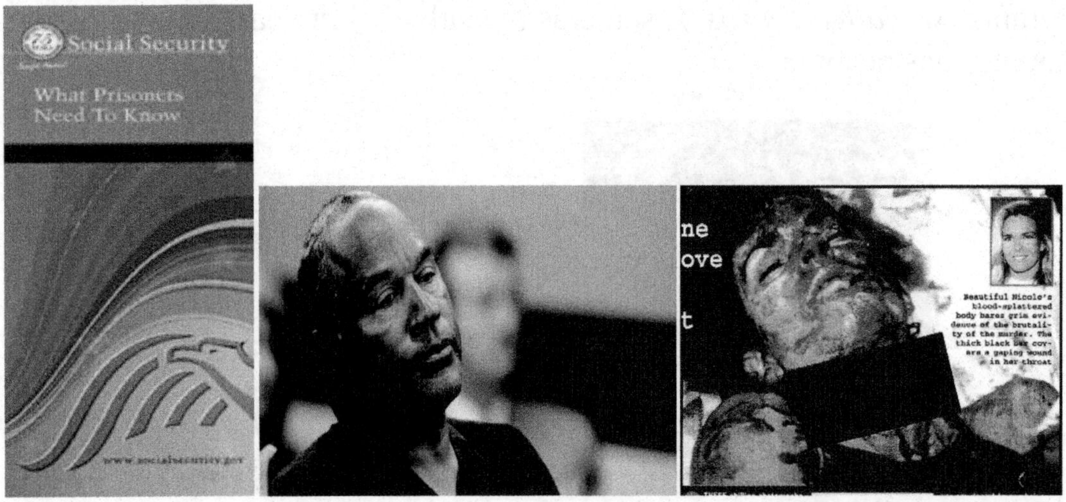

Double murderer O J Simpson will be eligible for Social Security benefits upon his 2017 release. Not so for German-American "Nazis".

**Simpson got away with murder but was arrested for robbery*

Why should an ex-"Nazi" who has worked hard for many years, paid taxes into the American system, and *never* broken any laws be denied his benefits? Well, we all know why. It's all because of "The Holocaust - **TM**". Nonetheless, apart from the fact that the HoloHoax Fairy Tale does not even make for plausible fiction, the few so-called "Nazis" left are all in their 90's. Enough already!

But the dirtiest part of this dastardly trick is that some of the elderly "Nazis" were originally approved for SS benefits only under the condition that they leave America. After being "persuaded" to accept the cruel cash-for-expulsion offer, **the NSSN Act of 2014 then betrayed the four remaining recipients by pulling their due benefits anyway!**

Who would vote for such an unjust, cruel and senseless betrayal of innocent AMERICANS as the ***"No Social Security for Nazis Act"***?

Answer: Every, and I mean *every*, single whore-fool in Congress, that's who.

December 2014 Vote

House: **420-0** Senate: **100-0**

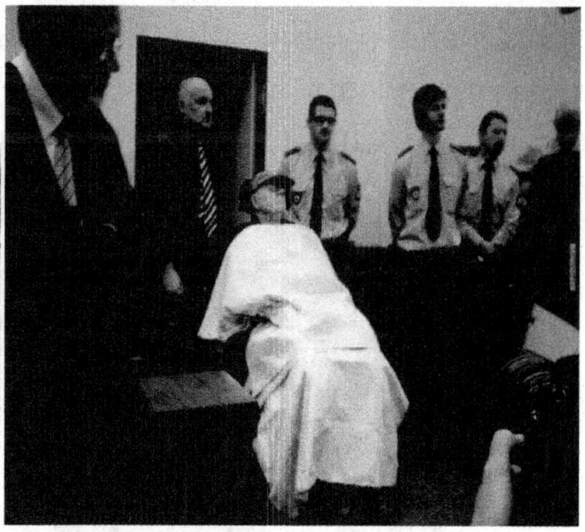

1- German SS men (especially blonds!) were singled out for special abuse because they were elite volunteers and committed to the ideology. Note the battered face of the prisoner above, the machete in the hands of his sadistic captor (a Jewish torturer?) and what appear to be missing fingers on the poor soul's left hand. Rest in Valhalla young man.
2- The heart-breaking courtroom abuse of elderly SS men continues to this day. Bastards!

JUNE, 2015

NY Times: China Says It Could Set Up Air Defense Zone in South China Sea

By EDWARD WONG

A Chinese admiral said Sunday that Beijing could set up an air defense zone above disputed areas of the South China Sea if it thought it was facing a large enough threat, according to Chinese news media.

REBUTTAL BY

The Anti-New York Times

Big bad Russia catches a propaganda breather from the dirty trouble-making demons at the New York Slimes. Today's hate-fest is instead directed towards Russia's close and mighty ally, China. The pretext for this attack is China's development of suddenly "disputed islands" which puppet Vietnam- with Secretary of Offense Asston Carter playing the role of Cyrano DeBergerac to Vietnam's Christian de Neuvillette - now claims belong to it.

"Tell her that only Lady Liberty can defend you from China."
In the classic play, the poetic Cyrano de Bergerac hides behind a bush and tells the simple Christian de Neuvillette what to say to the lovely Roxanne. Likewise, Vietnam's claims to the "disputed islands" and its stated fear of China are actually just sounds emanating from Uncle Sams' talking anus.

Following are a few unsettling excerpts from today's China-bash:

"Speaking to reporters afterward, Mr. Carter said that the United States and Vietnam would sign a "joint vision statement" on Monday after he met with his counterpart in Hanoi. The purpose of the statement was to "modernize" the growing ties between the United States and Vietnam, Mr. Carter said, adding that the United States was also planning to give Vietnam $18 million to help buy patrol boats."

And does this *"joint vision statement"* strike fear into China's Dragon-heart? Let's ask Chinese Admiral Sun:

"China and the Chinese military have never feared the devil or an evil force, and we are convinced by reason but not by hegemony," Admiral Sun said on Sunday, according to a transcript of his speech posted by the Chinese Defense Ministry. "Don't ever expect us to surrender to devious heresies or a mighty power. And don't ever expect us to swallow the bitter fruits that would harm our sovereignty, security and development interests."

Obongo with puppet Vietnamese President. US and Vietnam begin joint Naval exercises.

If Carter and friends don't back off , this could get ugly. But that's the whole point, isn't it Asston? As for Vietnam, one has to wonder in amazed confusion as to why a weaker nation such as Vietnam would be foolish enough to provoke powerful China. Well, it's for the same reason that Poland provoked a much stronger Germany in 1939, and why nations like Georgia and Ukraine continue to provoke the Russian Bear. These little thug regimes are fronting for a much stronger bully that "has their back" - the United States, aka "The West".

In order to shed more light on this question, your ever-snooping reporter here at **The Anti-New York Times** took the Google surfboard out for a wave-run and came up with some very damning data for your consideration. For 2014, Vietnam ***surpassed*** extortionist Israel, yes *Israel*, as the Number #1 recipient of Globalist "Foreign Aid" coming from all international sources! *(most of which are heavily funded by the US & EU)* *

***Afghanistan's top ranking is only a temporary aberration due to the destruction and rebuilding of the country.**

Vietnam's total haul of $4.1 Billion for 2014 tops it's 3.6 Billion from 2013. For a country with government revenues of only about $30 Billion, such a Globalist "gift" surely buys a lot of influence, no, *obedience*. Who knew that the AVPAC Lobby *(American Vietnam Public Affairs Committee)* was so powerful?

This level of open treachery and dangerous warmongering is really hard to watch, but it shouldn't be so hard for people to figure out. If only *Boobus Americanus* would spend less time worshipping the Electronic Idiot Box and just an hour a day seeking alternative news via the miracle of the Internet, Satanic scum such as Asston Carter, Mr. & Mr. Obongo, McCain the Insane and George Sorrows would all be out of business in no time. Instead, we continue our long sleep-walk towards God-knows-what.

So frustrating.

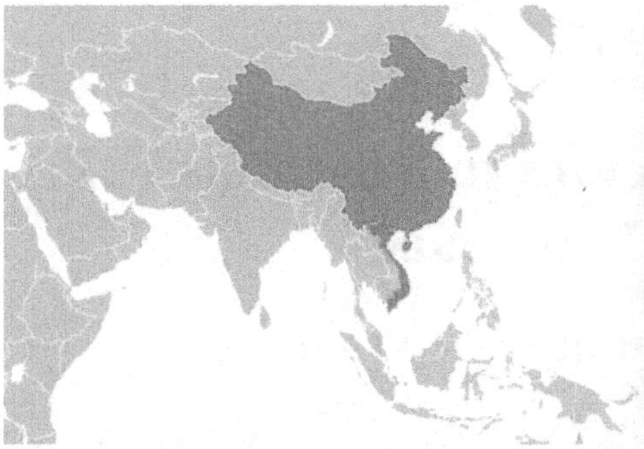

China has neither threatened nor attempted to subvert its southern neighbor in any way. Above: CIA flash mobs in Vietnam (with the usual English language banners) are used to poison relations between the former Asian allies.

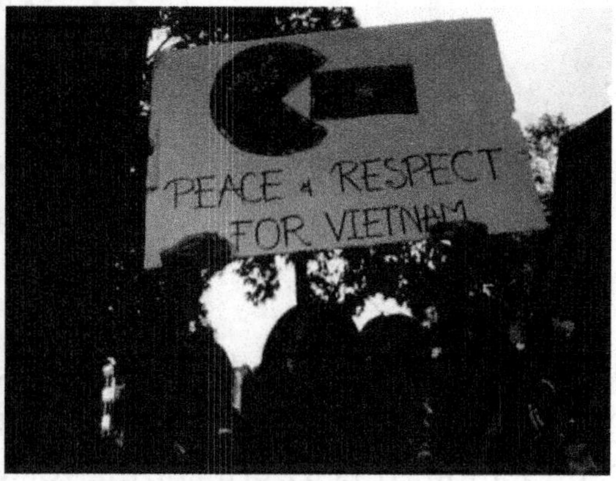

The Hildebeast in Vietnam. / CIA stoogette holds up English language sign falsely accusing peaceful China of trying to swallow up Vietnam.

Peaceful Russia and China are also wargaming joint combat scenarios. Are we on the brink of World War III?

JUNE, 2015

NY Times: Sepp Blatter Decides to Resign as FIFA President in About-Face

By SAM BORDEN, MICHAEL S. SCHMIDT and MATT APUZZO

Four days after he was re-elected, Mr. Blatter said that he would resign his presidency of world soccer's governing body in the wake of a corruption inquiry.

REBUTTAL BY

The Anti-New York Times

Well, they got him. It took only one week for International Jewry to tear down the long-time Emperor of International Football *(Soccer)* and cast him aside like a used-up lemon. It is awe-inspiring to watch how these greasy gangsters operate on a subordinate who has gotten "too big for his britches". Let us review the sudden fall of King Blatter:

July 2013:

Blatter threatens to expel Israel from FIFA: ***"If Israel is not careful, the only team it will be able to play is Camaroon (a FIFA-banned country)."***

April 2015:

- Thirteen U.S. Senators pen a letter to Blatter requesting that Russia be stripped of the 2018 World Cup.
- Blatter responds forcefully, stating that politics and sports should not mix and that Russia will host one of the best tournaments ever. *"I am proud that Russia is getting ready to host the World Cup."*, said Blatter.

Early May 2015:

- Bibi Satanyahu personally lobbies Blatter to have the expulsion vote against Israel stopped.

- Blatter states that although he is opposed to expelling Israel, he may not be able to stop the FIFA Congress from voting to expel Israel.

Blatter to Satanyahu: *"I love Israel! But I may not be able to stop the expulsion vote. I'll see what I can do and get back to you."*
Blatter to McCain: *Screw you. Russia will host the 2018 Games.*

Late May 2015

The U.S. Justice Department and Sulzberger's Slimes unleash hell on Blatter. The rest of the piranha press follows. After finally caving-in and killing the vote to ban Israel, Blatter appears to weather the storm for a few days before suddenly "resigning". God knows what they had on him, or what they threatened him with!

Although the *conveeeenient* "scandal" forced Blatter to kill the vote to expel Israel; the next step in the one-two punch is to take the games away from Russia. The Globalists and their coming FIFA stooge *(Michel Platini of France, most likely)* won't move on this front right away, for that would be too obvious. Expect the drive to strip Russia to unfold slowly, climaxing sometime during 2016 *(assuming we aren't already at war by then)*.

As it is with American Presidents, so too it is with FIFA Presidents. The words of Henry Ford:

"And if after having elected their man or group, obedience is not rendered to the Jewish control, then you speedily hear of "scandals" and "investigations" and "impeachments" for the removal of the disobedient."

-Henry Ford. The International Jew: The World's Foremost Problem

JUNE, 2015

NY Times: Inequality Troubles Americans Across Party Lines, Times/CBS Poll Finds

By NOAM SCHEIBER and DALIA SUSSMAN

A strong majority says steps need to be taken urgently to assure that the fruits of the economic recovery are shared among income classes, according to the New York Times/CBS News poll.

REBUTTAL BY

The Anti-New York Times

Ah yes; the tried and true trick of "Let's-Take-Our-Own-Manipulated-Poll-and-Then-Report-That-the-American-Public-Supports-*(fill in the blank)*".

SCENARIO:

Ring - Ring

Boobus Americanus: "Hello"

CBS/Slimes Pollster: "Good evening sir. Do you have a moment to participate in a brief opinion survey?

Boobus Americanus: "Yeah. Sure."

CBS/Slimes Pollster: "Great! Here's the question: Don't you think it would be really nice if *everybody* in America could earn a good income?"

Boobus Americanus: "Well...uh... yeah. I could sure use a raise."

CBS/Slimes Pollster: "Thank you for your time. Bye."

Click

"Would I like a pay-raise? Definitely!"

Jew York Slimes Headline (next day):
"AMERICANS DEMAND BIGGER GOVERNMENT!"

Perhaps that's a bit of an oversimplification, but not too far off the mark. That's how these crooked journalistic shysters operate. Lost in the whole discussion of "income inequality" is the fact that **the poor man cannot be lifted up by taxing the rich, or even the middle class man.** That's not how economics works. The Jewish mafia controllers at the top of the pyramid know this, but their loyal libtard legions do not. Libtards, and even many non-political ordinary people, view this thing we call "the economy" as if it were a group pizza-pie lunch wherein someone who hogs up 5 slices leaves the others with just 1. It doesn't work that way.

In reality, there are limitless amount of dough, tomatoes and cheese for *everyone* to make their own pizza-pies, regardless of how fat a particular individual is getting *(We are talking about wealthy men in the free market here, not to be confused with the damaging looting engaged in by the Fed and its cronies)*. Moreover, the investment capital and charitable donations managed by those "evil" millionaires and billionaires fulfills an important and beneficial role in the wealth creation of others. As long as people have two hands with which to work, a brain with which to think, and a heart with which to care for others, everyone has the innate ability to make a decent life for himself. **God built self-sufficiency into the natural system of things.**

The reason why so many good *working* people are struggling - amidst all this vast wealth, industry and technology that should be making all of us comfortable - is due to Marxists, Globalists and assorted libtard followers *destroying* that natural system - i.e., the free market and the natural laws of morality. It's quite a damnable trick. First, they crush the private economy with massive taxation, inflation *(Fed money printing)*, usury and excessive regulation. This effort goes hand-in-hand with their destruction of the nuclear family and religion / morality. Then, they present themselves as the benevolent saviors of the very "downtrodden classes" *(proletariat)* which they created in the first place!

And what are the Left's "solutions" for the problem? Answer: *More* taxation, *more* regulation, *more* currency debasement, *more* usury and *more* social degeneracy.

And what is the result of these "solutions"? Answer: *More* "income inequality" and *more* poverty!

And what is the next solution to the next wave of economic hardship? Answer: *More* taxation, *more* regulation...

It's an endless circle-jerk of moral and economic destruction that has been cycling ever since that wretched fiend Lyndon Baines Johnson unleashed "The Great Society" upon a country that had been steadily advancing towards universal prosperity, or at least, universal self-sufficiency.

Lyndon Baines Johnson and Marxist Loser King worked to "solve" the problem of "economic inequality" 50 years ago. How's that workin' out?

nswer to "income inequality" is to **drastically** reduce the size of the vernment and its massive military, kill the Income Tax, kill the Capital , kill the Federal Reserve counterfeiting and loan-sharking operation, t-free, hard asset-backed currency from the U.S. Treasury, abolish consumer lending *(in phases)*, dramatically deregulate the private economy, impose reasonable tariffs to protect American manufacturing as we restore it, deport all foreign-born welfare recipients, pause legal immigration and end illegal immigration, end the subsidization of unwed baby-factories, and begin the long process of restoring traditional morality and families.

This is pretty much what Hitler did to restore Germany in the 1930's; which is exactly why he was "whacked" by the Globo-Zionist Mafia. If we could only implement such bold actions, then soon enough, even low-wage workers would find themselves able to buy modest homes, support families, enjoy a middle-class lifestyle, and still have a few bucks left over to help a brother who has fallen down and needs a temporary lift. **The natural system of economy and morality works.** The controllers *know* this. But they don't want their slaves to know.

Within just a few short years of Hitler's rise to power, previously starving paupers were working full time and taking Scandinavian and Mediterranean cruises through Germany's public 'Strength Through Joy' program (a good form of socialism). Germany's economic miracle was achieved mainly through currency reform, public debt repudiation, tax cuts, pro-business policies, and good old fashioned hard WORK.

JUNE, 2015

NY Times: Data Breach Linked to China Exposes Millions of U. S. Workers

By DAVID E. SANGER and JULIE HIRSCHFELD DAVIS

The Obama administration on Thursday announced what appeared to be one of the largest breaches of federal employees' data, involving at least four million current and former government workers in an intrusion that officials said apparently originated in China.

REBUTTAL BY

The Anti-New York Times

The non-stop barrage of simultaneous anti-Russia and anti-China horror stories is reaching fever pitch now as both the frequency and intensity of the hatred ramp up to levels not seen since pre-World War II. Once again, the breathless scribblers of Sulzberger's Slimes qualify the latest filthy smears from the Obongo administration with the unmistakable legalistic language that *always* accompanies a baseless he-said / she said accusation.

A line-by-line review of the finely-minced legalistic words:

Paragraph 1: "**appeared** to be" - "officials said" - "**apparently** originated"

Paragraph 2: "the official said" - "it **appears** to have begun"

Paragraph 3: "The target **appeared** to be" - "but it was **unclear**"

Paragraph 4: "There **seemed** to be" - "little doubt" - "but it was **unclear** if state-sponsored" - "difficult to attribute the source without compromising classified data"

Paragraph 5: "**apparently** obtained"

Paragraph 6: "hackers **appeared** to have targeted"

Paragraph 7: "**seemed** clear" - "**appeared** to havc involvcd"

Paragraph 8: "the objective **seemed** less clear"

Paragraph 9: "a **potential** compromise" - "a spokesman said"

Paragraph 10: "**potential** threats"

Paragraph 11: "breach **might have** affected"

Paragraph 16: "Determining the source of cyber-attacks is notoriously difficult" - **"the most sophisticated attacks often look as if they were initiated from inside the U.S."**

Paragraph 18: "One official said" - "it was **not clear**" - "**If** the attribution to China holds"

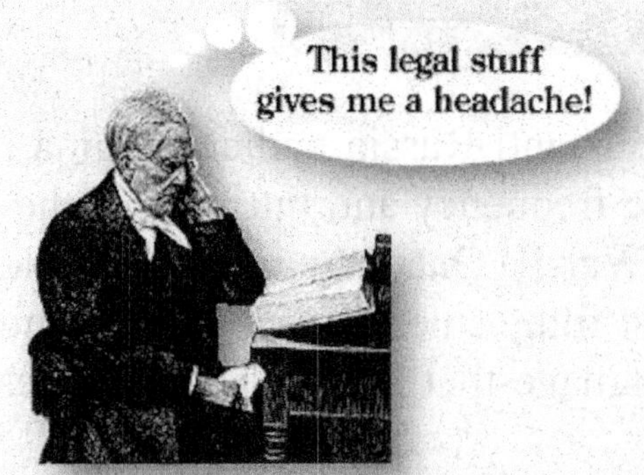

Legalistic qualifiers; he-said / she-said; and invisible sources.

"Psssst. Mr. Newspaper Man; let me tell you a secret about the Chinese hackers."

This legalistic mumbo-jumbo is what passes for journalism these days at America's oh-so-prestigious "paper of record": "appears" - "seems" - "unclear" - "apparently"

- "potential" - "might have" - "unclear" - "if". If your detail-oriented reporter here at **The Anti-New York Times** were an Editor at a major newspaper; and one of my writers brought a story infested with such parsed and legalistic language, it would be ripped up and shoved down his throat. ***"Eat it punk!"***

(Hearsay and minced words are pet peeves of mine.)

The saddest part is, very few will actually read this story with a critical eye and an inquiring mind. Instead, millions of seduced specimens of *Boobus Americanus* will today gather round water coolers, cafeteria tables and coffee shop counters; and obediently regurgitate the headlines:

Joe: *Hey Bill. You see what the Chinese hackers did?*

Bill: *Yeah. They're also hooked up with Putin now.*

Joe: *And probably North Korea too.*

Bill: *That's right! This reminds me of how Hitler teamed up with Japan and Italy.*

Joe: *Yeah. And Chamberlain appeased them at Munich.*

Bill: *Scary stuff. I'm worried they will take down our power grid one of these days.*

Though stinging and sarcastic humor is one of the favorite rhetorical weapons here at **The Anti-New York Times**; the above conversation, as most of you well know, is not a joke. It is exactly the type of "national conversation" that will occur in the wake of this latest bit of Sulzbergerian Slime.

"I read a rather disturbing article in The New York Times this morning. It appears as though China is....."

JUNE, 2015

NY Times: U. S. Was Warned of System Open to Cyberattacks

By DAVID E. SANGER, JULIE HIRSCHFELD DAVIS and NICOLE PERLROTH

The inspector general at the Office of Personnel Management issued a report in November that essentially described the agency's computer security system as a Chinese hacker's dream.

REBUTTAL BY

The Anti-New York Times

The Anti-New York Times generally does not cover the same subject two days in a row. But this particular piece of propaganda builds on yesterday's featured item in a way that really magnifies the deliberate libeling of China. The three authors - Hirschfeld, Sanger & Perlroth - sound like a Jew York City law firm. That's very appropriate given the comical level of 'legalese' language that is *again* sprinkled throughout this follow-up story. So, here we go, again!

A line-by-line review of the finely-minced legalistic words:

Paragraph 1: "**essentially** described"

Paragraph 3: "an official *(unnamed)* **painted a picture**" -

Paragraph 5: "could **potentially** have"

Paragraph 6: "Hackers in China **apparently**" - "a breach **appeared** (to be) aimed at"

Paragraph 7: "**apparently** obtained"

Paragraph 8: "attack **apparently** started" - "information was **apparently** downloaded" - "(attacks) are **likely** to grow"

Paragraph 9: "official who **would not speak on the record** said"

Paragraph 10: "the Chinese group was **probably**" - "exact affiliation with Chinese government **is not known**"

Paragraph 12: "government officials *(unnamed)* believe"

Paragraph 13: "officials *(unnamed)* said"

Paragraph 14: "administration officials *(again, unnamed)* said" - "a number of officials *(unnamed)* **painted a picture**" - "Chinese **appear to be**"

Paragraph 18: "Michael Daniel - White House's top cyber-official **declined to comment**" - "Lisa Monaco *(another Obama cyber-official)* **declined to be interviewed.**"

The Slimes slueths find more "official sources" every day!

This level of sloppy lying is truly a sight to behold. Even more shocking is the degree of gullibility manifested by the imbeciles who kneel in Sulzberger's cesspool every day. Can they not see through this legalistic mincing of words? Does it not strike Slimes readers as odd that none of these "officials" will actually go on the record with a definitive accusation?

It does "appear" that the New York Lie Firm of Sulzberger, Hirschfeld, Sanger & Perlroth is pre-conditioning *Boobus Americanus* for a ***real*** false-flag cyber-attack of war-starting proportions. Indeed, the term "cyber Pearl Harbor" now yields 453,000 results, and counting. Oy vey.

Boobus Americanus 1: *"I read **another** disturbing article in The New York Times this morning. Speaking off the record, officials painted a picture which essentially made it appear that there is a high degree of apparent probability that China may potentially be cyber-attacking sensitive U.S. systems, or so it seems."*

Boobus Americanus 2: *"That is very disconcerting news."*

JUNE, 2015

NY Times: George Soros Bankrolls Democrats' Fight in Voting Rights Cases

By MAGGIE HABERMAN

The billionaire has agreed to invest up to $5 million in litigation contesting limits to early voting and ID requirements that Democrats consider onerous.

REBUTTAL BY

The Anti-New York Times

Quick! Somebody call the Anti-Defamation League! Sulzberger's Slimes is spreading "anti-Semitic-**TM**" conspiracy theories linking **George Soros** and inner city "get-out-the-vote" drives!

1 - 2008: Ron Jones of Philadelphia tells CNN: "I voted a couple times."
2 - Obongo does very well with dead voters

Here:

"A Democratic legal fight against restrictive voting laws enacted in recent years by Republican-controlled state governments is being largely paid for by a single liberal benefactor: the billionaire philanthropist George Soros, ***the Hungarian-born*** *investor whose first major involvement in American politics was a voter-mobilization drive in the 2004 presidential race."*

Oh those naughty, naughty "Hungarians".

This decrepit creature is truly a demonic fiend straight out of Dante's Inferno. His trail of finance-subversion *("investment" as the Slimes calls it)* extends from Eastern Europe to Georgia to Ukraine to Malaysia to Burma to China to Latin America to Ferguson, MO to Mr. & Mr. Obongo and so much more. There hasn't been an American-based Globalist operator as powerful as George Soros (*Schwartz*) since the days of the American-born son of "Prussian immigrants", **Bernard Baruch**.

Oh those naughty, naughty "Prussians".

Baruch with Zionist faggot Churchill / with Communist lesbian Eleanor.

This article just confirms what "conspiracy theorists" have said all along about Soros and his support of "voting rights". Although the article describes Soros as "Hungarian", the fact that Sulzberger's Slimes would even allow the story to be printed, let alone front-paged, just goes to show how arrogant and confident the **Jafia** *(Jewish Mafia)* has become. One day there is a story about **Norman Braman** buying Republi**can't** Marco Rubio; the next it's about Republi**can't** Jeb Bush kneeling before **Sheldon Adelson**; the next it's about **Harvey Weinstein** or **Haim**

Saban throwing some Hollywood cash-bash for the Demonrat Party; and on and on it goes. And nobody seems to notice nor care that the Jafia is running the American Freak Show.

At this point, Sulzberger's scribblers could probably get away with running top-front page headlines: ***"Protocols of Zion True After-all. Secret Jafia Rules U.S. and Europe. Hitler was good. Holocaust was a Hoax".***

Seriously, would *Boobus Americanus* even object?

Let us hope that the continuation of such brazen arrogance may yet prove to be the Jafia's downfall. But don't get your hopes up too much. Nonetheless, keep fighting the good fight for truth, justice, and the distant future.

Boobus Americanus 1: *"I read a very interesting story in The New York Times this morning. Evidently, a small handful of Jewish Billionaires pick U.S. Presidents, finance voter fraud, foment world wars, engineer depressions & stock market crashes, incite civil unrest, control world events, corrupt our children, and seek to gradually wipe the White Race from the face of the Earth."*

Boobus Americanus 2: *"Wow. I never knew that. That's interesting."*

Boobus Americanus 1: *"Yep. Say, did you see the ballgame last night? Yankees won in 10 innings."*

Boobus Americanus 2: *"I missed it. I was watching 'Dancing With the Stars."*

JUNE, 2015

NY Times: Transgender Children's Books Fill a Void and Break a Taboo

By ALEXANDRA ALTER

Mainstream publishing houses are increasingly giving visibility to transgender authors and their books, which are aimed at broader and younger audiences.

REBUTTAL BY

The Anti-New York Times

In saner times, an article such as this would have spontaneously generated an angry lynch mob that would have stormed Sulzberger's Head-Quarters on 8th Ave in Manhattan and thrown some people out of skyscraper windows. As recently as just 10 years ago, such borderline child pornography would have horrified even many liberals and surely cost The Slimes more than a few cancelled subscriptions. That's assuming, of course, that the public didn't mistake the stories as satire, which they very well might have in the past.

But in this dark age of Mr. & Mr. Obongo, nothing is satire. There are no logically fallacious "reductio ad absurdum" *(reduce to the absurd)* arguments. Two plus two really *is* believed to be five. As a blogger named Matt Barber recently observed, Anderson's 'Emperor's New Clothes' has merged with George Orwell's '1984'. Nothing shocks nor angers *Boobus Americanus* anymore - **nothing!** *(except if the referee makes a bad call that causes their favorite sports team to lose.)*

Though we here at **The Anti-New York Times** do not condone heavy drinking, you might want to sit down and have a few glasses of some really hard stuff before we get into this freak show.

OK. Here goes:

"Sam Martin, 43, started transitioning to male from female after he bought the book (Transgender Photo Book). When I was growing up, I never saw people like me in movies or books.

Mr. Martin is now on a mission to change that. He belongs to a small group of emerging authors who are writing ***children's literature*** *that centers on transgender characters, hoping to fill the void they felt as young readers. His debut work of fiction — a semi-autobiographical story about a transgender teenage boy who falls in love with an older boy on the beach in Cape Cod — will be published in a collection this month by Duet, a new young adult publisher that specializes in lesbian, gay, bisexual, transgender and queer fiction."*

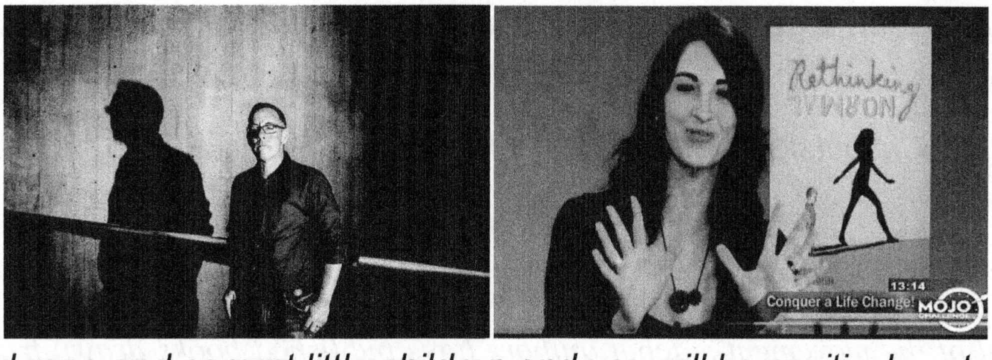

Mind-rape and corrupt little children and you will be positively noted by Sulzberger's Slimes. Degenerate psychopaths Sam Martin and Katie Rain Hill now have big-name Jewish publishing houses behind them.

Continued:

"My goal was to write stories that would have helped me feel less alone at that age," said Mr. Martin, who works as a Starbucks barista in Washington and writes at night.

A few years ago, gender fluidity was rarely addressed in children's and young adult fiction. It remained one of the last taboos in a publishing category that had already taken on difficult issues like suicide, drug abuse, rape and sex trafficking. But ***children's literature*** *is catching up to the broader culture, as stereotypes of transgender characters have given way to nuanced and sympathetic portrayals on TV shows like "Orange Is the New Black" and "Transparent."*

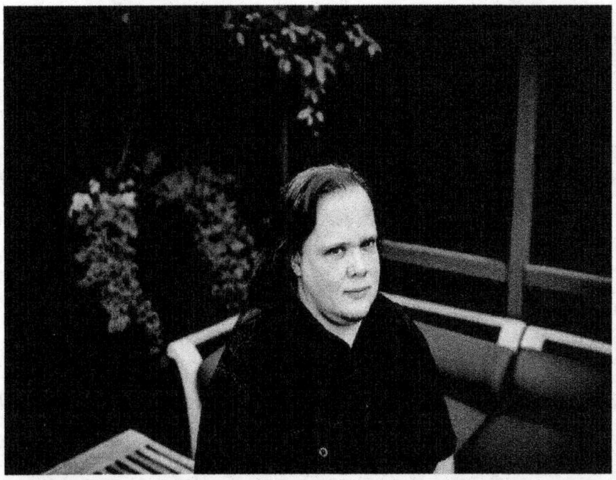

From the article: *"Alex Gino (above), the author of "George", identifies as gender-queer, a* ***gender identity that falls outside of the male/female binary.****"*

("outside of the male-female binary".....WTF ?!?!)

More filth and insanity:

"Several of the movement's debut authors have published books drawn from their own experiences. Last fall, a transgender teenager named Jazz Jennings published "I Am Jazz," a picture book she co-wrote about a transgender girl. ***Simon & Schuster*** *released dual memoirs by Katie Rain Hill and Arin Andrews, two transgender teenagers from Oklahoma who met and fell in love....*

In August, ***Scholastic will publish "George,"*** *a middle-grade debut novel about a boy who knows he is a girl but doesn't know how to tell his family and friends.*

George decides to try out for the part of Charlotte in a school production of "Charlotte's Web" in hopes that it will help others see him the way he sees himself.

Scholastic (Books) is facing resistance from some teachers and librarians who question whether ***third and fourth graders*** *are ready for the discussion."*

*

Other than to say that these demon-possessed mental molesters ought to all be strapped into electric chairs and zapped to death on live TV; what else is there to add to such mental and moral insanity? Is this article even necessary to rebut?

Between the obvious death march towards World War III abroad and the economic, moral and cultural **murder** taking place domestically, your heart-broken reporter here sometimes wishes he could just walk away from the emotionally taxing daily immersion in Sulzberger's Satanic filth. Unfortunately, or fortunately depending how one wishes to look at it, I can't. That would be like an exasperated battlefield medic throwing his hands up in despair and declaring, *"I can't take it anymore!"*

These demonic monsters are now *openly* devouring **millions** of vulnerable, innocent children. As weak as our bulbs may be, we are called to shine the light of truth upon these heinous hounds of Hell until Putin's ICBM's arrive. God damn you Sulzberger! And Soros, and Bloomberg, and Rockefeller etc. Damn you all!

Those who would mentally and morally molest God's little angels deserve to be strapped to an electric seat of dishonor.

JUNE, 2015

NY Times: Over Beer, Obama and Merkel Mend Ties and Double-Down on Russia

By **JULIE HIRSCHFELD DAVIS**

President Obama sought to smooth over tensions with a crucial ally, bonding on Sunday with Chancellor Angela Merkel of Germany over beer, sausages and their shared determination to confront Russia.

REBUTTAL BY

The Anti-New York Times

The G-7 pygmies of **The New World Order** are now in full agreement on "confronting Russia". Wonderful.

Technically speaking, the true consensus here isn't really about "confronting Russia", a dangerous idea that none of these puppets seem to passionate about. The *real* consensus - especially in the wake of the recent "hit" on FIFA boss Sepp Blatter; and the assassination or attempted assassination of John Kerry, is this: *"Friends, like it or not, we all must do what Mr. Rothschild and Mr. Soros say."*

The U.S. civilian population is *possibly* immune to the physical effects of a shooting war - ***if*** it stays regional. The pathetic leaders of Europe, however, are knowingly placing their respective peoples in imminent danger. What manner of explosive dirt must the true "powers that be" and their NSA - CIA - MI6 - Mossad have on these miserable little Marxist miscreants to force them to go along with this madness? The cast of shady characters who misrule the dying nations of 'G-7' resemble "the Seven Dwawfs", only with zero morals.

"Look, I'm not crazy about fighting Russia and China either; but if my wife ever finds out about the little boys that I'm buggering, she'd kill me!"

- Cameron: UK
- Renzi: Italy
- Hollande: France
- Obongo: USA
- Merkel: Germany
- Abe: Japan
- Harper: Canada

What a spineless supine bunch! All of them ambitious liars and traitors; each one a bigger scumbag than the other. Hitler sure had "Democracy" figured out when he wrote:

"The devastation caused by this institution of modern parliamentary rule is hard for the reader of Jewish newspapers to imagine, unless he has learned to think and examine independently. ***It is, first and foremost, the cause of the incredible inundation of all political life with the most inferior, and I mean the most inferior, characters of our time.***

The more dwarfish one of these present-day leather merchants is in spirit and ability, the more clearly his own insight makes him aware of the lamentable figure he actually cuts - that much more will he sing the praises of a system which does not demand of him the power and genius of a giant, but is satisfied with the craftiness of a village mayor, preferring in fact this kind of wisdom to that of a Pericles.

And this kind doesn't have to torment himself with responsibility for his actions. He is entirely removed from such worry, for he well knows that, regardless what the result of his 'statesmanlike' bungling may be, his end has long been written in the stars: one day he will have to cede his place to another equally great mind, for it is one of the characteristics of this decadent system that the number of 'great statesmen' increases in proportion as the stature of the individual decreases.

With increasing dependence on parliamentary majorities it will inevitably continue to shrink, since on the one hand ***great minds will refuse to be the stooges of idiotic incompetents and bigmouths, and on the other, conversely, the representatives of the majority, hence of stupidity, hate nothing more passionately than a superior mind."***

The Great One had the "Democracy" scam all figured out and honestly explained it to the German people.

Picking the most "lamentable figure" of the G-7 would make for quite a pageant. For my money, the award would have to go to the Frumpy Frau from Germany. Her nation was wiped out not once but twice by the ghastly ghouls of Globo-Zio NWO-US-UK. To see her throw Germany's fate into the hands of its historical tormentors is even more shocking than what Obongo is doing to America.

Angie on America:

"Although it is true we sometimes have differences of opinion today from time to time, the United States of America is our friend, our partner and, indeed, an essential partner."

Some folks in Hamburg, Dresden and other places would beg to differ, bitch:

Angela's American "friends" and "essential partners" have done sooooo much for Germany.

JUNE, 2015

NY Times: Evangelicals Open Door to Debate on Gay Rights

By LAURIE GOODSTEIN

Encouraged by younger Christians and cultural shifts, some church leaders are having what they describe as unprecedented discussions about homosexuality.

REBUTTAL BY

The Anti-New York Times

Some of the mainline Protestant Churches sold out to the Sons of Sodom years ago. Ditto for the Anglicans of Britain. Most recently, under the tyrannical rule of the Poofter Pope, even the Roman Catholic Church is already halfway down that same road to hell-on-earth. Now comes word that Evangelical leaders are *"opening the door to debate"* on homosexuality.

Ah yes, there goes that magic buzz-word of the Left - "debate". But time and time again, history teaches us that "debating" with Marxist-Libtard demons soon degenerates into no debate, *at all*! Just ask those bakery owners and photographers who are being sued and fined out-of-business for refusing to provide services for those lunatic abominations commonly referred to as "gay weddings". *(barf)*

Sorry to have to put this so graphically, but "opening the door" to a "debate" with anus-licking homosexuals who demand the "right" to alter millenniums-old moral / religious doctrine, re-write laws regarding marriage, and adopt newborn babies *(gasp!)*, is like inviting Satan into your living room just to hear his point-of-view.

"Well, Mr. Satan. I can't say that I agree with you, but in the spirit of tolerance, I respect your position and am willing to "open a debate".

1- "Aw come on Jesus! Chill out man. Stop being so intolerant. I just want to have a debate, that's all."
2- Gresham, Oregon: There is no "debate" here. "Sweet Cakes by Melissa" may *be forced to pay as much as $135,000 to a pair of angry lesbians who want their cake, and lots of cash too!*

These weak-willed and weak-minded church leaders are supposed to be leading the young people of their flock *away* from the popular madness of the modern world. Moral resistance to the temptations and decadence of a fallen world is the very foundation of every moral, philosophical and religious code ever known. Religion is about doing "what's right" - not "what's popular". It's about *defeating evil*, not debating it. Otherwise, the institution serves no purpose.

Whatever happened to the idea of *"Many are called but few are chosen?"* (Matthew 22) Though there are many preachers who are holding strong, more and more we learn about the weaker ones, the pretenders, the attention-seekers, the money-grubbers who are being "encouraged by younger Christians and cultural shifts". In the eyes of **The Anti-New York Times**, these irreverent reverends are just as vile as Sulzberger's scribblers, if not worse. Preachers! If you ain't got the balls to stand strong in the face of Satan's heavy artillery, then don't put on the damn robes!

And even if some of the preachers featured in today's article "debated" merely as a courtesy while holding firmly to their ground *(as appears to be the case)* , the legitimacy now bestowed upon the homosexual activists - and duly front-paged by Sulzberger's Slimes - has already done enormous damage to the flock. Mission accomplished! In the simplistic ignorance of the public mind, the "debate" itself was already won *(by the sodomites)* the moment these pusillanimous preachers "opened the door" and deigned to even speak with them about things such as "same sex marriage". Fools!

"Honey, I just want to open the door to a debate!

Who else should these mealy-mouthed ministers "open the door" for and engage in "debate"? Adultery activists? Tranny activists? Gambling activists? Drunkard activists, Druggie activists, Animal fornication activists? Child Molesting activists? Can you imagine? - *"Reverend Jones. As a proud heroine user and serial adulterer who seeks God, I'd like to "open the door to a debate" with you about softening up your Church's culturally outdated positions against drugs and adultery. When can we discuss this? Is it OK if we invite the New York Times?"*

Ironically, one "debate" that these Evangelical ministers won't be "opening the door to" anytime soon is the one about their fanatical support for the terrorist state of Israel - but we digress.

DEBATING WITH MARXISTS: A FLOWCHART

An innocent-sounding request to "open a debate" - A debate and compromise - Getting their cake and eating it too - Expanding their demands - No more debates - Hate Speech laws

*

Oh ye weak and unholy "men of the cloth"! **Do you not know the difference between an open mind and a malleable mind?** Take heed of the admonition from the 1973 classic film 'The Exorcist'. Recall the scene in which Father Merrin, the senior priest, sternly cautions the younger, inexperienced Father Karras to avoid engaging in any debate or conversation with the devil that is possessing the little girl. Here is the line:

"Especially important is the warning to avoid conversations with the demon. We may ask what is relevant but anything beyond that is dangerous. He is a liar. The demon is a liar. He will lie to confuse us. But he will also mix lies with the truth to attack us. The attack is psychological, Damien, and powerful. So don't listen to him. Remember that - do not listen."

Be he physical or metaphorical, this is how the Devil operates. First, he gently pleads for a small "door-opening" - a "debate". Then, by mixing truth with lies, he sows the seeds of confusion where there shouldn't be any confusion at all. Unfortunately for Father Karras, he allowed the words of the cunning demon to get into his head and rattle him, with tragic consequences for both priests. And that is exactly what is happening with these foolish Evangelical leaders who are allowing the first few cancer cells of "debate" to enter their churches.

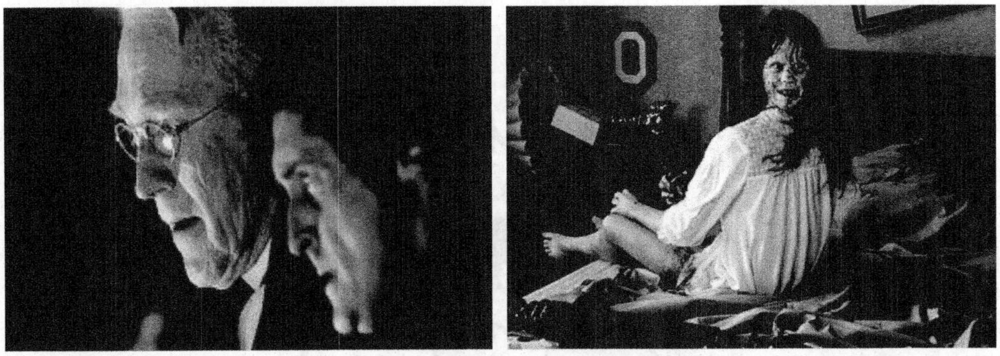

NO MORE "DEBATES"!

The Exorcist teaches us not to debate with liars and demons.

JUNE, 2015

NY Times: McKinney, Texas Police Officer Resigns Over Incident Caught on Video

By ASHLEY SOUTHALL

A police officer in McKinney, Tex., who was seen on video pulling his gun on teenagers in swimsuits and shoving a young black girl's face in the ground at a pool party has resigned, the police said Tuesday.

REBUTTAL BY

The Anti-New York Times

With cops nationwide being closely monitored by Attorney General Loretta Lynch Mob *(aka Al-Sharpton-in-drag)* it seems like a few weeks have passed without some 'dindoo nuffin' being killed by some evil "racist" White cop. But that won't stop Sulzberger's seditious scribblers from cherry-picking a total non-event and front-paging it *(albeit near the bottom)*.

One would think, given the sheer amount of coverage this insignificant incident has garnered from the Juden Press, that the female 'dindoo nuffin' in question must have been severely beaten, pepper-sprayed, or even killed! But no one died; no one was injured; and no one was even slapped. A close review of the "shocking video" reveals a White cop holding a loud-mouthed 'dindoo nuffin" down on the grass as a Black mob stirs about. Big frickin' deal! Your formerly mischievous reporter here at **The Anti-New York Times** received harsher treatment than that from his 1st Grade Catholic nun-teacher!

At one point, the cop, ***who has since been fired****, tries to calm the hysterical 'dindoo nuffin' down.*

The real "crime" here is that Mr. & Mr. Obongo have expanded the 'Section 8' free-rental program so that more and more of these 'dindoo nuffins' can be imported into the quiet, predominately White suburbs of America. Soon after arrival from the ghetto, the *nouveau riche* start throwing loud house and pool parties, announced beforehand via Twitter and Facebook *(this was the case with our screaming bikini-clad princess in the grass)*. When the boys-in-blue arrive to restore peace and quiet to the concerned community, it's always the same old song: *"I dindoo nuffin! The neighbors be racist!"*

The residents of this Texas neighborhood have indeed claimed that this was a Section 8 case that started the trouble. The **Anti-New York Times** has not been able to confirm this, but it is known that many other such incidents, as well as 'civil rights' lawsuits against various towns, are beginning to mount nationwide. Thanks to Mr. & Mr. Obongo - and their Jewish-Marxist masters to be more precise - rowdy 'dindoo nuffins' may soon be coming to a Cul de Sac near you.

The trouble began when an older White woman tried to break-up a cat fight between two female 'dindoo nuffins'. The White woman was then threatened (allegedly).

Free apartments in the projects wasn't good enough for the 'dindoo nuffins'. Free house-rent in lower income neighborhoods wasn't good enough. Now, the baby-factories and their fatherless litters get to live in 4-bedroom homes with 2-car garages and community swimming pools; while suburban working families struggle to afford their mortgage, groceries and the very taxes which pay for the Section 8, Medicaid and Food Stamps of their new neighbors!

*"Buy your own f%*5^#g litter box!"*

(Understandably, Sugar is very upset about the War on Whites)

The always-prophetic **Anti-New York Times** wrote about this unfolding disaster *(which is still in its early stages!)* about a month ago. Here's the flashback / excerpt:

****

Of course, at the highest levels of America's PRC *(Predatory Ruling Class)*, the "anti-poverty" spin for this totalitarian scheme has a much darker motive. The Globo-Zio elite couldn't give a rat's arse about the sanctified "poor". **The goal here is the obliteration of White America** *(and Mother Europe)*. And this "study" fits in perfectly with what we already know about Obongo's plans to flood the suburbs with free-loaders. From U.S. News & World Report, 2013 - Read it and weep:

HUD Proposes Plan to Racially, Economically Integrate Neighborhoods

The Department of Housing and Urban Development has proposed a rule to desegregate U.S. neighborhoods.

"The Department of Housing and Urban Development has proposed a new plan to change U.S. neighborhoods it says are racially imbalanced or are too tilted toward rich or poor, arguing the country's housing policies have not been effective at creating the kind of integrated communities the agency had hoped for.

The proposed federal rule, called "Affirmatively Furthering Fair Housing," is currently under a 60-day public comment period. Though details of how the policy would specifically work are unclear, the rule says HUD would provide states, local governments and others who receive agency money with data and a geo-spatial tool to look at "patterns of integration and segregation; racially and ethnically concentrated areas of poverty; access to education, employment, low-poverty, transportation, and environmental health."

Oh *Boobus Caucasianus Americanus (and Europithecus, Canadius and Australopithecus)*! Has the mind-numbing and soul-crushing din of the Devil's Loud-speaker (TV) so dulled your mind and desensitized your heart to the point that you cannot hear the death-bells tolling, nor see the grim reaper of genocide approaching? Evidently so.

1- "Yo! Snow White. Ya'll want some of diz, neighbor?"

2 - Meanwhile, Snow White's father has more important things on his mind

****

Nailed it! ..... Unfortunately.

JUNE, 2015

NY Times: Pope Urges Putin to make a 'Great Effort' to Resolve the Crisis in Ukraine

By JIM YARDLEY

Mr. Putin met privately with Pope Francis at the Vatican, his second audience with the pope in the past 18 months.

REBUTTAL BY

The Anti-New York Times

At this point, it would not surprise **The Anti-New York Times**, *at all*, if the Pinko Pope of Poofterism were indeed to join the anti-Putin parade of deceit and hatred. He is, after all, the man they call, "The New World Pope". Nonetheless, Sulzberger's Slimes has a long history of mistranslating words and/or taking them out-of-context in order to create a misleading headline. With both the precedent of this horrible bigmouth Pope *and* the precedent of this horrible newspaper in mind; your impartial analyst here dug deeper into the Slimes article, as well as other sources, to see if Frankie the Fake really did "urge" or dress down Vlad the Bad, as the headline is meant to imply.

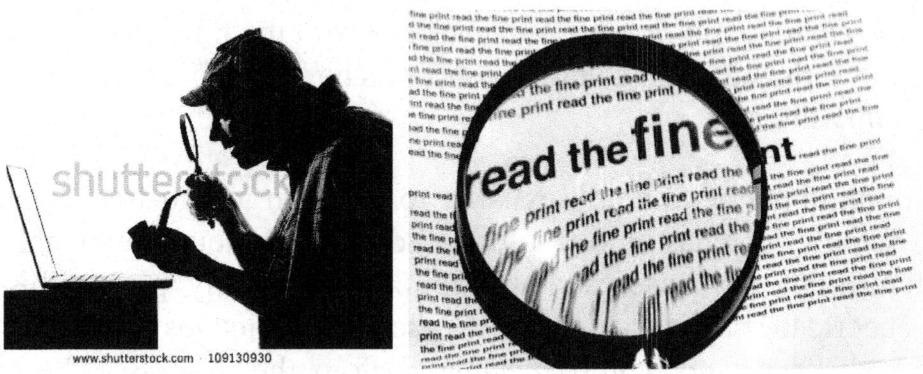

When it comes to sleazy Sulzberger's Slimes, always read the fine print!

In our search for actual quotes; the best we can come up with, from the Slimes, as well as some other media sources we checked into, is the following:

"Vatican officials said Francis told Mr. Putin that ***"a sincere and great effort"*** *was needed to achieve peace and called for all parties to comply with the Minsk accords."*

That's it? Just five little words? Nothing other than, "*a sincere and great effort*". Even taken out-of-context, as this mere 5-word quote clearly was, there is still nothing extraordinary about such a generalistic remark. Hence, the headline's subtle misuse of the strong word "urge" constitutes a bit of unnecessary drama.

1- Like Germany's Merkel, Italy's bigmouth Prime Minister Renzi is stuck between the Italian business class who want the anti-Russian sanctions lifted, and his US-EU masters who want them expanded.
2- Frankie's remarks to Putin on Ukraine are only vague generalizations blown out of proportion by the press.

A Google search of the term, "Pope **urges** Putin" already yields 1,700,000 results, proving yet again that The Slimes truly is, as the writer Gore Vidal so aptly put it, *"the typhoid Mary of American (and world) journalism"*. This barely noticeable manipulation of words and quotes leaves millions of superficial specimens of

Boobus Americanus and *Boobus Europithicus* with the false impression that the Unholy Father ripped Putin a new arse-hole as he "urged" him to make peace. He most certainly did not!

From economic policy to homosexuality to abortion to anti-traditionalism to open borders; Satan's Pope has indeed said, and done, many outrageous things that have shocked millions of conservative Catholics; yet greatly pleased his Globo-Zio-Marxist cheerleaders. His soon-to-be released papal dictates on "Global Warming"-**TM,** as well as his upcoming speeches before the godless U.N. and the U.S. ~~Knesset,~~ I mean Congress, promise to be real hard drink-inducing doozies. *However*, in this particular case, there is not a shred of evidence that Frankie the Fake has blamed Putin or "urged" him to do anything. Though he really ought to be loudly condemning warmongers Homo Obongo and Porky Poroshenko from the balcony of his Vatican apartment, Frankie's evident neutrality on the matter simply *does not* support the implied, almost subliminal message of the Slimes headline. Typical.

Boobus Americanus 1: *I read in The New York Times today that the Pope just told Putin off.*
Boobus Americanus 2: *This Pope is awesome. I may start going back to church.*

JUNE, 2015

NY Times: Russian Groups Crowdfund the War in Ukraine

By JO BECKER and STEVEN LEE MYERS

Several groups are running online campaigns to brazenly raise money for rebels in eastern Ukraine, helping succor a conflict that has killed thousands.

REBUTTAL BY

The Anti-New York Times

The breathless tone of this self-proclaimed, self-important piece of "investigative journalism" is designed to excite the gullible readers who kneel in Sulzberger's seditious cesspool each day. Note the drama:

"An examination by The New York Times of the groups' websites, social media postings and other records found more than a dozen groups in Russia that are raising money for the separatists..."

Ooooh. Imagine that. The Slimes' sleuths have discovered that private citizens in Russia are sending donations to their besieged brothers in Donbass *(eastern Ukraine)*. Wow! Who would have ever imagined such a thing? Give those Slimes reporters a Pulitzer Prize!

"....aiding a conflict that has killed more than 6,400 people and plunged Russia's relations with the West to depths not seen since the Cold War."

Liars! It wasn't *"the conflict"* that *"plunged Russia's relations with the West to depths not seen since the Cold War"*. It was the **New World Order's violent overthrow of the elected government** in Kiev that so angered the Russian Crimeans and Russian-speaking east Ukrainians. More than ninety percent of the people in Donbass voted for President Yanukovich; the guy who was forced to flee Kiev for his life. Just days after Yanukovich fled, Washington's new vassal-gansters in charge decreed an end to the policy of recognizing Russian one of the official languages of eastern Ukraine. **Those are among the justifable reasons why Donbass rebelled.** Putin's Russia had nothing to do with it!

1- December, 2013: US Senator John 'Insane' McCain incites the Kiev mob to overthrow the duly-elected government.
2- Under-Secretary of State Vicky Nuland poses with her hand-picked puppets - the so-called "opposition".

Continued:

"The groups have relied on social media — including YouTube and the Russian version of Facebook — to direct donations through state-owned banks in Russia and through a private system of payment terminals owned by a company called QIWI that is affiliated with Visa and traded on the Nasdaq."

We see the real game here. The Slimes is trying to "shame" You Tube and Visa into cutting off Russian videos and donations to Donbass.

*"These organizations are part of an online campaign that is **brazenly** raising money for the war in eastern Ukraine."*

"Brazenly"? Why such a loaded word? From Websters Dictionary:

Brazen: acting or done in a very open and shocking way without shame or embarrassment.

What would donors to east Ukrainian groups have to be "ashamed" of to begin with? What is so "shocking" or "embarrassing" about helping your oppressed

Russian brothers? Speaking of "brazen", let us not forget that the U.S. government "brazenly" poured 5 Billion of our tax dollars into Ukraine for the purpose of "promoting democracy" *(buying puppets)*. Vicki Nuland *(Nudelman)* Kagan "brazenly" admitted as such. By the way, this wretched wench is the wife of Robert Kagan; a high ranking Zionist neo-con who, in 1999, joined other neo-cons in "brazenly" stating that a "new Pearl Harbor" was needed to kick-start the U.S. war machine.

More recently, the broke U.S. has been "brazenly" giving taxpayer money to its terrorist thug-puppet Porky Poroshenko in Kiev, while "brazenly" positioning troops and missile bases in eastern Europe.

At a Chevron event, neo-con Nuland-Kagan "brazenly" admitted:

"Since Ukraine's independence in 1991, the United States has supported Ukrainians as they build democratic skills and institutions, as they promote civic participation and good governance, all of which are preconditions for Ukraine to achieve its European aspirations. ***We've invested over $5 billion*** *to assist Ukraine in these and other goals that will ensure a secure and prosperous and democratic Ukraine."*

More:

"The network features a disparate yet overlapping cast of characters that includes a mustachioed former Russian military intelligence officer credited with starting the uprising, ***Igor*** *Girkin, who uses the nom de guerre* ***Igor*** *Strelkov".*

Double wow! One of the "cast of characters" from this aid "network" has a mustache, and a code name of "Igor" - just like the notorious sidekicks who assisted Dr. Frankenstein and Count Dracula!

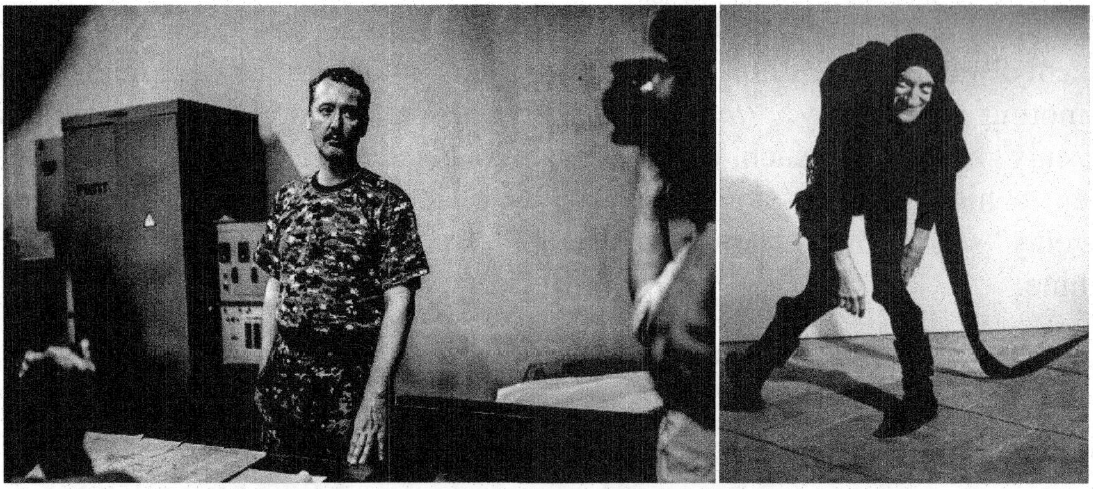

A "mustachioed" ex-spook code-named "Igor" is said to be running this operation. Be afraid, America. Be very afraid!

More:

"On April 20, a group called Batman noted on its social media page that all but its Sberbank account had been blocked. But by May 18, it had updated the page to include a new QIWI account number and a plea: "Donbass needs your help!"

Now Batman is hooked up with the Rooskies too?!

Holy Russian Rubles Batman!

Your historical researcher here at **The Anti-New York Times** has spent many hours analyzing the pre-World War II propaganda found in old issues of Sulzberger's Slimes. It is most interesting to observe that the distortions of 1936-1939 were nowhere near as ridiculous as what Sulzberger's spoiled-rotten grandkids are pumping out today. Indeed, some of those old articles are remarkably objective and even useful, all things considered.

Back then, the pre-war spin was subtle, almost undetectable at times. Evidently, today's swallowers of Sulzbergerian slime are so dumbed-down that subtlety is no longer needed. There is nothing subtle, *at all*, about so many of today's anti-Russia and anti-China hit-pieces. To the contrary, propaganda poop-pies such as this article are, well, a bit "brazen", and actually a bit funny too.

Boobus Americanus 1: *I read in The New York Times today that people in Russia are brazenly funneling terror money through a spooky separatist with a mustache. And, get this, his name is Igor!*

Boobus Americanus 2: *Igor? Wow. That's very intriguing. It almost sounds like a Hollywood movie script.*

"It *isss* a movie script, dumbasss!"

(Sugar, be nice.)

JUNE, 2015

NY Times: In Europe, Leaders Take Note: Jeb Bush Isn't His Brother

By MICHAEL BARBARO

After emerging from a 45-minute meeting here with Jeb Bush, the foreign minister of Germany, Frank-Walter Steinmeier, told colleagues that what struck him most about the American was not the strength of his opinions but something simpler: the depth of his curiosity

REBUTTAL BY

The Anti-New York Times

By this time next year, we expect that Jeb Bush, with the help of Sulzberger's Slimes, will *probably* be the Republi**can't** nominee for the QFS *(Quadrennial Freak Show)*. To that end, today's article does its best to separate Jeb from his much reviled brother, George W Bush. Evidence of this "difference" is provided in the form of impressions from European politicians.

Those who recall George W Bush's 2000 campaign will note that he too had to differentiate himself from his liberal President father, ex-CIA boss George H. Bush, by falsely branding himself as a "compassionate conservative" *(as opposed to us non-compassionate conservatives who, presumably, want to starve children, beat women, lynch Blacks for fun and throw old people off of cliffs).*

The success of Bush 43 in 2000 was due, in large part, to his devious differentiation from his unpopular father, Bush 41. If goofy Jeb hopes to become Bush 45, he will have to pull off a similar trick.

With that Year 2000 precedent of false differentiation in mind, your rebutting reporter here at **The Anti-New York Times** dove into this propaganda puff-piece expecting to find lies to the effect that Jeb is ideologically different from George, perhaps more of a fiscal conservative and less of a warmonger. But there are no such claims of the kind. Instead, we learn that the great sibling "difference" that these oh-so-sophisticated Europeans perceive is that Jeb is much more intelligent than George. That's just wonderful, isn't it? This means that Jeb will be an even more cunning and effective Globalist warmonger than his smirk-faced brother!

From the article:

"When Mr. Bush's brother George first ran for president, he erroneously referred to Greeks as 'Grecians,' flubbed the name of India's leader and confused Slovenia with Slovakia, offering the world an unabashed portrait of provinciality.

But across Europe this week, Jeb Bush revealed himself to be a very different kind of Bush: well traveled, almost encyclopedically knowledgeable about foreign countries, and possessing the genuine inquisitiveness that his brother had so notably lacked."

OK. Fine. We already knew George W Drunk wasn't the sharpest knife in the draw. But what about policy positions?

The Bush political dynasty began with Senator Prescott Bush (shown above with President Eisenhower). Grandpa Bush was a golfing buddy of the war criminal Globalist Eisenhower. Under Eisenhower's hidden hand, Grandpa Bush played a leading role in killing Senator Joe McCarthy's investigations into Communist infiltration and the Globalists who allowed it - a fact that the Bushes remain very proud of.

Another excerpt:

"Unlike the gaffe-prone former president, who referred to Africa as a nation during his first trip overseas after moving into the White House, the younger Mr. Bush criss-crossed Europe without a public blunder. His hosts politely noted the contrast."

Again, no mention of any difference between the brothers other than in intelligence and "curiosity". Truth be told, Jeb isn't all that smart either. He's just not as stupid as his idiot brother. But The Slimes and the European mouthpieces would have us believe that just because Jeb spent a whole hour in a Warsaw Museum dedicated to the Jewish-Communist "Warsaw Ghetto Uprising" of 1944; he is some sort of "intellectual".

Barf on this:

"Mr. Oldakowski said he was struck by Mr. Bush's decision to linger inside the museum for an hour, asking about the tactics of the Warsaw Uprising, the long-term impacts of German and Soviet occupation and modern Poland's standing in Europe. 'It was clear that he wanted to learn about that', Mr. Oldakowski said."

Like bother - like brother.

Ironically, the article does confirm, albeit unintentionally, that Jeb is every bit as much of a warmongering psychopath as his hated brother. On Russia:

"Mr. Bush told Mr. Oldakowski that the United States could not tolerate further Russian incursions into former Soviet-bloc nations "because it was this city, Warsaw, that was at stake."

And further down, we read:

"He (Bush) probed leaders in Germany and Poland about what type of military hardware, if any, they might supply to Ukraine as it tries to beat back Russian territorial ambitions."

The Bush campaign slogan for 2016: "Jeb 2016: A Better-Educated and Sober Warmonger".

No thanks!

Boobus Americanus 1: *I read in The New York Times today that Jeb is not at all like his brother. He's actually quite educated and intellectually curious.*

Boobus Americanus 2: *Indeed. My understanding is that the Europeans are rather impressed with his level of gravitas. Totally unlike George.*

"You frickin' idiots! The Bushes are all Globalist scum!"

(Sugar, be nice.)

JUNE, 2015

NY Times: U.S. Is Poised to Put Heavy Weaponry in Eastern Europe

By ERIC SCHMITT and STEVEN LEE MYERS

The proposal, if approved, would represent the first time since the end of the Cold War that the United States has stationed heavy military equipment in Eastern Europe.

AND…

NY Times: Pope Francis to Explore Climate's Effect on World's Poor

By JIM YARDLEY

When Francis releases his first major teaching letter on the theme of the environment and poverty, he may redefine a secular topic as a matter of morality.

REBUTTAL BY

The Anti-New York Times

At first glance, the above listed stories seem unrelated. Only when one is in possession of the "Rosetta Stone" of New World Order knowledge can he see that the respective stories about Poop Frankie's phony war on "Global Warming"-**TM** and Homo-Obongo's ever-escalating provocation of Russia are actually two fronts of the same evil effort to impose "global governance". With our NWO "decoder rings", we can pretty much link *any* major geo-political event to the usual suspects, and the usual motives.

Though the de-balled Judaized Popes of the Roman Catholic Church have been slowly going "downhill" for several decades; now, for the first time ever, the Globalists have seated an actual full-blown subversive agent on St. Peter's throne.

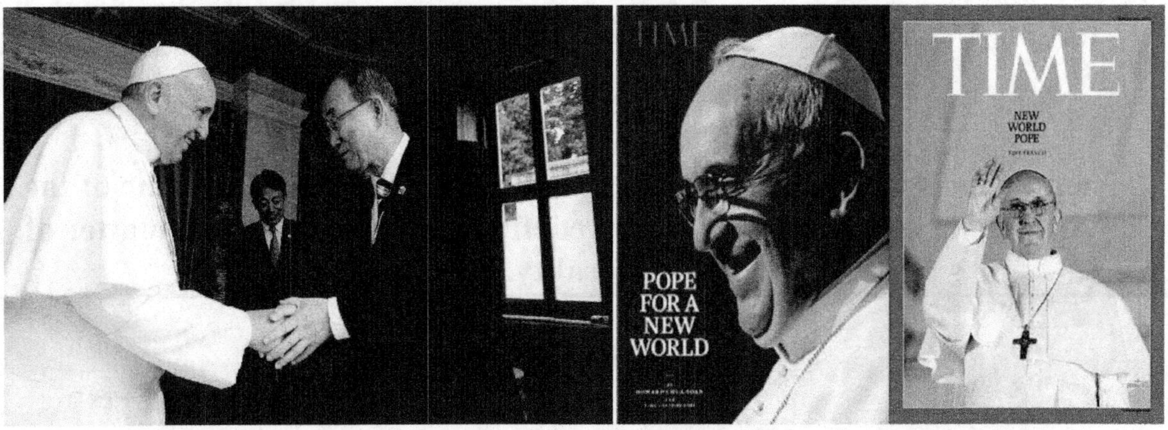

The 'New World Pope' is a big fan of the godless Communist United Nations. Above, Poop Francis makes eyes with Ban Ki-moon, the U.N. Secretary General.

What makes Frankie the Fake's environmental activism all the more disgusting is that it comes at the precise moment in time in which the world is headed towards confrontation - as the other referenced story about the U.S. military build-up in the Baltic States reveals. More than 5,000 people have already been killed in East Ukraine, the vicious thugs in Kiev grow bolder by the day, a Western / Israeli - engineered humanitarian disaster continues to unfold in Syria and Iraq, the U.S. - NATO war machine continues its eastward march towards Russia's doorstep, China is being threatened with force, and, as even the diabolical George Soros has hinted, World War III is now a very real possibility. Yet the only "crises" that this pro-homosexual "Catholic" clown from Argentina wants to lecture us about are "income inequality" and ***harmless*** carbon emissions *(plant food)*!

Compare and contrast Poop Frankie's shocking indifference towards World War III to the serious attempts made by Pope Pius to avert World War II in 1939 and a subsequent mediation effort in 1940; and we see how far this once important institution of world stabilty has fallen. By the way, it was the British, not Hitler, that killed both of those Papal peace plans.

Even as recently as 2003, a frail and aging Pope John Paul II tried his very best to prevent the Gulf War. It was George W Bush, not Saddam Hussein, who ignored the Pope, **even putting a personal letter from John Paul on a side table without opening it!**

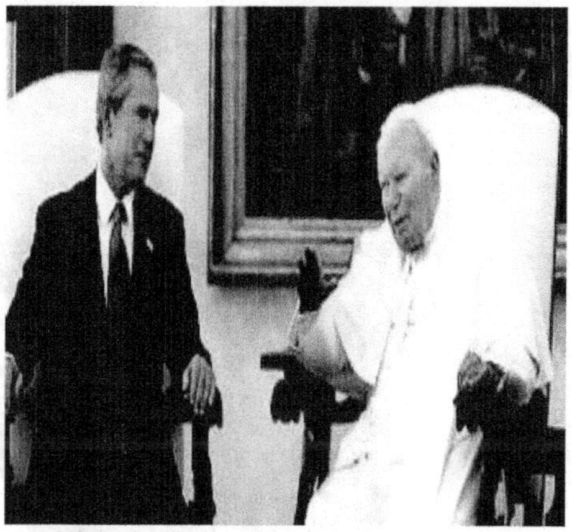

1 & 2- For his efforts to keep the peace of Europe, Pius has been dubbed "Hitler's Pope" (a wonderful compliment in our book!).
3- John Paul II openly opposed Bush's war in Iraq and told Bush to his face.

Russian President Vladimir Putin has visited with Frankie *twice* over the past 18 months. Most certainly, the peace-making Putin discussed the severity of the situation in Ukraine with him. Yet, unlike previous Popes, Frankie the Faker fiddles while the world burns. The best the Pinko Pope of Poofterdom can muster is a few vague words about "making sincere efforts for peace" while refusing to point the righteous finger of blame at anyone.

1- Putin to Frankie: "When you get a chance, Father, do you think you can say a few words about the genocide taking place in Ukraine and Syria? If it's not too much to ask. Maybe?

2- Poop Frankie to Homo-Obongo: "Is that a gun in your pocket or are you just happy to see me?"

*

I know, Jesus. I know.

Boobus Americanus 1: *I read in The New York Times today that the U.S. is going to place heavy weaponry in Eastern Europe.*

Boobus Americanus 2: *That's a smart move. We can't afford to appease Putin like Neville Chamberlain did Hitler.*

"If I hear that ssstupid-asss Neville Chamberlain cliche again I'm gonna ssscratch sssomebody's frickin' eye-ballsss out!"

(Sugar! Stop threatening the Boobuses!)

JUNE, 2015

NY Times: (A Letter to Editor)

Re: The June 7 Article: Pluses and Minuses of a Carbon Tax

By MARY SELKIRK / Berkeley, CA

REBUTTAL BY

The Anti-New York Times

Your ever-innovative reporter here at **The Anti-New York Times** is trying something new today. Rather than rebut the nonsense spewed forth by a Slimes reporter, let us have a bit of fun with a typical libtard Slimes reader who has so graciously shared her ignorance with the general public in the form of a "Letter to the Editor".

Mary Selkirk's letter in standard text, *your rebutting reporter in italics*:

Re: “The Case for a Carbon Tax” (letter):

Mary: A national fee on carbon assessed at the point of extraction is the most powerful, non-regulatory way to demonstrate that fossil fuel energy is no longer a good investment, not for oil companies or for human beings.

First of all, Mary, stop playing sneaky word games. It's not a "national fee". It's a national ***tax****. Say it, wench!*

Oh, and Mary, if "fossil fuel" is "no longer a good investment for oil companies", then why are they still drilling? If it were a bad investment, they wouldn't be doing it.

Mary: Returning all of the revenues to American households will create jobs ..

What "revenues"? You just said oil extraction was a bad investment. And how exactly would such a tyrannical confiscation of "all revenues" serve to "create jobs"? Wouldn't we be destroying jobs by "returning all revenues to American households"? You do understand that businesses with no revenues must shut down and discharge their employees? Make sense, Mary?

Mary: .. reduce deaths from emissions

"Deaths"??? What deaths? Mary, these "emissions" which you speak of consist of a natural element known as carbon dioxide (CO2) - also known as ***plant food****. Can you name for me one person who has ever died of CO2 emissions? Sweetie, it appears you have mistaken carbon dioxide for carbon monoxide (CO), which is indeed toxic. Better brush up on your chemistry.*

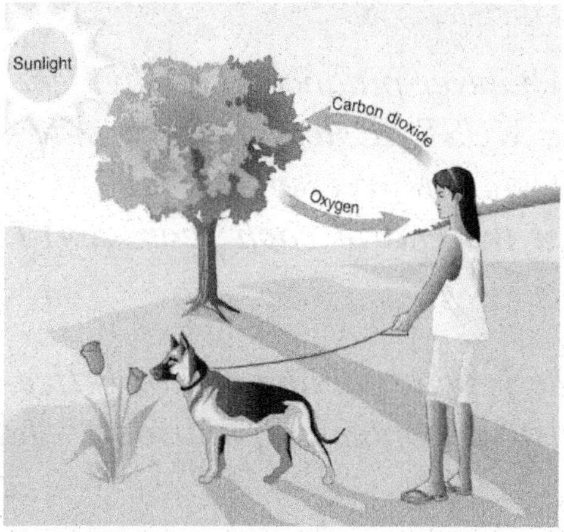

Back to High School Special Needs Class, Mary.

CO = Death / CO2 = Life

Evidently, Mary Marxist believes CO2 is "2" times deadlier than CO1.

Mary: ... and put money back into the pockets of two-thirds of American households, through a carbon fees trust fund.

Mary, you are as woefully ignorant of basic economics as you are of chemistry. A heavy carbon tax will not "put money back into the pockets of American households. ***To the contrary, it will extract money from American households.***

You see, Marxist Mary, your punishing carbon ***tax*** *will increase the overhead costs of oil and coal companies. If you had ever operated a front lawn lemonade stand as a child, you would understand that overhead expenses have to necessarily be embedded in the final cost of goods and services.*

Mary: Recent polls by Yale and Stanford show that almost twice as many Americans support a carbon fee and dividend as oppose it.

Yeah. Recent polls also show that Americans are far less literate and educated that 30 years ago. Your stupid platitude-filled letter and your ***Appeal to Authority Fallacy*** *(Yale / Stanford) offer further evidence of just how brain-dead the average American "citizen" has become.*

As for this "dividend" nonsense; first of all, only a libtarded fool would actually believe that a carbon tax would go back to "the American public". Uncle Sam will keep that money for his perpetual welfare and warfare machines.

And finally, whatever pittance of a "dividend" (our own money) that comes back to us will be, no, MUST BE, less than the indirect, passed-on fees that we will have to pay. Tell you what, Mary; send a "fee" of $100 to The Anti-New York Times each month, and at the end of each year, ANYT will send you a "dividend" check of $500. Deal?

Mary, not only is your parsing of words (fee-tax / dividend) unethical, but you also suck at chemistry, economics, philosophy and even basic math!

This Bolshevik Broad from Berkeley fails ethics, chemistry, economics, philosophy and math. The worst part; she actually thinks she's smart!

Mary: Once again, the American public is showing that it is more forward-thinking than its elected leaders.

My dear Ms. Poop-for-Brains. You have contradicted yourself. If the public is as "forward-thinking" (an empty platitude) as you say, then how is it possible that leaders, chosen by this very same "forward-thinking" public, are as deficient as you say?

Furthermore, Mary, even if the brain-dead public actually did understand or even care a rat's arse about this issue (which they don't), you committed yet another grave philosophical error - the ***Appeal to Popularity Fallacy.*** *Polls don't determine truth, Mary. Facts do!*

Mary: Over the next few months President Obama and Congress are in a position to transform the global energy economy and stabilize our planet ......

"Stabilize the planet with a tax increase", eh Mary? You know, Mary, your chivalrous reporter here would never hit a woman. So pardon me while I summon the ghost of Joan "Mommy Dearest" Crawford.

"Joannie. Smack some sense into this bitch, will ya?"

"No carbon taxes!"

Mary: ...by promoting a revenue-neutral carbon tax...

Check out Mary Marxist trying to sound like an financial intellectual - "revenue neutral". Shut up Mary, just shut up!

Mary: ... at home and at the United Nations climate talks in Paris in December.

I don't what grade you are in, Mary; but please don't let it be the case that you are actually an adult. Please, please, pleeeease be a 7th grader whose commie-pinko social studies teacher gave her class the talking points to write letters to the editor in advance of the big Climate Confab in Paris. Because if you truly are an adult, and perhaps even a college graduate, then boy-oh-boy America may be in even deeper, and more imminent trouble than feared.

Let's see what we can find out about "Mary Selkirk". Google time....

****

Mary Selkirk

- Collaborative public policy consultant
- San Francisco Bay Area
- Alternative Dispute Resolution

Current	1. Collaborative Natural Resources Solutions
Previous	1. Center for Collaborative Policy 2. CalFed Bay Delta Program
Education	1. University of California, Berkeley

Previously a guest lecturer in the graduate program of Urban and Regional Planning, UC Berkeley, and graduate program in Public Policy and Administration, CSU Sacramento. Former elected member of the Board of Directors of a major Northern California water utility.

****

Oh God, no! Mary Marxist of Berkeley is ***not*** a 7th grader. This dope not only has a college "education", but she serves on Boards and gives college lectures too. That's the "sophisticated" readership of Sulzberger's Slimes for you - diploma-decorated dorks - aka LIBTARDS!

The Boobus Brothers catch a break today; because even by their own standards of stupidity, they come off as Tesla-like geniuses compared to Marxist Mary Selkirk.

"Mary Mary dumb and hairy. Your abject ssstupidity is very ssscary!"

(Sugar! That is absolutely uncalled for!)

JUNE, 2015

NY Times: Spanish Official Apologizes Over Twitter Joke About Holocaust

BY RAPHAEL MINDER

A member of Madrid's new City Council, who had been set to become the councilor in charge of culture, resigned Monday amid a storm over jokes he posted in 2011 on Twitter about the Holocaust.

REBUTTAL BY

The Anti-New York Times

This past Saturday evening, a Spanish politician named Guillermo Zapata posted an Internet apology, insisting that he was not "anti-Semitic-**TM**". The controversy erupted over a recently discovered 2011 "Holocaust-**TM** joke" that Zapata had posted on Twitter, at a time when he had not even entered politics yet.

Zapata's obedient groveling act was as pathetic as it was disingenuous. He described his joke as an example of his penchant for *"dark and cruel humor,"* and as a *"healthy expression to laugh at the horror that we human beings create."* He again noted that the joke was made before he had entered politics.

Zapata's knee-crawling continues:

"I firmly condemn all forms of racism, and, of course, anti-Semitism. I believe the Jewish Holocaust teaches us a lesson that humanity must never forget so that it is never repeated".

Still, opposition politicians, Spanish libtards and Jews wasted no time in calling for his ouster. As expected, Zapata, a member of Madrid's new City Council who had been set to become the councilor in charge of culture, has just resigned. *(A "culture councilman"? WTF?)*

  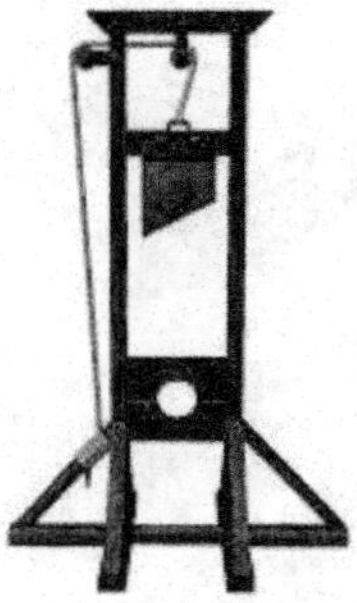

Too late for groveling, Senor Zappy.

"Off with his cabeza!"

Oddly enough, Sulzberger's Slimes does not reveal the contents of the Twitter joke - neither in its first story about this "controversy" *(last Saturday)*, nor in this follow-up story about the "resignation". All we are told is that Zapata's "anti-Semitic"-**TM** Twitter post alluded to the incineration of Holocaust-**TM** victims.

Regular readers of **The Anti-New York Times** are well aware of our position on this greatest hoax-of-all-hoaxes. Nonetheless, to *publicly* joke about the 270,000 people, some of them just victims of circumstance, who died in what were meant to be temporary wartime internment camps isn't really advisable for someone aspiring to be a public figure. But it should not be a "fireable" offense and it damn sure does not merit so much as a blip in a major newspaper.

Not all of the dead were Communist subversives. Some were just ordinary low-level Jews caught up in events that they could neither understood nor control - tragic events dictated not by Hitler *(blessed be his name)*, but by the Evil 3 *(FDR, Churchill & Stalin)* and the Globo-Zio power structure above them. Truth activists should, by all means, spread jokes about the ridiculous Holocaust Fairy Tale itself; but not about victims of horrible typhus - at least not the innocent ones. It really doesn't help us truth-tellers in opening up people's minds -which is already a tough task.

Of course, had Zapata told a joke about the 100's of 1000's of Germans suffocated to death or incinerated alive during the Dresden firebombing of 1945, not only would Sulzberger's Slimes not care a rat's arse, but Zapata would probably be puffed-up to become Spain's next Prime Minister!

That being said; here's a better Holohoax joke, and a much more effective one as well:

"How do you fit the spectators of 13 full NFL stadiums into a 'gas-chamber' the size of a 3-car garage?

Answer: By using your imagination.

Nonetheless, why didn't Sulzberger's Slimes reveal Zapata's joke to its readers? Why is it that whenever someone makes the most vile and offensive remarks about Muslims, Christians or Whites, the Slimes, though perhaps not stating agreement with the comments, will not hesitate to print them? You know the routine: *"It's not us saying these horrible things. We're just reporting."*

But that's not the case here. Why not? Let's all hear Zapata's joke!

Google time!.....Found it in the Times of Israel *(for Jews only to hear)*

Question: “How do you fit five million Jews in a SE 600 *(a Spanish small car)*?

Answer: "In the ashtray”

OK....OK. Confession time. Your humor-loving reporter here did ever-so-slightly crack just a wee-little virtually undetectable subdued smirk at that one. But it's still not appropriate. Nor is destroying people's careers and lives over politically incorrect "Tweets" and Facebook posts!

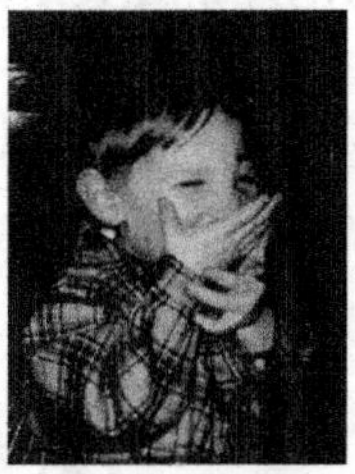

("In the ashtray")

Boobus Americanus 1: *How do you fit 6 million Jews in a car?"*

Boobus Americanus 2: *How?*

Boobus Americanus 1: *In the ashtray.*

Boobus Americanus 2: *I'm reporting you to H.R.!*

(Sugar! It's not funny!)

JUNE, 2015

NY Times: Nine Killed in Shooting at Charleston Church

By ASHLEY SOUTHALL

A white gunman opened fire Wednesday evening at a historic black church in downtown Charleston, S.C., before fleeing, the police said, and nine people were killed.

REBUTTAL BY

The Anti-New York Times

Oh dear. This is bad news - very, very bad news. Though it is way too early to make a call on this one; it will not matter if it was another Sandy Hook fake shooting with fake victims; or a 'false-flag' with real victims; or an actual White "lone gunman" who really did just lose his mind and started killing Black folks in a church *(doubtful, but possible)*.

Just before firing, the killer is said to have declared: *"You rape our women and you are taking over our country. You have to go."* He allowed on person to live, instructing him/her: *"Go tell the world what you saw."* It all sounds a bit Hollywood-ish, doesn't it?

Time will reveal if these are 'crisis actors' or actual mourners.

Let the dust settle and the hard data emerge before making a definitive judgement. But the truth is secondary because we all know what's probably coming:

- Retaliatory Black on White actions
- Massive White guilt trips
- Renewed push for gun control

The vomit-inducing "national conversation" on race sure to come out of this may last for years - with annual commemorations and vigils similar to the 9/11 memorial services in terms of self-righteousness and overall cheesiness. Get the barf bags ready folks, and keep your powder dry, White Man!

Now, don't misunderstand. If indeed it should turn out, unlike Sandy Hook and the Boston Smoke Bomb, that actual people died in this church; our condolences go out to the families. But when are we going to ever recognize, let alone grieve for, the ever-growing list of White people murdered and tortured in "hate crimes"? Don't "White lives matter" too?

Time and time and time again, Sulzberger's Anti-White Slimes has ignored some of the most ghastly Black-on-White crimes imaginable. For example, how many Americans know that **the 2nd worst mass-murderer in U.S. history was a Black-on-White 'hate-criminal'**? That's right; a single bigot killed not nine, but ***forty three*** White people in a 1987 suicide-hijacking. Oh, you didn't hear about that one? Don't feel stupid. Neither has 99% of America.

What a story!

Sulzberger's Slimes did run a few initial stories on the strange incident, but when investigators began piecing together the crime and pointing towards a Black man, Sulzberger and the rest of the media suddenly dropped the story. In 2014, **The**

Anti-New York Times did a special piece on this astonishing 1987 event. Keep this mass-murder story in mind, and do share it, as the coming "national conversation" about the South Carolina church killings unfolds over the coming days and weeks and months and years.

FLASHBACK - EXCERPT

****

As the aircraft cruised at 22,000 ft over the California coast, the cockpit voice recorder of the relatively small plane recorded the sound of someone entering, and then exiting the lavatory. The timing of the lavatory door sounds, Burke's seating proximity to Thomson, and the two quick gun shots heard just after the 2nd door closing sound, suggest that Burke entered the lavatory in order to discreetly draw his gun. The captain and the co-pilot were speaking to air traffic control when the Cockpit Voice Recorder **(CVR)** picked up the sound of the first two shots being fired.

The most plausible theory as to what happened was deduced from the pattern and audible volume of the shots on the CVR. It appears that Burke first shot Thomson twice. Though Thomson's own seat was never recovered, part of a serial numbered seat that was identified from the wreckage as being directly behind Thomson's was found to have two bullet holes in it. Due to the power of the Magnum .44, the bullets must have traveled through Thomson's body, his seat, and then through the seat behind.

The co-pilot immediately reported that a gun had been fired and no further transmissions were received from the crew. At that point, the CVR recorded the cockpit door opening and a female flight attendant telling the pilots, *"We have a problem!"* The captain replied, *"What kind of problem?"* A shot was heard as Burke shot the flight attendant dead, and announced *"I'm the problem."* He then fired two more rounds. Most likely, he shot the pilot and copilot once each, incapacitating or killing them on the spot. Several seconds later, the CVR picked up increasing windscreen noise as the airplane pitched sharply downward and accelerated. The remains of the flight data recorder (FDR) indicated Burke had pushed the control column forward into a dive.

David Burke was born May 18, 1952, to Jamaican parents living in Britain. He was, as you can see, Black. If you are a regular reader, you should know by now where your author is going with this. Is it really even necessary at this point to ask the question, *"Why was this story suddenly spiked and then buried for eternity?"*

After spending 2 days as one of the front page stories of the New York Times, *(December 8 & 9)*,the story dropped down to page A-28 as soon as it was learned who the shooter-hijacker actually was (December 11). **Burke's photo was never published.** By the following day, the historic mass murder drama was gone from Sulzberger's Times, and the TV media, altogether.

The San Bernardino County Times *(a small local paper)* offered an honest glimpse into Burke's animosity towards White people *(which all, or nearly all, of the passengers certainly were)*. From its December 12, 1987 issue:

"Burke, who was black, had alleged to state authorities long before he was fired that Thomson had passed him over for promotion because of race."

"On July 15, Burke went to the state Department of Fair Employment and Housing and said he had been passed over twice for promotion to customer service supervisor. Burke alleged white workers with less experience were promoted to the supervisory positions he deserved, said Annabella Hwa, the department's district manager in Los Angeles. Burke, although investigated several times for alleged drug involvement and auto theft in New-York, was never charged."

You see, in the warped mind of the racist-bigot David Burke, being passed over for a promotion couldn't possibly have had anything to do with company suspicions that he may have once been involved with a Jamaican drug-smuggling ring, or that he was clearly a troubled head-case. No. It was "racism" that got White people promoted over him. Of course! And it was "racism" that got him fired after he was caught stealing money- *on camera!*

David Burke was a violent abusive man who fathered 7 children out of wedlock with multiple "baby mommas". And, make no mistake, he hated White people. We can imagine the great delight which Burke took in blowing that White Flight Attendant's brains out, just after offing Mr. Thomson, and just before blasting the White pilots.

The unknown dirty work of a White-hating monster named David Burke.

****

Yes, Sulzberger. Let's have that "national conversation" about race and about "hate crimes". We can start with David Burke.

Boobus Americanus 1: *What happened in South Carolina was shameful. We have got to have a national conversation about race in this country.*

Boobus Americanus 2: *Indeed. And also about gun control.*

"White cats matter too, you pathetic self-hating libtards!)

(You tell em Sugar!)

JUNE, 2015

NY Times: 60 Million People Fleeing Chaotic Lands, U.N. Says

By SOMINI SENGUPTA

The United Nations refugee agency finds that war and persecution have displaced a record number of people.

REBUTTAL BY

The Anti-New York Times

Whether the issue is high unemployment, low wages, high crime, rising health care costs, student debt, racial conflict, social unrest, foreign wars or pick your favorite socio-economic dysfunction; members of the Marxist-Globalist-Zionist Left will always wring their hands in dismay over the very crisis which their policies caused in the first place. The Global refugee crisis, which adversely impacts both the refugees and the host nation which they are fleeing to, is no different.

Let us break out the hip-waders and dissect this bit of front-page rubbish:

"The U.N. report states that the global distribution of refugees remains heavily skewed away from wealthier nations and towards the less wealthy."

Translation: Europe and North America are still too White.

"For now, the European Union has shelved its plans to get approval from the United Nations Security Council to target human smugglers......

Translation: World Government is already in effect. The U.N. will not allow Europe to protect its sovereignty and borders.

......who operate in lawless Libya and to destroy the ships they use to bring migrants across the sea."

Comment: And whose decision was it to blow up Libya, murder Qaddafi and plunge the previously stable nation into a "lawless" state? The U.N., with the support of Sulzberger's Slimes; that's who!

*Upon learning of the murder of Qaddafi, Killary Clinscum cackled: **"We came. We saw. He died"**. As a result, many refugees are now also dying, as will many European victims of the incoming crime wave. The Slimes misses the connection.*

"Instead, the European Union is scheduled to meet on Monday to discuss whether it will start military operations in the international waters of the Mediterranean Sea, for which it does not need the Council's blessings."

Translation: Europe will use its military forces to act as rescue workers and welfare case managers. The all mighty U.N. is 'OK' with that.

"Australia has felt no such compunction. Its prime minister, Tony Abbott, has pledged to turn around migrant boats before they enter Australian territorial waters."

Translation: Australian public opinion has compelled the generally ball-less Abbott to protect what little is left of Australia's sovereignty.

"Amnesty International, in a report issued this week, accused governments and smugglers alike of pursuing "selfish political interests instead of showing basic human compassion."

Translation: A Globalist-CIA front group makes a ridiculous moral equivalence between vicious human traffickers and any politician who dares to stand up against the invasion of Europe or Australia.

Don't be fooled by the holier-than-thou posturing. Amnesty International is a U.S. State Department / CIA front, all the way!

"The war in Syria is the largest source of displacement."

Comment: Brought to us by Globalists, Zionists and their "rebel" proxies. *(now repackaged as 'ISIS')*

"The latest of 15 new conflicts to erupt in the last five years has arisen in Yemen."

Comment: Brought to us by Globalists, Zionists and their Saudi proxies.

"Older conflicts, like the ones in Somalia"....

Comment: Brought to us by Globalists, Zionists and their "rebel" proxies.

"...the Darfur region of Sudan"...

Brought to us by Globalists, Zionists and their "rebel" proxies.

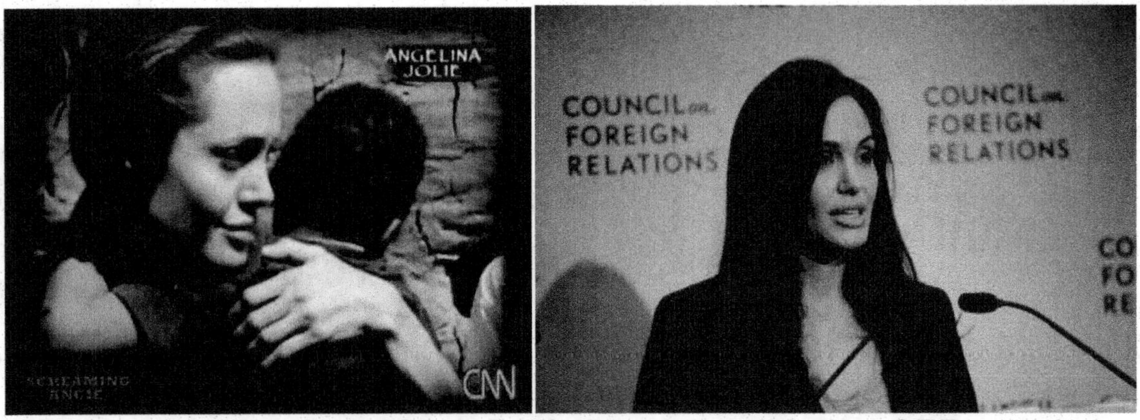

You know that whole "Save Darfur" cause-celeb that CFR member Angelina Jolie has so publicly promoted? That was a Western-Israeli engineered crisis designed to break up Sudan in two countries and cause problems for Chinese businesses operating there. Whether Jolie is a stupid tool or a conscious agent is open to debate.

"....and Afghanistan"

Comment: Brought to us by Globalists, Zionists and the 2001 invasion which was based on the idiotic Fairy Tale of 9/11; featuring Osama Bin Laden, an Afghan cave fortress, Al Qaeda, skinny hijackers with box-cutters, melted steel, pulverized skyscrapers, heroic passengers etc.

"...are no where close to a lasting peace."

Yes; no peace. Thanks again to the usual suspects!

Find a "hot spot" or even just a minor upheaval anywhere on this troubled planet; gently scratch the facade of the official explanation with the edge of a dime, and time and time and time again the experienced student of the New World Order will discern the unmistakable fingerprints of the same old invisible Globo-Zionist hand. And the index finger of that hideous hand is always Sulzberger's seditious Slimes with its fake explanations of causes; and its equally fake whining about the plight of the poor victims.

What a dirty, damnable trick. And the bastards get away it every time - which is why **The Anti-New York Times** is here to expose them.

Boobus Americanus 1: *I read an article in the New York Times about the horrible human tragedy of the international refugee crisis.*

Boobus Americanus 2: *I know. It's heart breaking. Western governments should really do more to take in these poor migrants.*

"Boobus! Western governments are the ones causing the problem! By the way, will you be adopting a migrant anytime soon?"

(Good comeback, Sugar!)

JUNE, 2015

NY Times: In Charleston, Raw Emotion at Hearing for Suspect in Church Shooting

By NIKITA STEWART and RICHARD PÉREZ-PEÑA

Relatives of people killed in a shooting at a black church addressed the suspect, Dylann Roof, in court on Friday, tearfully offering forgiveness, and hope that he would confess and repent.

NY Times: Black Church Is Target for Deadly Strike at the Heart

By RACHEL L. SWARNS and CAMPBELL ROBERTSON

After the Civil War, black churches became what the scholar W. E. B. Du Bois and others have described as the "first social institution fully controlled by black men in America." And before long, those institutions became targets.

NY Times: Outrage vs. Tradition, Wrapped in a High-Flying Flag of Dixie

By ALAN BLINDER and MANNY FERNANDEZ

The debate has been renewed on social media and beyond about whether the flag should be displayed, and whether politicians should continue to defend it.

REBUTTAL BY

The Anti-New York Times

Barf bags and Pepto-Bismol are flying off of store shelves as Day 3 of the Charleston Circus rolls on. As expected, Sulzberger's Slimes continues to dedicate its entire front-top page to the event. There is, however, a bit of very good news to report. Our initial suspicion and subsequent hypothesis are now confirmed. **The Anti-New York Times** is "happy" to declare that no one died.

- Let us take comfort in the fact that, due to the obstinate gullibility of *Boobus Americanus*, the CIA has come to realize that killing real people in real 'false-flag' attacks *(such as Oklahoma City 1995, 9/11 attacks of 2001, London 7/7 train bombing of 2002, etc)* is no longer necessary. Why shed innocent blood when it can all be faked with crisis actors and CIA journalists? *(Sandy Hook School, Boston Marathon Bombing, ISIS "beheadings" etc)* Heck, at this point, the Feds & Media could probably get away with a fake nuclear bombing of a fake American town!

Mourn not for the murdered Bible-studying Black Folk of the Emanuel African Methodist Episcopal Church, for they are alive and well, presumably enjoying their new identities and wads of CIA cash. Following are just a few of the "tells", as they say in poker parlance.

CRISIS ACTORS *(bad ones too!)*

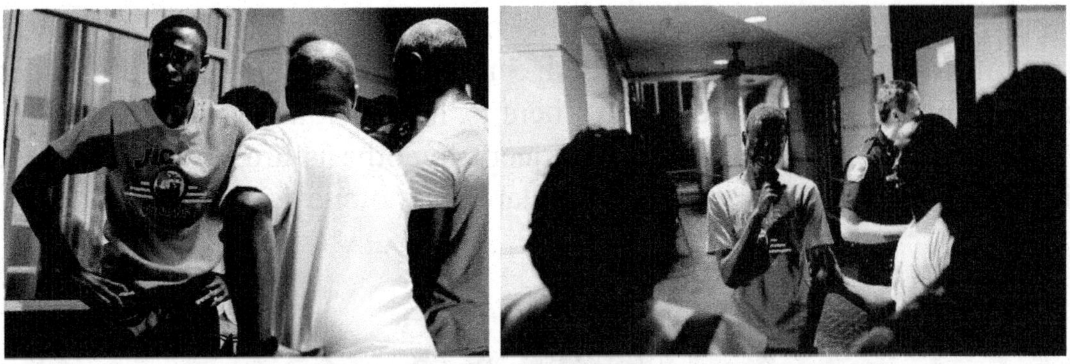

Fake grief, followed by smiles and laughter.

*

This boy's mother was just murdered and he's giving press conferences? He claims he feels "weak in the knees" with grief, but then cracked a smile! Immediately after the "massacre", all he could think of was "tweeting" out about his mother: "Pray for my mom please."

Then we have the "heroic" White lady, *(there must always be "heroes" with these scripted events)*, the one who conveniently spotted the fake suspect in North Carolina after watching 'Fox & Friends". Fox News says so.

"I'm not the hero. God is the hero. He just used me." Sure He did, Debbie. Sure He did.

Grieving faces and tissues, but where are the tear tracks?

*Cut it out, Obongo! You and your scripted little "racist-**TM**" White "psycho" aren't fooling anyone....On 2nd thought, you actually are.*

"Oh I wish I were in the land of cotton. Old times there are not forgotten. Look away -- look away -- Look away DixieLand."

UPDATE:

An alert reader has just informed us that the day after the fake massacre, with the nation distracted, the House of Representatives voted to grant "fast-track" authority for Obongo's stalled sovereignty-busting TPP deal.

Boobus Americanus 1: *You know, if it wasn't for the quick thinking of that brave woman in North Carolina, this racist psycho would have gotten away.*

Boobus Americanus 2: *Indeed. God put her in the right place at the right time.*

"And you freakin' idiots actually believe that bull-sh!t?"

(I'm afraid they do, Sugar. I'm afraid they do!)

JUNE, 2015

NY Times: A Hectic Day at Charleston Church, and Then a Hellish Visitor

By RICHARD FAUSSET, JOHN ELIGON, JASON HOROWITZ and FRANCES ROBLES

The visitor arrived around 8 p.m. Wednesday, asking for the minister. It was unusual for a stranger, much less a white one, to come to Bible study, but the pastor welcomed him.

REBUTTAL BY

The Anti-New York Times

The Anti-New York Times received mostly positive feedback over our Charleston non-shooting coverage. Unfortunately, some nasty feedback and even a few cancelled subscriptions also trickled in. Here's one:

"You have discredited yourself with this! I will no longer support your work."

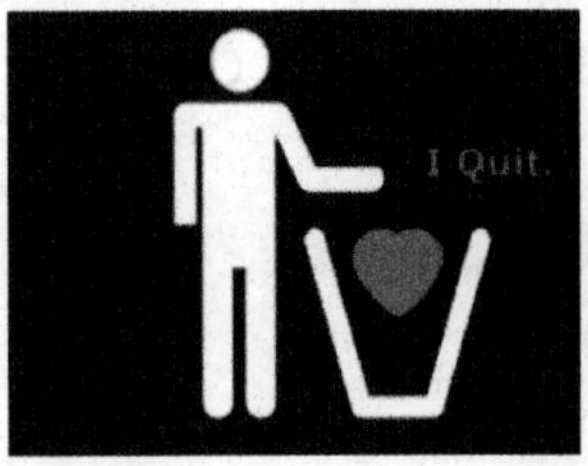

The Anti-New York Times

You'll be back.

Sorry to see you go, mate. But once the emotional reaction passes, you'll come around to the truth. No offense taken. That being said, the **Anti-New York Times** would like to take this opportunity to double-down and again declare that the Charleston non-shooting was a Sandy Hookish hoax. Indeed, this Hollywood script is so 'Grade B' that it doesn't even make for plausible fiction.

From the article:

"When the shooting was over, nine congregants were dead, including Mr. Pinckney and two of the newly ordained ministers, each shot multiple times with a .45-caliber handgun."

To shoot nine people "multiple times" requires a bit of time and aiming *(and reloading!)*. Yet nobody thought to bum-rush our Confederate killer - or run away? Fight or flight, there is no way that 'Dylann Storm Roof' could have accurately fired 30 or more times and not have some of the adrenaline-rushed victims either run away or attack him.

Apart from such an unrealistic scenario, the obvious 'crisis actors', and the scripted Confederate and Rhodesian (?!) flag props; the most damning piece of evidence against this non-event lies not so much in what is seen, phony as it all is, but rather, in what is *not seen*- **the bodies / crime scene**.

Sherlock Holmes and Lt. Colombo solved crimes by looking for the things that should have been visible - but were not.

As it was in Sandy Hook, as it was with the fake killing of 'Osama Bin Laden', there are no photos of dead bodies, no bloody aftermath, and no one being rolled out on gurneys. Nine people bleeding to death would have left quite a pool and quite a wall-spattering of blood. And oh how the press and the anti-gun Demonrats could use such photos to incite for their agendas! So, where are the bloody photos? Theatrical yellow tape proves nothing.

Now, before some of you subscription-cancelling naysayers *(whose E-mails have not yet been removed from the subscriber list)* retort with something like: *"the crime scene photos of Sandy Hook and Charleston weren't released because the images are too graphic."* - please explain why the grisly and gory crime-scene photos of the most notorious murders / mass murders of past decades are *all* readily available on the Internet.

Because the gruesome scenes may be too disturbing for some of our readers, they are linked (Google Terms) below, but not posted.

Nasty stuff - Enter at your own risk!

Google: Charles Manson Crime Scene

Google: Jeffery Dahmer Crime Scene

Google: John Wayne Gacy Crime Scene

Google: OJ Simpson Crime Scene

Google: Son of Sam Crime Scene

Google: Hillside Strangler Crime Scene

Google: Richard Speck Crime Scene

Google: Ted Bundy Crime Scene

Google: Zodiac Killer Crime Scene

Google: Green River Killer Crime Scene

There are plenty more high profile crime scenes available for viewing. And yet, not a single image of the bloody Sandy Hook "crime scene" has either been released or leaked. It's the same with the Charleston Church. And don't hold your breath waiting for any to be released in the future either.

Oh, and 'one more ting' as Detective Colombo used to say. From Reuters New service:

*"WASHINGTON (Reuters) - The Justice Department will fast track the sending of **$29 million** to South Carolina to help families of victims of the mass murder of nine churchgoers at a historic black church in Charleston, a Justice Department spokesman said."*

That ought to "ease the pain" of the families - and buy some silence and new lives as well.

Boobus Americanus 1: *The media is to be congratulated for not showing the crime scene images from South Carolina.*

Boobus Americanus 2*: I agree. That would be disrespectful to the victims' families.*

"Come on dad! Posst the Mansson murder photos of that blood-ssoaked pregnant lady for these idiotss."

(Sugar; you're a real psycho sometimes.)

JUNE, 2015

NY Times (Editorial Board): The Fantasy Mr. Putin is Selling

By THE EDITORIAL BOARD

President Vladimir Putin of Russia is not veering from the mythology he created to explain away the crisis over Ukraine.

REBUTTAL BY

The Anti-New York Times

The Editorial Board of Sulzberger's Slimes *(Andrew Rosenthal doing his loud 'Wizard of Oz' act)* weighs in today on "Mr. Putin's Fantasy". The rant is accompanied by a cartoon image of a pad-locked Russian doll which bears a very subtle resemblance to Adolf Hitler *(above)*.

Behind the curtain, the pathetic little worm Andrew Rosenthal pretends to be the great and mighty "Editorial Board".

The boldness with which ~~Rosenthal~~ - er, I mean, "the Board" lies calls to mind Hitler 's famous description of "the Big Lie" - which Rosenthal's synagogue buddies have always misrepresented as Hitler advocating the use of the lie, when, in actuality, he was describing Jewish-owned newspapers. Tell it, chief:

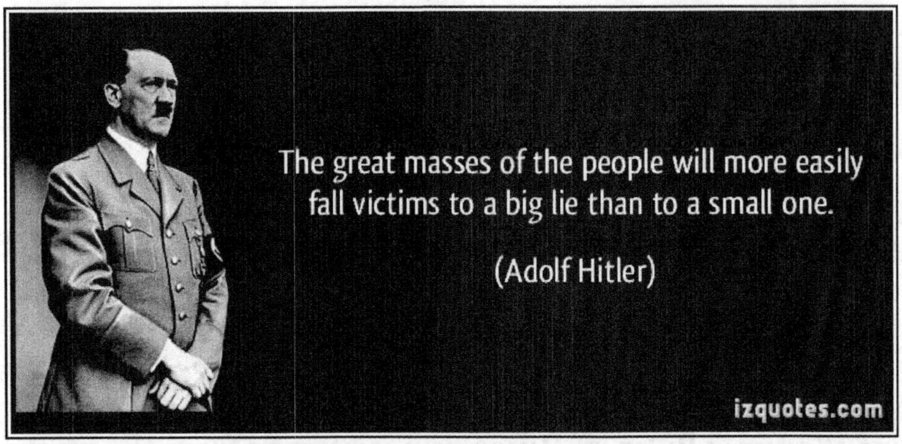

The great masses of the people will more easily
fall victims to a big lie than to a small one.
(Adolf Hitler)
izquotes.com

"But it remained for the Jews, with their unqualified capacity for falsehood, and their fighting comrades, the Marxists, to impute responsibility for the downfall precisely to the man who alone had shown a superhuman will and energy in his effort to prevent the catastrophe which he had foreseen and to save the nation from that hour of complete overthrow and shame.

By placing responsibility for the loss of the world war on the shoulders of Ludendorff they took away the weapon of moral right from the only adversary dangerous enough to be likely to succeed in bringing the betrayers of the Fatherland to Justice.

All this was inspired by the principle—which is quite true within itself—that in the ***big lie*** *there is always a certain force of credibility; because the broad masses of a nation are always more easily corrupted in the deeper strata of their emotional nature than consciously or voluntarily; and thus in the primitive simplicity of their minds they more readily fall victims to the* ***big lie*** *than the small lie, since they themselves often tell small lies in little matters but would be ashamed to resort to large-scale falsehoods.*

It would never come into their heads to fabricate colossal untruths, and they would not believe that others could have the impudence to distort the truth so infamously. Even though the facts which prove this to be so may be brought clearly to their minds, they will still doubt and waver and will continue to think that there may be some other explanation. For the grossly impudent lie always leaves traces behind it, even after it has been nailed down, a fact which is known to all expert liars in this world and to all who conspire together in the art of lying."

With that "Big Lie" technique in mind, let's dissect ~~Rosenthal's~~, er, I mean "the Board's" egregious editorial.

~~Rosenthal,~~ Board: President Vladimir Putin of Russia is not veering from the mythology he created to explain away the crisis over Ukraine. It is one that wholly blames the West for provoking a new Cold War...

~~Mike King,~~ Anti-New York Times: What "mythology"? It was western agents who openly incited Kiev mobs against a duly elected Russia-friendly President. The New York Times even ran photos of McCain and Nuland agitating the mob! Were these images "mythical"?

A few weeks after McCain's agitation in Kiev, the CIA provocateurs and rent-a-mobs overthrew a duly elected government.

~~Rosenthal,~~ Board: ....and insists that international sanctions have not grievously wounded his country's flagging economy.

~~Mike King,~~ Anti-New York Times: It's not only Putin claiming that Russia has weathered the sanctions storm. A Google Search for the term "Russia economy resilient" yields 458,000 results, many from anti-Russian western outlets such as Bloomberg and Fortune. Are your elite media colleagues also living in "fantasy land"? Have a look.

~~Rosenthal,~~ Board: He told the story again on Friday at a business forum whose purpose was to give weight to that fantasy.

~~Mike King,~~ Anti-New York Times: "Fantasy" in the title - "Mythology" in the opening paragraph - "fantasy" in paragraph # 2. How about we skip the childish *ad hominem* logical fallacies and provide some actual empirical data?

~~Rosenthal~~, Board: Despite Mr. Putin's skill at using foreign executives as props, he is looking more desperate than confident that he will win the confrontation with the West.

~~Mike King,~~ Anti-New York Times: "Props" - "desperate". Again, where's the economic data to support your thesis?

~~Rosenthal~~, Board: It will be a big setback for Mr. Putin if, as expected, European Union foreign ministers formally extend sanctions on Russia by six months when they meet this week in Luxembourg.

~~Mike King,~~ Anti-New York Times: Before ~~you~~ the Board can declare from Mt. Olympus that, *"It will be a big setback for Mr. Putin"* - the Board must first establish how the original round of sanctions crippled Russia. Again, where's the bloody data to contradict the aforementioned 458,000 Google results?

~~Rosenthal~~, Board: Ever since Russia's 2014 annexation of Crimea forced NATO and the European Union to react...

~~Mike King,~~ Anti-New York Times: Wrong again! It was not the annexation of Crimea - supported by 97% of Crimeans, by the way - that "forced NATO and the European Union to react." To the contrary, it was U.S. arm-twisting. Project much, ~~Rosie~~, Board members?

But don't take our word for it. A 2014 headline from the Globalist 'Der Spiegel' of Germany:

US Loses Patience with Europe: Washington Wants Tough Russia Sanctions

By Gregor Peter Schmitz in Brussels

~~Rosenthal~~, Board: The Europeans are indeed divided....but Mr. Putin's aggression so far has ensured their unity when it counts.

~~Mike King,~~ Anti-New York Times: Exactly what "aggression" is Mr. Putin guilty of? No one has ever defined this "aggression". The evidence of this Russian "aggression" is as scant as evidence for the Russian economic collapse. It's all, shall we say, a "fantasy"?

Speaking of aggression - how about that Porky Poreshenko tearing up civilan neighborhoods, eh? *(sound of crickets)*

~~Rosenthal~~, Board: Although Mr. Putin insisted on Friday that Russia had found the "inner strength" to weather sanctions and a drop in oil prices, investment has slowed, capital has fled the country and the economy has been sliding into recession.

~~Mike King,~~ Anti-New York Times: The sanctions have had an adverse impact, as even Putin admits. But the hoped-for crisis simply has not materialized, *at all*! Savvy investors such as the legendary Jimmy Rogers are betting heavily on a Russian rebound; and even Globalist Newsweek Magazine carried a story entitled:

What Sanctions? The Russian Economy Is Growing Again

By Bill Powell

Jimmy Rogers: April, 2015: ***"I'm very optimistic about the future of Russia. Certainly one of the most attractive stock markets in the world these days for me is Russia."***

~~Rosenthal~~, Board: One of the most alarming aspects of the crisis has been Mr. Putin's willingness to brandish nuclear weapons.

~~Mike King,~~ Anti-New York Times: ~~I,~~ we evidently missed that scary spectacle. How exactly did Bad Vlad "brandish" these nukes? Did he, like, wave them about in the air like some cowboy from an old Western?

"Yippee Kie Yay Americanski!"

Rosenthal, Board: the confrontation could end if Mr. Putin withdrew his troops and weapons from Ukraine

Mike King, Anti-New York Times: Again, what troops? What weapons? Over the past year or so, neither Sulzberger's Slimes nor the U.S. State Department has even attempted to offer the slightest bit of evidence to support this claim. The best "evidence" The Slimes has presented is this bit of bull-sugar from one Sgt. Panko of Ukraine, published on August 28, 2014:

".....a soldier with the Ukrainian border patrol unit, said he had seen tanks drive across the border, although they were marked with flags of the Donetsk People's Republic. "I tell you they are Russians, but this is what proof I have," said Sgt. Aleksei Panko, holding up his thumb and index finger to form a zero."

Thanks for the insight, Sgt. Zero!

Rosenthal, Board: Given Mr. Putin's aggressive behavior, including pouring troops and weapons into Kaliningrad, a Russian city located between NATO members Lithuania and Poland, the allies have begun taking their own military steps.

Mike King, Anti-New York Times: Dirty lying rat! The sequence of those events is in the wrong order. The recent reinforcement of Kalingrad came *after* - many months after to be precise - NATO beefed up its eastern "defenses".

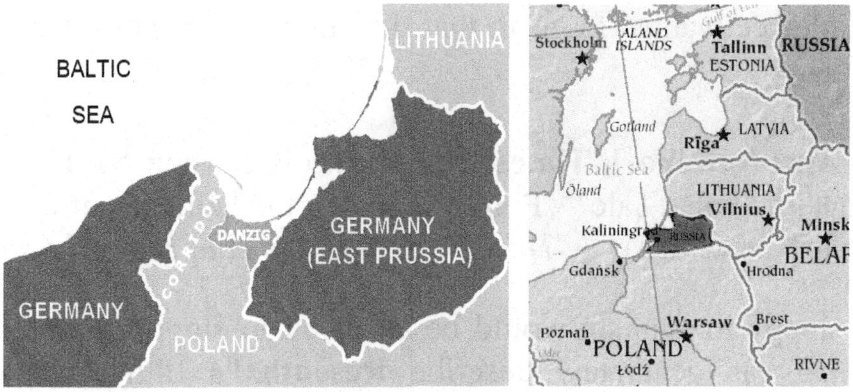

1939 vs 2015

Ominous parallels between unattached German East Prussia / Danzig in 1939 - and unattached Russian Kalingrad today. Perfect isolated hot-spots to force Putin's hand.

~~Rosenthal~~, Board: In recent months, NATO approved a rapid-reaction force in case an ally needs to be defended.

~~Mike King,~~ Anti-New York Times: "In recent months"?! **Liars!** NATO's "rapid-reaction" schemes aimed at peaceful Russia date back to **2011. TomatoBubble** did a whole article on it.

2011: Paratroopers from (left to right) the U.S. Army, Canada, the United Kingdom, Belarus, Poland and Ukraine embrace for a photograph to commemorate Rapid Trident 2011.

~~Rosenthal~~, Board: If he is not careful, Mr. Putin may end up facing exactly what he has railed against — a NATO more firmly parked on Russia's borders — not because the alliance wanted to go in that direction, but because Russian behavior left it little choice.

~~Mike King,~~ Anti-New York Times: So *Russia* is causing NATO to prepare for war? Now that's a "Fairy Tale" - Pure projection, the hallmark of all true psychos. As the old Polish proverb says; *"The Jew cries out in pain before he strikes you."*

To call this sloppy journalism would be an insult to sloppy journalists. There is only word that can accurately describe **Rosenthal's** filthy, wicked, libelous, warmongering editorial - **treason.**

Boobus Americanus 1: *"The New York Times Editorial Board just said that Putin is spreading Fairy Tales about the state of the Russian economy as he brandishes nuclear weapons."*

Boobus Americanus 2: *"He's just like Hitler. We can't appease him."*

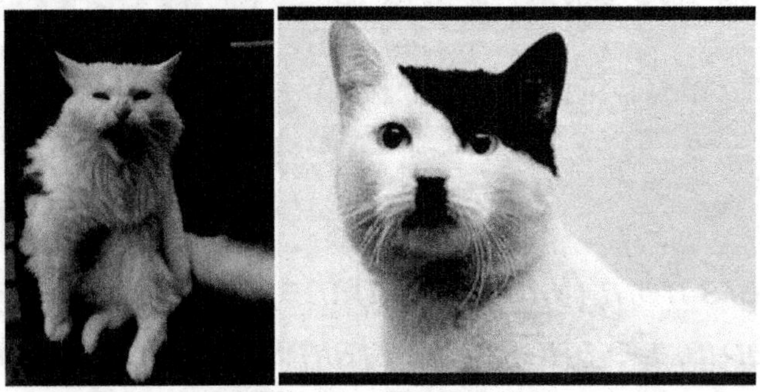

"Hey dumb-asses. Say hello to my little friend!"

(Nice find, Sugar!)

JUNE, 2015

NY Times: Nikki Haley, South Carolina Governor, Calls for Removal of Confederate Battle Flag

By FRANCES ROBLES, RICHARD FAUSSET and MICHAEL BARBARO

Gov. Nikki Haley's call to remove the flag from Capitol grounds came in the wake of the killing of nine people in a Charleston church.

NY Times: Making a Point, Obama Invokes a Painful Slur

By MICHAEL D. SHEAR

In a podcast interview, President Obama drove home his point that slavery still "casts a long shadow" on American life.

NY Times: Council of Conservative Citizens Promotes White Primacy, and G.O.P. Ties

By MICHAEL WINES and LIZETTE ALVAREZ

The massacre in Charleston, S.C., has propelled the organization back onto the national stage and embroiled the Republican Party in new questions about its ties to the group.

REBUTTAL BY

The Anti-New York Times

The Anti-White Tsunami of slime and slander continues to spew forth from Sulzberger's seditious cesspool with not just one, not just two, but *three* inflammatory front page poop-pies. We have the Republi**can't** Indian-American Governess of South Carolina banning the Confederate flag of which she knows nothing about; followed by Homo-Obongo's deliberately provocative use of the word, "nigger" *(damn!)*; followed by a hit piece on the gutsy 'The Council of Conservative Citizens'.

The sorry spectacle of Republi**can't** bed-wetters trembling before the illusionary Oz-like power of Sulzberger's Slimes and the rest of the piranha press is quite a sorry sight to behold. In addition to the Haley capitulation, Senator Ted Cruz *(who talks oh-so-tough when it comes to defending terrorist Israel)*, Rancid Paul *(whose own father was slandered as a "racist" by these very same devils)*, and circus clown Donald Trump have obediently lined up to either denounce the flag of old Dixie or, in the case of GOP Presidential contenders Cruz and Paul, announce that they would be refunding campaign donations received from the big bad Council of Conservative Citizens - the Left's newest bogeyman.

When the mighty 'Oz" of Manhattan blew its horn, the supine Senators were quick to soil their panties and wet their beds.

Will no one stand up for scores of millions of our vilified southern countrymen? Are there enough real men left *in the south* itself who are willing to even stand up for themselves and their cultural heritage? Is there not one among the Senate who will step-up to openly, boldly and logically denounce the pinko press and Mr. & Mr. Obongo as the vile stinking provocateurs that they are?

If the rebel flag is so indecent, then why did CBS, as recently as 30 years ago, carry "The Dukes of Hazzard", a hit show which featured a car dubbed the "Robert E. Lee", with a horn that blurted out the opening notes of "Dixie", and a Confederate flag for a rooftop?

Why did Viacom's country music-themed cable network CMT then air daily re-runs from 2005 to 2007?

"Just the good ole boys."

And if his holiness St. Abe Lincoln, upon winning the Civil War, could order a band to play Dixie, then why are southern college football bands now banning the awesome tune?

The words of St. Lincoln, April, 1865:

"I have always thought `Dixie' one of the best tunes I have ever heard. Our adversaries over the way attempted to appropriate it, but I insisted yesterday that we fairly captured it. I presented the question to the Attorney General, and he gave it as his legal opinion that it is our lawful prize. ....Now let the band play ' Dixie; It belongs neither to the South, nor to the North, but to us all.' I now request the band to favor me with its performance.'"

Is there not a single public figure or Republi**can't** candidate who can forcefully make these logical points and then counter-accuse the press and Obongo for trying to stir up racial animosity? This nonsense is *sooooo* easy to neutralize and throw back. A bit of logic and a bit of balls and watch the piranha press scurry into Oz-like panic mode. Because courage is contagious, the first leader to do so would instantly find millions of frustrated Americans lining up behind him.

But therein lies the problem. There are no leaders in Congress. In an unlimited "democracy", the real men work at real jobs while the untalented and the unscrupulous rise to the top of the political world. Politicians of all stripes have a good thing going. Who needs controversy?

Boobus Americanus 1: *I read in the New York Times today that the Governor of South Carolina has courageously called for the removal of the Confederate flag.*

Boobus Americanus 2: *Brave woman! It's about time too. It's an offensive flag that represents slavery.*

The ssslavery of 150 yearss ago offendss you, eh libtard? Yet you'll hand over 50% of your income to Fed, ssstate and local government without even batting a frickin' eye-lassh -- dumbassss!"

(Good logic there, Sugar! And let's not forget the government-caused price inflation that he is paying for too.)

JUNE, 2015

NY Times: Trade Accord, Once Blocked, Nears Passage

By JONATHAN WEISMAN

President Obama's ambitious trade push is back on track, after several near-death moments, in large measure because top Republicans stood by him.

REBUTTAL BY

The Anti-New York Times

Well, well, well. Look at what we have here. With the piranha press all frenzied over the South Carolina shooting **hoax** and the subsequent controversy over the Confederate Battle Flag; Obongo's favorite Republi**cant's** appear to have saved his Globalist "legacy" from that "stinging rebuke" *(staged innoculation)* of a few weeks ago; and will indeed push us into an advanced form of world government - the TTP *(Trans-Pacific Partnership).*

The article actually spells it out for us in chilling detail; and even goes on to explain that merger with Europe is next on the Globalist agenda! Check it out:

"With Congressional support for "fast track" authority, the president can press for final agreement on the Trans-Pacific Partnership, a legacy-defining accord linking 40 percent of the world's economy — from Canada and Chile to Japan and Australia — in ***a web of rules governing Pacific commerce.***

His administration can also ***bear down on a second agreement with Europe*** *— known as the* ***Transatlantic Trade and Investment Partnership*** *— knowing that lawmakers will be able to vote for or against those agreements but will not be able to amend or filibuster them."*

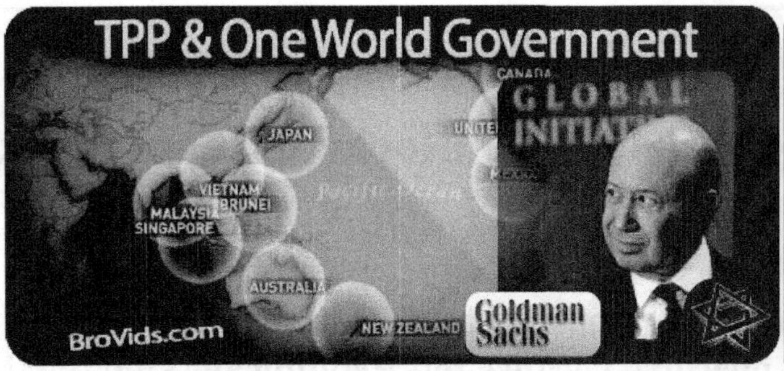

TTP = Novus Ordo Seclorum (New Order of the Ages)

America is on its way to being reduced to the lead vassal state of **The New World Order**. First, we merge with the Pacific Rim - then comes Europe. Trade rules, environmental regs, immigration quotas, military cooperation and internal social policies can then be harmonized by Presidential decree. Only Russia and China stand in the way of final One-World consolidation - but the Globalists have plans for them!

QUOTES TO REMEMBER:

"The UniPolar world refers to a world in which there is one master, one sovereign, one center of authority, one center of force, one center of decision-making. This is pernicious - At its basis there can be no moral foundations for modern civilization."

- Vladimir Putin

*

"We must respect the right of each country in the world to independently choose its path of development and oppose interference in the internal affairs of other countries."

- Jin Ping (China)

*

"All nations must come together to build a stronger Global regime."

- Obongo

Those quotes tell you all you need to know about the world situation and the coming confrontation; and TPP fits right into this NWO puzzle.

By the way, has anyone heard from Homo-Obongo's Democrat "nemesis" on trade policy? You remember the "populist", Lizzie ~~Borden~~ Warren, don't you? Why isn't she shooting off her massive Massachusetts mouth over this outrage? The Slimes articles doesn't even mention her. Has the hideous hag from Harvard suddenly lost interest in protecting America from the TTP? Say it ain't so, Lizzie.

Exactly as **The Anti-New York Times** forecast in May, Lizzie ~~Borden~~ Warren's "woman of the people" act was actually a deceitful controlled-opposition **inoculation** all along.

Anti-NY Times Flashback - Sunday, May 10, 2015:

****

Wily Warren: just a "regular gal" in a diner who taught only one class and raked-in $400,000 per year at Harvard - as some of her lesser affluent students are left to choke on student loan debt.

Knowing that the bosses of the Republi**can't** Party *(McConnell, McCain, Boehner, Ryan et al)* are "all in" for the sovereignty-killing TPP, Obongo can easily afford to lose, and actually *wants* to lose as many Demoncrap votes as possible and have the deadly deal still fly. **This is exactly how Bill Clinscum played the big NAFTA vote in 1993.**

These types of sneaky manipulations are the typical hallmarks of sociopaths and criminals. Obongo is "in on it". The phony "populist" Wench Warren is "in on it". And Harry Reid, the Republi**can't** leadership, and, of course, Sulzberger's Slimes are also "in on it" .

The joke is on you, "Blue Collar" America!

Bend over and grab your ankles, American working man. The "Bi-Partisan" TPP Express is coming.

****

Nailed it -- unfortunately.

What we could not have predicted, however, was the critical role that the fake shooting in South Carolina played in enabling TTP to sail beneath everybody's radar. The TTP 'fast-track' narrowly made it through a House vote that took place the *very next day* after the fake shooting. With attention since diverted towards "racism" and "N-words" and Rhodesian flags and Confederate flags - the greatest single power grab since the establishment of the Federal reserve in 1913 *(no exaggeration!)* just took a huge step forward. Lizzie ~~Borden~~ Warren - save us!

Boobus Americanus 1: *I read in the New York Times today that the Republicans helped Obama get closer to that Pacific free trade deal.*

Boobus Americanus 2: *It's nice to see bi-partisanship. Perhaps the tragedy in South Carolina will serve as the catalyst to unite the political establishment for the common good.*

"You corny-asss sstupid %#%$ ^/&#@ ! They are sselling us down-the-river!"*

(Sugar! Come here and take your meds. Now!)

JUNE, 2015

NY Times: Supreme Court Ruling Makes Same-Sex Marriage a Right Nationwide

By ADAM LIPTACK

In a long-sought victory for the gay rights movement, the Supreme Court ruled by a 5-to-4 vote on Friday that the Constitution guarantees a right to same-sex marriage.

The New York Times
'EQUAL DIGNITY'
5-4 Ruling Makes Same-Sex Marriage a Right Nationwide

When images of a rainbow-lit White House first surfaced online, the reaction here at **The Anti-New York Times** was a subdued chuckle over the creativity and graphic skill of the Internet community's latest joker. Lo and behold - it is ***not*** a joke! Mr. & Mr. Obongo actually lit the house of John Adams, Thomas Jefferson, James Madison, Andrew Jackson, William McKinley and Warren Harding on rainbow fire. At least the sexual predator, Bill Clinton, kept his perversion within the realm of "heterosexuality".

From front to back, the Judaized White House has been corrupted.

As the rainbow flags of faggotry flutter in our faces, the honorable Battle Flag of the South is being torn down and phased out everywhere. Even as recently as just five years ago, few could have foreseen that such madness would take hold in such a short period of time. But that's what happens when cancer - in this case, the moral and mental cancer of liberalism - metastasizes. The final stages of the fatal disease are accelerated.

The 'Cross of St. Andrew' battle flag comes down. The sodomy, tranny, pedophilia flag goes up.

*

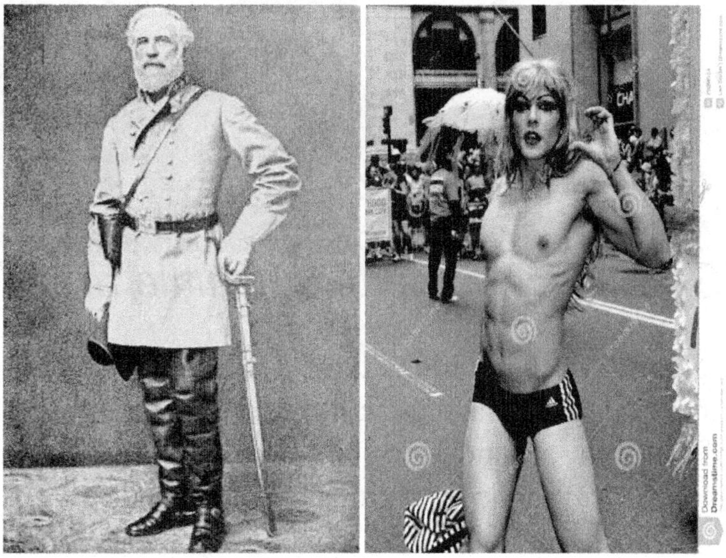

Robert E Lee is out / Bobby-Ann Lee is in

Whether one believes that God, in due time, consciously and directly metes out harsh justice to decadent peoples; or that the violation of the Creator's natural laws for living bring about the crash on its own - much like an attempted violation of a law of physics - the end result for America *("The West")* will still be the same. There is only so long that Nature's God can tolerate scores of millions of human middle fingers in His face.

Now the insane perverts and their Marxist / libtard enablers aren't the only ones at fault here. As disgusting as Sulzberger's front page full of kissing couples may be, the "normal" people who shrug their shoulders at this stuff and say to themselves: *"What freaks! But as long as they don't bother me, who cares?",* are also to blame. The problem with such moral indifference is that it's similar to saying, *"The plague is a horrible thing. But as long as I'm not infected, I'm not worried."*

It doesn't work like that! A sick, twisted, degenerate society will ultimately consume itself as the moral rot spreads everywhere. No family, no matter how decent, can, in the long run, remain immune to this epidemic. We do not live in a vacuum and nor do our children. When the final crisis and collapse comes, a heavy price will be paid by all.

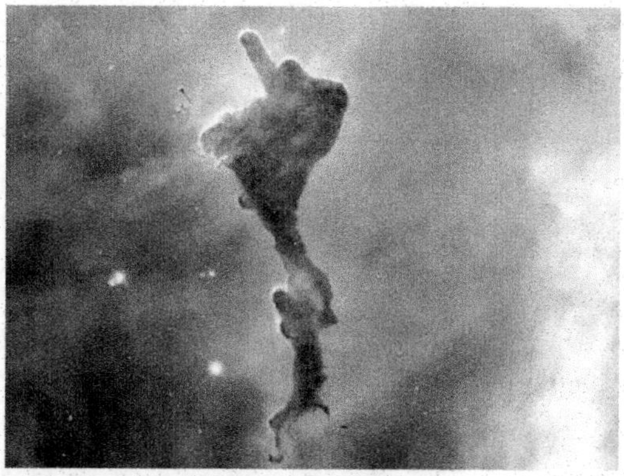

God: *"The same to you, little man."*

Were it not for the good people in immediate circles *(as well as our readers!)* one would almost be inclined to embrace the coming chastisement of God & Nature with an attitude of "Kill-em-all-and-let's-start-over." - but alas, there are still many millions of good people and innocent children who will get caught up in the engineered crash of western civilization.

And make no mistake, it's coming. One of God's more recent prophets said it best:

"Man's effort to build up something that contradicts the iron logic of Nature brings him into conflict with those principles to which he himself exclusively owes his own existence. By acting against the laws of Nature he prepares the way that leads to his ruin."

Right on, chief. Right on!

More recently, another wise man stated:

"A policy is being conducted of putting on the same level multi-child families and single-sex partnerships, belief in God and belief in Satan. The excesses of political correctness are leading to the point where people are talking seriously about registering parties whose goal is legalizing the propaganda of pedophilia. This is the path to degradation."

Right on, Vlad. Right on!

As far as the more short-term consequences of Supreme Court ruling mandating "same-sex marriage" *(barf)*; this vote means that any baker, photographer, band, florist, town Mayor and, in due time, even Priests and Pastors who refuses to accommodate these sodomite spectacles could face Federal discrimination lawsuits, fines and perhaps, one day, imprisonment!

This sorry situation - this country - will not stand in the long run. Believe it! All **Anti-New York Times** readers are hereby invited aboard Noah's ark.

Remember when the rainbow was a symbol of beauty and new beginnings?

Boobus Americanus 1: *This was a landmark ruling by the Supreme Court. It would otherwise have taken decades for the southern redneck states to individually legalize same-sex marriage.*

Boobus Americanus 2: *I agree. Best decision since Brown vs. Board of education in 1954. Tolerance and equality must be enfoced at the Federal level.*

"I am absolutely NOT getting aboard that ark with all those ssmelly-asss animalss!"

(Sugar. You really need to get some humility.)

NY Times: South Sudan's Agony

By THE EDITORIAL BOARD

South Sudan must rank among the most astounding failures in Africa, if only because the country is not even four years old.

REBUTTAL BY

The Anti-New York Times

From high up above the cloud line of 8th Avenue, the modern Moses of Manhattan, Andrew Rosenthal, *(speaking in the Oz-like voice of "The Editorial Board")*, wrings his grubby hands in dismay over the sad state of affairs in the 4-year old nation of South Sudan.

Behind the curtain, the pathetic little worm Andrew Rosenthal pretends to be the great and mighty "Editorial Board".

From the oh-so-humanitarian ~~Rosenthal~~, er Editorial Board:

"A report in The Times last week describes unspeakable atrocities against children and civilians. It describes how more than 1.5 million people have been forced to flee their homes and how almost half the population of 12 million is facing hunger, often because aid workers cannot reach them through the fighting.

What makes the South Sudan tragedy all the more astounding is that the country was initially hailed as a triumph of American foreign policy."

The collapse of South Sudan, despite billions in American aid, offers a stark lesson on the limits of American state-building powers. South Sudan was a long shot from Day 1, and despite Republican charges that Mr. Obama could have prevented its unraveling, it is not clear what Washington could have done. South Sudan had virtually no government institutions or infrastructure at independence, its population was fragmented into diverse ethnic groups and it had oil revenue to tempt the greedy."

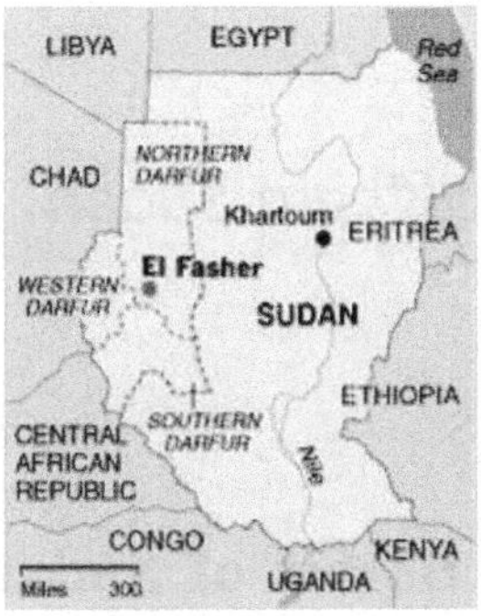

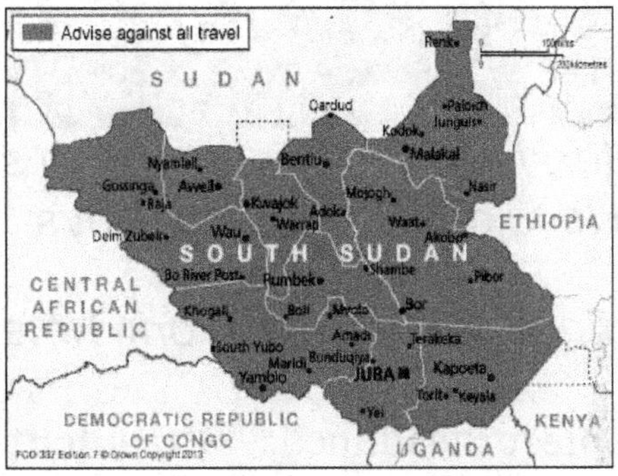

After breaking away from Sudan (according to Globalist-Zionist plan), South Sudan is now in crisis. Many refugees are fleeing to Europe by way of Libya (another once-stable nation whose destruction was also cheered by Sulzberger's Slimes).

~~Rosenthal's~~, The Editorial Board's analysis of the chaotic situation is correct. But what ~~Rosenthal~~, The Editorial Board doesn't tell you is that Sulzberger's Slimes was supportive of the push to split the new nation of "South Sudan" away from the predominantly Muslim North. Not only did this move weaken a Muslim state which Israel considers an enemy; but the subsequent destabilization of both North and South was problematic for the big bad Chinese - who conduct a ton of mutually beneficial business in the Sudans.

How quintessentially Slimes-ish! First, Sulzberger, Rosenthal et al. support a major Globalist propaganda assault against Sudan. Then, when the situation blows up - as planned - they blame it "policymakers", or Republicans - in this case, Bush.

For example, a November 27, 2010 Slimes piece gushed over the secession vote - headline: **"For Lost Boy, Vote on Sudan is Homecoming"**.

Joseph Gatyoung Khan, center, returned this month to southern Sudan after 22 years. He is one of the Lost Boys. -

Credit Sven Torfinn for The New York Times

Earlier that year, in May, a hit piece headlined: **"President Bashir of Sudan Can't escape Isolation"** ripped Sudan's President to shreds.

Still earlier in that pre-secession period of 2010, in April, another piece entitled, **"Obama Backs Down on Sudan"** took Obongo to the woodshed for not being tough enough on Sudan *(The North)*.

From January, 2010, atrocity propaganda regarding Darfur *(Western Sudan)*: **"Fragile Calm Holds in Darfur After Years of Death"**

Headline from 2009:

"Court Issues Arrest Warrant for Sudan's Leader"

"Fears of More Misery in Darfur"

"Trailing George Clooney *(Darfur activist)*"

"Aid Groups' Expulsion, Fears of More Misery"

Take it from your probing ~~reporter~~ Board of **The Anti-New York Times,** these anti-Sudan articles can be dug up by the scores going back for at least 12 years! The Sulzbergerian smear campaign, along with the orchestrated *cause celeb* antics of **actors** Angelina Jolie and George Clooney, served to support the CIA / Mossad subversion of Sudan. More than that, Slimes stories were *essential* in creating the pressure which finally brought about the idiotic partition of Sudan.

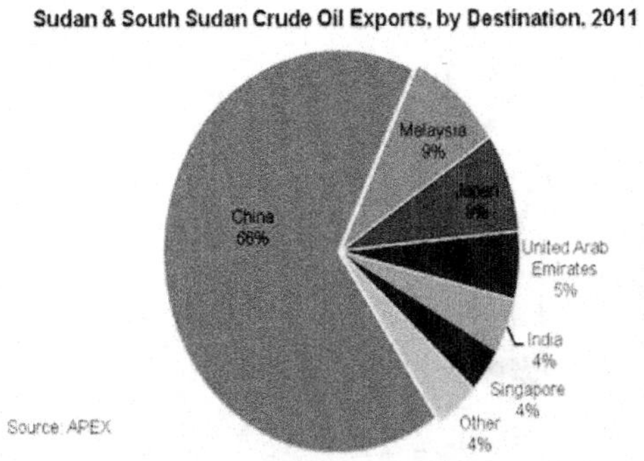

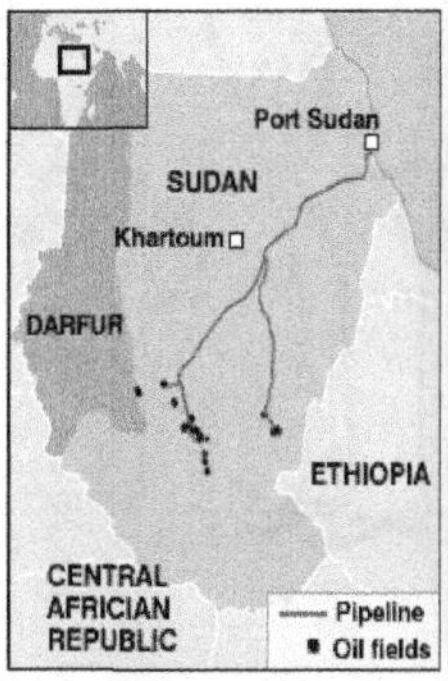

The airhead Angelina Jolie may have been sincere in her efforts to help "the children of Darfur"; but the Darfur "cause" was really all about the Judeo-Globalists wanting to destablize Sudan and then push Chinese business out of oil rich nation altogether, nothing else!

It was the Zio-Globalists, with their phony "Save Darfur" scheme in the Sudan which helped to break up that oil rich nation into two. The new nation of "Southern Sudan" is where most of the oil fields are; and where China gets most of its oil. Now that South Sudan is an NWO puppet state facing turmoil and counter revolution, China is hedging its bets and making deals with Russia.

Now that the new nation is in a state of chaos and mass suffering *(a la Iraq, Syria, Libya),* ~~Rosenthal,~~the Editorial Board passes the full blame onto some vague "policymakers" while walking away with its hands clean. Due to the short memories and stupidity of its readership; ~~Rosenthal~~, the Editorial Board will get away with this big lie too.

Boobus Americanus 1: *I truly admire Angelina Jolie for doing so much for the children of Darfur.*

Boobus Americanus 2: *Indeed. I understand that George Clooney is also heavily involved in that noble cause.*

"You frickin' idiotsss! Those Hollywood narcissssists couldn't give a cat'ss assss about Darfur!"

(An astute cat, you are.)

JUNE, 2015

NY Times: Climate Marchers gather to Show Rousing Support for Pope

By ELISABETTA POVOLEDO

When Pope Francis appeared on the balcony of the Apostolic Palace, where he delivers an address each Sunday, he was met by the usual cheers and by an unusual forest of bright green oversized paper leaves.

REBUTTAL BY

The Anti-New York Times

Pope Francis' encyclical
Laudato Si'
(Praise be to You)
ON THE CARE OF
OUR COMMON HOME

Given how Frankie the Fake was installed via a "Vatican Spring" operation which overthrew his predecessor *(first Papal "resignation" in 600 years!)*; it is not surprising that the 'New World Pope" would be given his own flash mobs with CIA-like props. From the article:

"The leaves were among the colorful props carried by a hodgepodge of organizations — mostly religious or environmental — that marched to the Vatican on Sunday to thank the Pope for his forceful message on climate change, and to demand that world leaders heed his call for environmental justice and climate action."

The Vatican march built upon the "People's Climate March" that brought 300,000 libtards out onto the streets of New York in September. The march at St. Peter's Square resonated beyond the Roman Catholic Church. Alongside nuns and priests and other Catholics were Buddhists, Jews, Atheists and Hindus. Only Rome's residents were conspicuously absent.

The story quotes Frankie:

"I encourage the collaboration between people and associations of different religions for the promotion of an integral ecology."

Rabbi Lawrence Troster, from Teaneck, N.J., one of the organizers of the march, applauded the "universality of the Pope's message":

" 'Laudato Si' (Praise be to You) is addressed to everyone. It is trying to create a consensus among all people, and not leave such an important issues to a small group of policy makers, leaders or diplomats."

GreenFaith
Interfaith Partners for the Environment

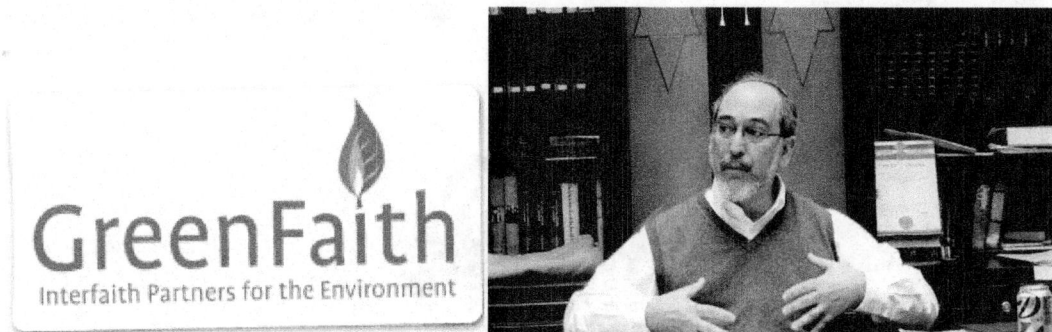

Rabbi Lawrence Troster of 'Green Faith' gushes with admiration for Frankie Faker and his Marxist "Encyclical"

More Marxist madness, quoted from Samantha Smith,leader of the Global Climate and Energy Initiative at World Wildlife Fund:

"It's an amazing document that brings together environmental science, social justice and religious teaching and asks us to think about economic policies. At the heart of the encyclical is a powerful message "that the way we are living on the planet is not sustainable or equitable. But it is also hopeful because it urges global mobilization."

It seems that the Earth-worshipping charlatan is in competition with Homo-Obongo to see who can inflict the most damage on the decaying remnants of once hallowed western institutions. The mere fact that radical Enviro-Marxists and so many Jews are so enamored of this venal viper in the Vatican should be enough to prove that he is an impostor. And yet, every time **The Anti-New York Times** lays a righteous smack-down on this loony "liberation theologist" from Argentina, a handful of Catholic die-hards *(though fewer and fewer as of late)* will write in apologizing for this clownish cleric who, they insist, is being deceived by others.

Nonsense! This evil-doing deceiver dubbed "The New World Pope" knows *exactly* what he is doing. The eye-popping manner in which the emissaries of International Jewry adoringly swarm about Satan's Pope like flies on feces constitutes all the visual evidence we need. If a picture is worth a 1,000 words, the following images are worth 1,000,000.

1- As an Argentine Cardinal, Jorge BERGoglio often visited synagogues and lit Menorahs.
2- Satan's Pope is given a Menorah by Satan's Prime Minister.

*

More gifts and hugs from the 'all-of-a-sudden' admirers of the Papacy

Bowing before Peres and the Holocaust-TM Remembrance Wall as Palestinians are slaughtered and Israel threatens to bomb Iran. How low can one go?

Reuters: Shimon Peres floats idea of U.N.-style "United Religions" with Pope Francis

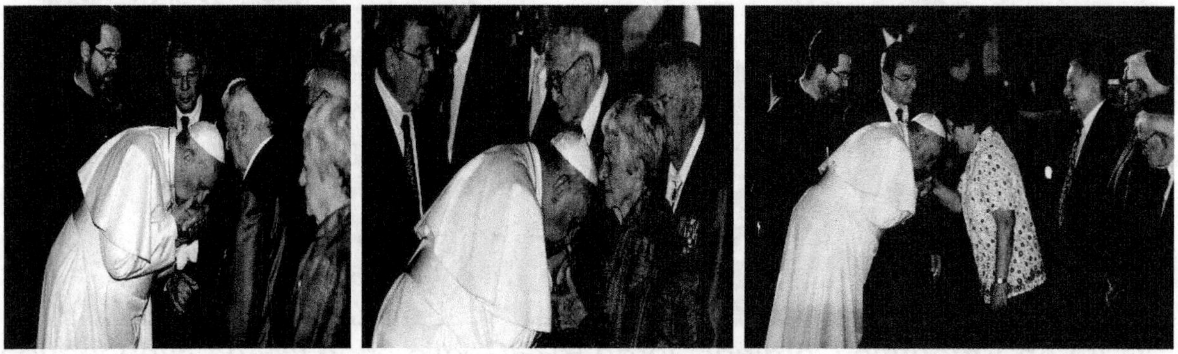

Frankie Fake goes down on the whole "Holocaust line - degrading his own church as he bows and kisses the hands of multiple "survivors". Oy vey!

*Hey Frankie Fakeout! How about some prayers and papal tears for the people of Dresden - **mostly Catholics** - fried and melted alive under orders from your 'chosen ones' on the Catholic holiday of **Ash Wednesday**, 1945 (someone's idea of a joke).*

Seen enough? It get's worse!

The Kosher Cleric tucks his crucifix in his belt so as not to offend his owners.

Please don't offend the blood-sucker with your crucifix!

Like we say: "Satan's Pope"

Boobus Americanus 1: *I read in The New York Times today that the Pope is gaining support from people of all faiths for his position on Climate Change.*

Boobus Americanus 2: *Yes. He is truly the 'People's Pope'.*

"Peopless's Pope my asss. He's a frickin' Commie!"

(Sugar. Tone it down a notch.)

CPSIA information can be obtained
at www.ICGtesting.com
Printed in the USA
LVOW03s2007061215
465638LV00028B/879/P